THE FIFTH DIMENSION

RELATED TITLES PUBLISHED BY ONEWORLD:

Avatar and Incarnation, Geoffrey Parrinder, ISBN 1–85168–130–2
Believing – An Historical Perspective, Wilfred Cantwell Smith, ISBN 1–85168–166–3
Concepts of God, Keith Ward, ISBN 1–85168–064–0
Faith and Belief: The Difference Between Them, Wilfred Cantwell Smith, ISBN 1–85168–165–5
God and the Universe of Faiths, John Hick, ISBN 1–85168–071–3
God, Chance and Necessity, Keith Ward, ISBN 1–85168–116–7
God, Faith and the New Millenium, Keith Ward, ISBN 1–85168–155–8
In Defence of the Soul, Keith Ward, ISBN 1–85168–040–3
Jesus and the Muslim, Kenneth Cragg, ISBN 1–85168–180–9
Muhammad and the Christian, Kenneth Cragg, ISBN 1–85168–179–5
Muslims and Christians Face to Face, Kate Zebiri, ISBN 1–85168–133–7
The Meaning of Life in the World Religions, ed. Joseph Runzo and Nancy M. Martin, ISBN 1–85168–200–7
Mysticism, Evelyn Underhill, ISBN 1–85168–196–5
On Being a Muslim, Farid Esack, ISBN 1–85168–146–9
Patterns of Faith Around the World, Wilfred Cantwell Smith, ISBN 1–85168–164–7
The Phenomenon of Religion, Moojan Momen, ISBN 1–85168–161–2
Religious Truth for our Time, William Montgomery Watt, ISBN 1–85168–102–7
The Sense of God, John Bowker, ISBN 1–85168–093–4
Sexual Morality in the World's Religions, Geoffrey Parrinder, ISBN 1–85168–108–6
Ultimate Visions, edited by Martin Forward, ISBN 1–85168–100–0

THE FIFTH DIMENSION

AN EXPLORATION OF THE SPIRITUAL REALM

JOHN HICK

O N E W O R L D
O X F O R D

THE FIFTH DIMENSION

Oneworld Publications
(Sales and Editorial)
185 Banbury Road
Oxford OX2 7AR
England

http://www.oneworld-publications.com

Oneworld Publications
US Marketing Office
160 N. Washington St.
4th floor, Boston
MA 02114
USA

A CIP record for this book is available
from the British Library

ISBN (hb) 1–85168–190–6
(pb) 1–85168–191–4

Cover design by Design Deluxe
Printed in England by Clays Ltd, St Ives plc

Dedicated to
the grandchildren,
Jonathan and Emily,
Rhiannon and Alexander,
who will find their own paths in the twenty-first century

PREFACE

This book is addressed to anyone interested in such questions as the nature of this mysterious universe of which we are a part; the meaning of our human existence with its unpredictable mixture of good and evil, happiness and misery; the significance of religious experience and of the extraordinary individuals called saints or mahatmas; the prospect of death and the possibility of further life beyond it. In response to these questions I argue for the radical insufficiency of a purely naturalistic, or humanist, understanding of life, and for the reality of a fifth, spiritual, dimension of the universe.

I have avoided technical terms as far as possible and when Hindu or Buddhist or other unfamiliar words are necessary I have adapted them into English, so that *saṃsāra*, for example, becomes *samsara* or even samsara. And I have also not engaged in debate with other scholars, because the concern here is not with the internal discussions of the academic world. However, the basic ideas are ones that I have developed over the last thirty years in a series of other books in which I do debate extensively with academic friends and foes. The aim now is to share the outcome of all that work with the general reader. If some find this helpful in their own thinking and living, the book will have served its purpose.

John Hick

ACKNOWLEDGEMENTS

I am grateful for permission to use in this book source material of my own that has appeared elsewhere.

Some of Part II first appeared in my book *Faith and Knowledge* (1st edn. 1957), and reappeared, together with new material, in a paper at a conference on 'The Meaning of Life in the World Religions' at Chapman University, California, in the spring of 1997. It is published in the volume arising from the conference, *The Meaning of Life in the World Religions*, edited by Joseph Runzo and Nancy M. Martin (Oneworld Publications, 1999). Some of the material on Gandhi was used in a lecture at Boston University's Institute for Philosophy and Religion in the spring of 1998 and published in *Religion, Politics, and Peace*, edited by Leroy L. Rouner (University of Notre Dame Press, 1999).

CONTENTS

Preface vii
Acknowledgements viii

INTRODUCTION: THE BIG PICTURE 1

Alternative pictures • The fifth dimension of our nature • The axial age • Sin or false consciousness? • Guilt or *dukkha* as the problem? • Transcategorial reality

PART I DRAWING THE PICTURE

1. WHERE WE START TODAY: THE NATURALISTIC ASSUMPTION 13

   Naturalism • An ambiguous universe • Science versus religion: a false opposition

2. NATURALISM AS BAD NEWS FOR THE MANY 20

   Hard and soft naturalism • No hope for the many

3. WINDOWS ON THE TRANSCENDENT 26

   Windows in the physical sciences • Windows in the social sciences • Windows in the natural world • Windows in human life

4. THE KEY TO UNDERSTANDING 32

   Perception as interpretation • Cognitive freedom . . . • . . . in religious awareness

5. TURNING THE CRITICAL REALIST KEY 39

The transformation of information • Critical realism

PART II THE MEANING OF LIFE

6. THE RELIGIOUS MEANING OF LIFE 47

Practical meaning • Religious meaning • Cosmic optimism

7. COSMIC OPTIMISM IN THE EAST 55

In Hinduism • In Buddhism

8. AND IN THE WEST 64

In Judaism • In Christianity • In Islam

PART III THE GODS AND ABSOLUTES AS MANIFESTATIONS OF THE REAL

9. THE REAL EXPERIENCED AS GOD 77

The pluralist hypothesis • Pseudo-Dionysius • Dionysius' dilemma • Meister Eckhart and others

10. THE REAL EXPERIENCED AS THE ABSOLUTE 91

In Hinduism • In Buddhism

PART IV RELIGIOUS EXPERIENCE AND MYSTICISM

11. ALTERED STATES OF CONSCIOUSNESS 99

Some distinctions • Altered states • Drugs and altered states • Self-transcendence • The influence of set and setting

12. RELIGIOUS EXPERIENCE 110

Preliminary distinctions • The sense of presence • Some examples

13. VISIONS – A CASE STUDY OF JULIAN OF NORWICH 118

The emergence of women visionaries • Julian herself • The historical setting • The visions

14. LADY JULIAN'S FRUITFUL HERESIES 129

The fall–redemption model • The lord–servant parable • The godly will within us • Universal salvation?

15. UNITIVE MYSTICISM: LITERAL UNITY 136

Literal or metaphorical? • Advaita Vedanta • An epistemological problem • Neoplatonism

16. UNITIVE MYSTICISM: METAPHORICAL UNITY 144

Christian Neoplatonism • Pseudo-Dionysius • Deification • The love poetry of the mystics • The Jewish Kabbala • The Sufis of Islam

17. THE DARK SIDE 155

The dark side of the cults • The dark side of the great religions • Harmless eccentricities

18. THE CRITERION 163

The fruits in human life • Operating the criterion • Trusting religious experience

PART V THE SAINTS COME MARCHING IN

19. ONE LIVING SAINT IS WORTH TEN DEAD ONES 173

Saints, mahatmas and others • The founders • Living saints • The profile of the saint • Modern political saints

20. GANDHI: A CASE STUDY 180

My life is my message • A very human saint • A rock-like integrity

21. THE POLITICS OF TRUTH 191

God is Truth, Truth is God • A Hindu critic of Hinduism • Non-violence

22. GANDHI'S TRUTH FOR US TODAY 199

Non-violent conflict resolution • Green thinking • The position of women • Religious pluralism

23. AN ACTIVIST AND A CONTEMPLATIVE 205

Kushdeva Singh • Nyanaponika Mahathera

PART VI TIME PRESENT AND TIME FUTURE

24. WHAT WE DON'T NEED TO KNOW 219

The beginning and the end • The Buddha's 'unanswered questions' • Living on a need-to-know basis • What then *do* we need to know?

25. LIVING WITHIN A TRUE MYTH 229

Myth and metaphor • The use and misuse of myths • The Jewish myth • The Christian myth • Living consciously within a true myth

26. DEATH AND BEYOND 241

Our contemporary confusion • Traditional possibilities • Many lives • What reincarnates? • Dying

CONCLUSION 253

BIBLIOGRAPHY 255

INDEX 268

INTRODUCTION: THE BIG PICTURE

ALTERNATIVE PICTURES

We are finite, fallible, fragile fragments of the universe. But because we have an inbuilt need to find meaning we inhabit the universe in terms of a conception of its character – a big picture – either consciously adopted or unconsciously presupposed. In so doing we are always, whether we realize it or not, living by faith, that is, moving in an immensely important area in which there is no certain knowledge and in which we cannot avoid the risk of being seriously mistaken.

To most of us within our highly technological western culture it has come to seem self-evident that a scientific account of anything and everything constitutes the full story, and that the supposed transcendent realities of which the religions speak must therefore be imaginary. Since at least the beginning of the twentieth century this naturalistic assumption has been an integral part of our culture, and any contrary hopes, dreams, intuitions, sensings of transcendence, intimations of immortality or mystical experiences have been overshadowed by its pervasive influence. But it is a fundamental error to think that the assumptions that our culture has instilled into us, and which we take for granted, are necessarily true. It was Einstein who said that 'common sense is what we are taught by the age of six', or perhaps, in the case of more complex ideas, by about fourteen. The beginning of wisdom is to become aware of our own presuppositions as options that can be examined and questioned. Otherwise we are wearing mental blinkers without even being conscious of them.

The full range of big pictures includes the naturalistic account, according to which our human existence is a fleeting accident within a universe ultimately devoid of meaning. And it includes the multitude of specific religious pictures, each offering its own detailed cosmology. But the contention of this book is that it also includes a new and yet very old global religious vision – new in that it is only now coming into prominence among us, but old in that it has long been there in the mystical strands of each of the great traditions.

From this latter standpoint, neither the naturalistic nor the traditional religious beliefs are sufficient and a more complete picture must include the truth within each. It must accept modern science in its entirety, as our current and ever-developing exploration of the physical universe, but it must also acknowledge the inherent limitations of the scientific method and be open to the transcendent dimension witnessed to by the global religious life of humanity.

THE FIFTH DIMENSION OF OUR NATURE

In outlining this larger picture we begin with ourselves. We are part of a species which emerged a hundred thousand years or more ago – the dating changes from time to time with new discoveries – within the evolution of life on earth. We exist within a single biological stream, but we differ from the other life forms in our much greater brain complexity and hence much greater intellectual capacity. Human life is continuous with the rest of animal life, and the mental and also emotional difference is one of degree, though so great a degree as virtually to constitute a difference in kind. Nevertheless, the other animals are our biological cousins since in the remote past we had common ancestors. In some cases – such as some domestic dogs, cats and horses, also some chimpanzees, elephants and dolphins – we can recognize a degree of mental and emotional affinity. But we should not treat even those animals with which we cannot empathize as mere 'things' totally unconnected with ourselves. We are all branches of the same tree of life.

As well as being intelligent animals we are also 'spiritual' beings. This is a vague term which is often defined in equally vague terms. I am using it here to refer to a fifth dimension of our nature which enables us to respond to a fifth dimension of the universe. In this aspect of our being we are – according to different versions of the religious big picture – either continuous with, or akin to and in tune with, the ultimate reality that underlies, interpenetrates and transcends the physical universe.

Another way of affirming our spiritual nature is to say that we are religious animals with an inbuilt tendency to experience the natural in terms of the supra-natural. It was the anthropologist R.R. Marett who first suggested that *homo sapiens* could better be called *homo religiosus*.[1] For as another anthropologist, Clyde Kluckhohn, wrote, 'Until the emergence of Communist societies we know of no human groups without religion';[2] and indeed, on a 'family resemblance' analysis of the concept of religion, communist societies also have their religious aspects. The great historian of religion Mircea Eliade puts a commonly accepted view when he says that 'the "sacred" is an element in the structure of consciousness and not a stage in the history of consciousness'.[3] Rudolf Otto even held that the idea of the holy is a priori, innate within the human mind.[4] For according to many anthropologists there are signs of a religious concern in the earliest evidences that we have of human behaviour. As far back as we can trace them we find that humans have done something that no other species does – they have buried or otherwise deliberately disposed of the corpses of their own kind. The Neanderthals, as long as a hundred thousand years ago, placed food and precious flint implements in the graves of their dead; and the Cro-Magnons of some twenty-five thousand years ago buried weapons, ornaments and food with their dead and sometimes dusted red ochre – presumably representing blood, itself a symbol of life – on the corpses or in their graves. These practices clearly express some notion of an afterlife, and such ritual behaviours, later crystallizing into consciously formed beliefs, are the earliest surviving expressions of humanity as a religious animal.

Let me add immediately, to avoid a possible misunderstanding, that this innate human religiousness leaves entirely open the crucial question of whether or not there is a transcendent reality to which religion is a response. That people have always believed in such realities does not prove that they exist.

We do not need to spend time arguing about whether something or someone is religious, because the term does not refer to a single definable essence but is what Ludwig Wittgenstein called a family resemblance concept. He took the example of games. They have no common essence – they can be individual or team activities; they can depend on skill or on chance; some can be won or lost, others not; they can be played for amusement, fame or monetary reward; some are played with balls, others with cards, marbles, chess pieces and so on. Each shares common features with some others but none with all others. And so we have a network, somewhat like a family, in which

1. Marett, p. 3.
2. Kluckhohn, p. v.
3. Eliade, 1978, p. xii.
4. Otto, 1958, chapters 14–20.

each member has points of resemblance to some members but not to others.[5] Likewise the various kinds and aspects of religion form a loose cluster of characteristics of which no one religion has all, but all have some. For example Christianity involves the worship of a supreme being whilst Buddhism does not; but they are alike in another way in that both offer comprehensive understandings of reality, of our highest good, and of the way to attain it.

Returning to our modern naturalistic worldview, the assumption that the idea of an afterlife began in fear of extinction and a desire for a better life beyond the grave is a good example of its influence. The archaeological remains by themselves cannot tell us what went on in the minds of those earliest humans. But if we project back from the primal or archaic peoples who were intensively studied by anthropologists in the last half of the nineteenth century, before their societies had been significantly changed by contact with the modern world, we find that generally speaking what survived was not thought of as mind or soul in distinction from body, but rather as a shadowy and insubstantial counterpart of the body inhabiting a dark underground region. This theme emerges into literature as the gloomy, bloodless, miserable half-life of Sheol or of Hades. For Job, in the Hebrew scriptures, the prospect of Sheol was even worse than the flood of earthly troubles engulfing him: 'Let me alone, that I may find a little comfort before I go whence I shall not return, to the land of gloom and deep darkness, the land of gloom and chaos, where light is as darkness'.[6] For the dead were cut off even from God: 'The dead do not praise the Lord, nor do any that go down into silence.'[7] The afterlife was like an advanced stage of Alzheimer's disease! Among the ancient Greeks, Hades was likewise regarded as a place of barely conscious shades: 'There remains even in the house of Hades a spirit and phantom of the dead, although there is no life in it', says Homer,[8] and the shade of the great Achilles, briefly energized by a goat's blood, says, 'I would rather live on the earth as the hireling of another, with a landless man who has no great livelihood, than bear sway among all of the dead who have departed.'[9] Clearly such thoughts did not arise as wish-fulfilments. The belief in a desirable afterlife – heaven, paradise, the happy hunting ground – came later as part of a moral conception of the universe in which there is a judgement of the soul and the rewards of heaven are balanced by the punishment of hell.

The studies of recently existing primal societies show that their afterlife conceptions were accompanied by belief in a multitude of spirits which were as real to them as the physical world and which had

5. Wittgenstein, paragraph 66, pp. 31–2.
6. Job 10:20–2.
7. Psalm 115:17.
8. Homer, *Iliad*, xxviii, line 103.
9. Homer, *Odyssey*, xi, lines 488–91.

power to benefit and harm. Mountains, sky, rocks, forests, streams, clearings, trees and totem animals were indwelt by unseen forces that had to be worshipped, placated with sacrifices, or cautiously negotiated with. Our rigid modern distinctions between humans and the other animals, and between the natural and the supra-natural, had not been formed, and the living universe was experienced as a seamless unity. The basic religious concern was stability, the need to keep fragile human life on an even keel – to ensure that the sun rose, that the seasons came round again, that the rain fell when it was needed, that the warriors were strong and the women fertile. And the practices expressing this concern reinforced the vital unity of the tribe or people. For what we now think of as individuals saw themselves, for all important purposes, as part of the social organism rather than as separate autonomous persons. Value and authority resided in the group as a whole rather than in its constituent parts.

THE AXIAL AGE

However, around the middle of the first millennium BCE (Before the Common Era[10]), in a band of time stretching from about 800 to about 200 BCE, remarkable individuals appeared across the world, standing out from their societies and proclaiming momentous new insights. In China there were Confucius, Mencius and Lao-Tzu (or the anonymous writers of the *Tao Te Ching*) and Mo-Tzu. In India there were Gautama, the Buddha; Mahavira, the founder of the Jain tradition; the writers of the Upanishads and later of the *Bhagavad Gita*. In Persia there was Zoroaster. In Palestine there were the great Hebrew prophets – Amos, Hosea, Jeremiah, the Isaiahs, Ezekiel. In Greece there were Pythagoras, Socrates, Plato, Aristotle. This immensely significant hinge in human thought has come to be known as the axial age. If we see Christianity as presupposing Judaism, and Islam as presupposing both Judaism and Christianity, all of the present major world religions trace their roots to this axial period.

Pre-axial or archaic people generally just accepted the given conditions of their lives. They did not stand back in thought to engage in critical reflection. They did not envisage alternatives that might lead to a fundamental dissatisfaction with the existing state of affairs. Life was for them, as one anthropologist puts it, 'a one-possibility thing'.[11] But during the axial age, in large areas of the world, there were several mutually reinforcing developments: the formation of cities; the

10. This term is not perfect but does reflect the fact that three major religious traditions, Christianity, rabbinic Judaism and Mahayana Buddhism, began at about the same time.
11. Stanner, p. 515.

emergence of individual as distinguished from communal consciousness, first in rulers and religious leaders and then increasingly widely; and a sense of the unsatisfactoriness, the felt incompleteness of our ordinary human existence, found somehow lacking in a higher quality that nevertheless stands before us as a real possibility.

These extraordinary individuals emerged, of course, within societies that had through long gradual change become ready to hear them. And because their messages were addressed to individuals, challenging them to a personal response, these messages were for the first time universal in scope. Instead of being concerned to preserve the existing framework of meaning, they were conscious of its deeply incomplete and unsatisfying character, and proclaimed a limitlessly better possibility for the individual, and thus ultimately for society.

SIN OR FALSE CONSCIOUSNESS?

In the Semitic religions this sense of incompleteness has a primarily moral focus. There is within our human nature an evil inclination (the *yecer ha-ra* of Genesis 6:5), which we have to resist and overcome; or we are fallen beings, bearing within us the original sin of Adam and Eve in whom the whole human race fell (I Corinthians 15:22); or we are made out of the dust of the earth (Qur'an 3:59) and are self-centred and prone to disobey God's commands (96:6–7). And evil, embodied in the malevolent figure of Satan, was always believed to be around to tempt and lead astray.

In the religions that originated further east, in India, the focus has been less upon sin and guilt and more upon false consciousness – of which false consciousness in the Marxist sense of class consciousness is only one aspect. The religious notion of false consciousness is expressed metaphysically in the closely connected Hindu concepts of spiritual ignorance (*avidya*) and illusion (*maya*). But the more psychological and moral aspect is classically expressed in the Buddhist analysis of the human condition. The Buddha's basic teaching is summarized in the Four Noble Truths, traditionally believed to have been first taught in his sermon in the deer park at Sarnath, just outside Benares (now Varanasi). The first of these is the truth of *dukkha*, of which there is no one entirely satisfactory English rendering but which is variously translated as unsatisfactoriness, suffering, unhappiness. Describing ordinary unenlightened human consciousness, the Buddha said, 'Birth is dukkha, age is dukkha, disease is dukkha, death is dukkha; contact with the unpleasant is dukkha, separation from the pleasant is dukkha, every wish unfulfilled is dukkha.' And its source is our self-centred way of participating in the process of life. Stemming from a biologically programmed instinct for self-preservation, it consists at the human level in seeing and valuing everything primarily as it affects oneself. This produces a distrust of strangers, a feeling of being threatened by the otherness of others, an apprehension about what the unknown future may bring, and a fear of death, all building up into a pervasive angst which deprives us of serenity and the deep joy of inner freedom. This in turn leads to individual greed, malice, cruelty, jealousy, resentment, cheating, untruthfulness, and to corporate selfishness in the forms of aggression, exploitation, war, slavery, institutionalized injustices. According to the Buddha, all this human misery, which evoked his compassion and led him to a strenuous life of teaching, flows from a false consciousness that renders us fundamentally insecure, seeing others as potential rivals and enemies, so that we have to safeguard ourselves by grasping at power and possessions. In Buddhist terms, we lack awareness of our own buddha nature and of the ultimate buddha nature of the universe, an awareness that would release us from the constant defensive self-concern that makes life a danger, the future a threat, and the human world a jungle of competing interests. When the buddha nature within us is released by eroding the hard shell of self-concern, its natural and spontaneous expression is a universal compassion (*karuna*) and love (*metta*).

But we do not have to think of this only in Buddhist terms. In speaking of *dukkha* the Buddha was pointing to a basic human insecurity which shows itself in a thousand ways. Within our own relatively stable and affluent society we see it, and participate in it, in the worried rush of life in which so many have to live, in 'strained time-ridden faces distracted from distraction by distraction',[12] in the anxious expressions, the quick tempers, the road rage, the envy and jealousy, the thoughtless selfishness and dishonesty, the animosities and resentments, the enveloping unhappiness, of so many. We see it in hard-faced businessmen intent on building their empires of wealth and power, regardless of the welfare of those whom they employ. We see it at all levels of society in resort to gambling and a wide range of drugs, in such contemporary communal chauvinisms as racism, anti-Semitism, Islamophobia, homophobia, lack of empathy with those who are different. We see it in the continuous agony of homeless refugees and helpless civilians trampled by opposing military powers. We see it in the developed world's monumental indifference to populations impoverished by the destruction of their living space, in the maiming of

12. From T. S. Eliot, 'Burnt Norton'.

men, women and children by land mines and other armaments manufactured for profit, and in the cumulative pollution of the atmosphere which we all breathe and the wanton destruction of the protective ozone layer above us. We see it in the progressive degradation of the natural environment as we dissipate the earth's basic resources to sustain our highly developed modern life styles. And we see it and participate in it in innumerable other ways, large and small, both in our individual lives and in the structures of our society. Most of us are aware of this, and yet collectively we continue heedlessly on the path of mutual destruction, for *dukkha* forms a self-perpetuating cycle that can only be broken by transformation into a radically different human outlook.

GUILT OR *DUKKHA* AS THE PROBLEM?

The 'western' religions call this general distortion of human life sin, thus identifying guilt as the problem. The 'eastern' religions call it spiritual blindness, thus identifying false consciousness as the problem. But whether we regard moral evil as the expression of false consciousness, or false consciousness as the expression of sin, the distortion itself is a manifest reality; and it is from this that the post-axial religions offer to free us. Their function is to be enabling contexts of the transformation of human existence, a transformation from sinful and/or deluded self-centredness to a radically new orientation centred in the Divine, the Transcendent, the Ultimate, thus freeing what they variously call the true or selfless self, the *atman*, the universal buddha nature, the image of God within us.

This radical change is a re-centring which produces an inner peace, serenity, joy, purity of heart, and clarity of moral vision. But it is obvious that this salvific transformation makes only very limited progress in most of us during this present life, so that the world faiths anticipate further spiritual growth beyond this life, although by no means necessarily in the forms that we most easily imagine. But the awareness of transcendence always brings us back into the present moment with its open possibilities. Here the outstanding examples of the great transformation, expressed in either inner contemplative or outer and political forms, are what Christianity calls saints and for which other traditions have other names, about which more in Part V.

TRANSCATEGORIAL REALITY

The fifth dimension of our nature, the transcendent within us, answers to the fifth dimension of the universe, the transcendent without. In speaking of this, the limitations of language create a problem to which there is unfortunately no satisfactory solution. We want to refer to that which, according to the religions, is the ultimate object of human concern. In a western context we speak of God. And it is possible to use this familiar term with the stipulation that it points to the ultimate reality without however defining it, and so without prejudging whether that reality is personal or non-personal or even such that this duality does not apply. But in practice the long-established associations of the word as referring to an infinite divine Person are generally too strong for this stipulation to be effective. And so we resort to such terms as the Ultimate, Ultimate Reality, Absolute Reality, the Real, the Transcendent, the Divine, the Holy, the Eternal, the Infinite – with or without capitals. I shall use all of these, and even the grammatically improper 'ultimately Real', as a reminder that no one of them is entirely adequate. But I shall tend to favour either the Transcendent or the Ultimate or, even more, the Real, because this latter is the rough equivalent of both the Sanskrit *sat* and the Arabic *al-Haqq*. However we shall be continually up against the fact that language has developed in our struggle to cope with the material environment and that when we use it to refer to the transcendent it inevitably has non-literal meanings (i.e. not in accordance with the ordinary dictionary meanings of words). It is now allusive, suggestive, metaphorical, poetic, pointing rather than defining. And so we have continually to try to focus, not on the pointing finger of language, but on that to which it points.

The mystics of the great traditions affirm almost unanimously that the Real is beyond human conceiving. It is ineffable or, as I prefer to say, transcategorial – outside the scope of the categories with which we think. It (though 'it' is as inappropriate as 'he' or 'she') is what it is, but what it is does not fall within the scope of our human conceptual systems. Our operative paradigms enable us to think about our physical and social environments; and going beyond this, mathematical concepts enable us to think numerically and logical concepts to think consistently. But the Real cannot be defined in terms of our conceptual repertoire. We can make purely formal, linguistically generated, statements about it (such as that it can be referred to), but we cannot properly either affirm or deny that it has any of the positive qualities captured in human language. We cannot say, for example, that it is personal or that it is impersonal; or again, that it is good or that it is evil, that it is a substance or a process, even that it is one or many. The binary dualisms in terms of which we think, although indispensable features of human thought, do not apply to the Ultimate.

This notion of concepts not applying to something is a familiar one. Philosophers speak of category mistakes. It does not make sense, for example, to ask whether a molecule is intelligent or stupid, because it is not the sort of thing that could be either. And nor is the Real. Indeed it is not a *kind* of thing at all. It is, using inevitably metaphorical language, the ground of everything. So human language can describe the various forms taken by the 'impact' of the Real upon us, but not the Real as it is in itself.

It follows at once that the descriptions of ultimate reality treasured by the different religions do not apply literally to the Ultimate in itself. And so, according to our big picture, the Holy Trinity of Christian teaching, and the God of Abraham, Isaac and Jacob revealed in the Hebrew scriptures, and the Adonai of rabbinic Judaism, and the Allah *rahman rahim* (God, merciful and gracious) of the Qur'an, and the Vishnu and Shiva of theistic Hinduism, and again Brahman, the Tao, and the Dharma or Nirvana of the Hindu, Taoist and Buddhist traditions, are forms which human awareness of the Real has been given by human consciousness. They are personae and impersonae (i.e. personal and non-personal manifestations) of the Ultimate as it impinges upon our different religious mentalities, with their associated spiritual practices, as these have developed within the great historical traditions. In the paradoxical words of an ancient Hindu text, 'Thou art formless: thy only form is our knowledge of thee.'[13]

Accordingly, that the different religions give such different accounts of the Ultimate does not mean that if one of them is correct the others must be incorrect. So far as the differences between them are concerned, they may all be authentic responses to the Transcendent, and their different theologies may be valid descriptions of the different ways in which that ultimate reality is humanly conceived, and therefore experienced, and therefore responded to in life from within the different cultural ways of being human (more about this on pp. 77–9).

All this raises a multitude of questions which will come to the fore as we proceed. But this has been a preliminary sketch of the big picture, a small-scale map of the territory to be explored in the following chapters.

13. *Yogava'sistha*, 1:28; Pansikar, p. 144.

PART I

DRAWING THE PICTURE

1

WHERE WE START TODAY: THE NATURALISTIC ASSUMPTION

NATURALISM

We start with the fact that we find ourselves existing – though this does not astonish us because we are so used to it! We have been, so to speak, thrown into existence with a given nature, each with our own unique genetic endowment, and at a time and place which we did not choose. And as we proceed through life, different voices, religious and naturalistic, tell importantly different stories about what kind of beings we are and what kind of universe we are part of.

Naturalistic teachers tell us that reality consists exclusively of the physical universe, including of course human brains, which are physical objects, and their functioning. Humanism, when not just an uncontroversial emphasis on human values but a dogmatic exclusion of the supra-natural, is another name for naturalism. So is materialism, the idea that nothing exists but matter/energy, including again animal brains. According to naturalists, or Humanists, or materialists, our existence as material organisms in a material world constitutes the whole story. They differ among themselves as to whether we have a real degree of free will or are totally determined, with only the illusion of free will. However in practice we can only assume that we have free will. For if someone's thought, 'My every thought is totally determined' is true, that thought itself is not the outcome of a process of free critical thinking but is determined by physical causes. There may well be an element of sub-atomic randomness within this causal process, but this does not affect the logical dilemma: if every thought is either rigidly or randomly determined, we could never be in a state of rationally believing that this is so! For rational believing presupposes a degree of intellectual freedom, the freedom to exercise judgement, and if we are totally determined we have no such freedom.

Naturalistic thinkers also disagree among themselves about whether consciousness is identical with cerebral activity, or is a new emergent factor, different in nature although dependent from moment to moment on the electro-chemical functioning of the brain. But we can pass over this difference at the moment, returning to it in chapter 3.

Naturalism, then, is the belief that reality consists exclusively in the multiple forms of discharging energy that constitute the physical universe. This includes our earth and the human and other forms of life on it, and hence the multitude of human brains and their functioning, which in turn includes the production of thought, language, feeling, emotion, and action. The status of such supposed non-physical realities as God, Brahman, Dharma, Tao, the soul or spirit, is that of ideas in the human mind, so that before there were human mind/brains to create them, they did not in any sense exist. Naturalism is thus equivalent to the qualified materialism which does not deny the existence of mentality, but holds that it is either identical with, or totally dependent from moment to moment upon, the electro-chemical functioning of the brain.

In our western world, beginning around the seventeenth century, the earlier pervasive religious outlook has increasingly been replaced by an equally pervasive naturalistic outlook, and during the twentieth century this replacement has become almost complete. Naturalism has created the 'consensus reality' of our culture. It has become so ingrained that we no longer see it, but see everything else through it. The main reason for this is clearly the continuing and most welcome success of the sciences in discovering how the physical world works, and in using this knowledge for our benefit in many fields, not least in medicine. (It is also alarmingly true that our use of highly sophisticated technology is eroding and poisoning the environment and has even put humanity in danger of destroying itself; but although obviously immensely important, this does not affect the present point.)

The rise and eventual dominance of the scientific point of view was in fact more than an intellectual revolution. The decades from about 1840 to about 1890 in Britain, during which science gained social respectability and then establishment status, saw 'the rise of the professional and the decline of the gentleman'.[1] There was a gradual shift in the class and power structure of the country. Indeed, the 'warfare between science and theology' was in part a 'professional

1. Desmond, p. 235.

territorial dispute'.[2] T.H. Huxley was a key figure in this development, starting as an outsider rejected by both church and state, and ending as President of the Royal Society, a Privy Counsellor, and internationally respected as one of 'the great and the good'.

To see how the naturalistic assumption colours our experience I must anticipate the analysis of awareness in chapter 4. The central point is that experience always involves the interpretive activity of the mind. The impacts upon us of our environment are interpreted by means of our operative conceptual system, so that the same impacts may be pre-consciously processed through different sets of concepts to create different conscious experiences. But in the case of events that can be experienced either naturalistically or religiously, the latter is precluded by the dominant faith of our culture. And when philosophizing about the history of religions a naturalistic interpretation is likewise routinely accepted as self-evidently more plausible than a religious one.

Thus for example, when we hear someone speak of a moment when they had a strong sense, or feeling, of God as an unseen, all-enveloping, benign presence, the naturalistic assumption automatically rejects this as illusory and points to psychological mechanisms that might have produced it. It is firmly assumed that there is no reality beyond the physical (including, once again, the functioning of human brains), so that the religious person's sense of a divine presence can only be some kind of self-delusion. That the presence of a transcendent reality might be mediated to us by means of our own innate psychological structure is not even considered as a serious possibility.

AN AMBIGUOUS UNIVERSE

If, however, we set aside preconceptions, we can see that the universe, so far as we are able to observe it, is ambiguous. As humanly conceived and experienced, it can have either a naturalistic or a religious character. It is possible to describe it, in principle completely, in naturalistic terms within which religious experience is included as imaginative projection and religious life as a response to that projection. But it is equally possible to describe it, again in principle completely, in ways that accept most of the naturalistic account but which set this in the context of a more encompassing spiritual reality, variously conceived and experienced as God, or Brahman, or the Dharma, or (in Chinese religion) Heaven, or the Tao, or in yet other forms.

In saying that the universe as known to us is religiously ambiguous, I am assuming that the various philosophical attempts to prove the

2. Ibid., p. 250.

existence of God (the traditional ontological, cosmological, teleological and other arguments), or to show that divine existence is more probable than not, either in some precise sense or in the vaguer sense invoked by the currently popular anthropic principle, do not succeed. This is the most common view today among philosophers.[3] What we are then left with are opposing indications, one set pointing towards and the other away from the existence of a transcendent-and-immanent divine reality. In this book we shall encounter both sets of indications.

The naturalistic assumption we are considering in this and the next chapter appeals to two main considerations. One is that the sciences can describe the physical universe in ever greater detail without at any point having to invoke divine agency – as Laplace famously said, he had no need of that hypothesis. And the other is the ever-present reality of pain and suffering due to human wickedness and to natural disasters. These provide powerful support for the naturalistic assumption, at least when this is focused upon an anthropomorphic concept of God. By this we mean a conception of God as human-like in the sense of being a personal being – as in Richard Swinburne's definition of theism as the view that 'there exists now, and always has existed and will exist God, a spirit, that is, a non-embodied person who is omnipresent'.[4] I shall address both of these negative factors, and the contrary religious indicators, in the course of these chapters.

To start with Laplace's 'I have no need of that hypothesis', the methods of the physical sciences – basically physics, astrophysics and chemistry – are not designed to recognize any non-physical reality that there may be. It is therefore quite proper for scientists, in their professional role, to assume that nothing but matter exists. But there is in fact no logical route from the absence of any non-material reality in the findings of the physical sciences to the conclusion that there *is* no non-material reality, for if there is, in the nature of the case, scientists would not encounter it in their scientific work.

This can be illustrated from Stephen Hawking's account of current cosmology in his widely read *A Brief History of Time*. Discussing the origin of the universe in a 'big bang' some fifteen billion years ago, he points out that anything prior to that lies outside the purview of science. It cannot therefore be a scientific conclusion that there was nothing before the big bang. For if there was, science can know nothing about it. As Hawking says, 'even if there were events before the big bang, one could not use them to determine what would happen afterward, because predictability would break down at the big bang. Correspondingly, if, as

3. I have discussed the theistic arguments at length in *Arguments for the Existence of God* and also in *An Interpretation of Religion*. For the contrary view, see, for example, Richard Swinburne's *The Existence of God* and *Is There a God?*
4. Swinburne, 1979, p. 90.

is the case, we know only what has happened since the big bang, we could not determine what happened beforehand. As far as we are concerned, events before the big bang have no consequences, so they should not form part of a scientific model of the universe. We should therefore cut them out of the model and say that time had a beginning at the big bang.'[5] This deliberate restriction is inherent in the scientific method and is entirely legitimate; but it says nothing about the possibility or otherwise of a further dimension of reality beyond the physical.

SCIENCE VERSUS RELIGION: A FALSE OPPOSITION

It follows that the entire science versus religion controversy, beginning in the nineteenth century with Lyall's discovery of the age of the earth and then Darwin's discovery of the basic mechanism of biological evolution, has been a gigantic mistake, even though it is a mistake that has inspired a torrent of books to which eminent writers are still enthusiastically contributing.

The mistake has stemmed mainly from the religious side of the debate. Before the development of modern science, the apparently innate religiousness of the human mind led people to invoke the supranatural to explain physical occurrences. In early societies it was often believed that thunder and lightning, storm and drought, volcanic eruptions and earthquakes occurred because a god was angry. Later, sickness was seen as divine punishment and death as God's ultimate control over the human creature. This thinking continued into the modern period. When the Spanish Armada was wrecked by storms around the Scottish coast, Queen Elizabeth had medals struck with the words, 'God blew with his winds and they were scattered.' The great Lisbon earthquake of 1755, which so traumatically challenged eighteenth-century optimism, was at the time regarded by many as a manifestation of God's wrath against a sinful city:

> Lisbon, the people were told, had been a very sinful city indeed. It was greedy, devoted to material wealth, immoral, licentious, and irreverent, the behaviour in some of its churches being, it was alleged, outrageously scandalous. For permitting this misuse of sacred buildings, the clergy had to, and did, take their share of the blame, and in doing so they were able to explain why God in His anger had destroyed so many churches, great and small . . . Thus, it was understandable that God should not only have destroyed His own churches, but spared a street full of brothels; for God pitied the miserable creatures that frequented such places, but could not pardon

5. Hawking, p. 46.

> those who profaned the buildings set apart for worship of Himself and for the religious instruction of the faithful'.[6]

Such thinking continues today in all manner of confused and inconsistent ways. After D-Day in 1944, when calm water in the Channel aided the allied landings in Normandy, many thanked God for the favourable weather. After the British–Argentinian Falklands war in 1982 there was an attempt, resisted by the leadership of the Church of England, to thank God publicly for the victory.

The trouble with that kind of thinking lies in its implications. Suppose someone 'miraculously' survives a car crash in which the other three people involved are killed. She might thank God for her deliverance. But if this is intended as thanks for a literal miracle, a special divine intervention without which she would have perished, it implies that God could have saved the other three but decided not to. And if God miraculously manipulated the weather over the Channel on D-Day, why did he not work a greater miracle to save hundreds of thousands from being killed in the ensuing battles? Or indeed, why did he not miraculously prevent the war, and its causes, in the first place? This is the insurmountable problem for the concept of God as a limitlessly powerful supernatural Person who is continually intervening, sometimes openly and sometimes secretly, in the course of human affairs. Such an anthropomorphic image pervades Judaism, Christianity and Islam in their traditional forms, and almost all western atheists have naturally enough pursued them into the same trap. They have accepted an anthropomorphic God as that which, quite reasonably, they reject. But many religious people are also atheists in relation to that particular concept of God. 'Atheism' is thus much too general a term to be useful, unless accompanied by a clear statement of the kind of God that one does not believe in. However, in this book we are exploring the non-anthropomorphic conception of the ultimately Real that has always been present within the mystical strands of the great traditions. This does not clash in any way with the sciences – unless one illicitly incorporates the naturalistic assumption into them – but it does go far beyond them.

Note at this point that a non-anthropomorphic understanding of the Ultimate does not entail that prayer – for example, for healing and for physical and mental well-being, whether of oneself or others – is useless. On the contrary, it can be a real force in the world. But it is not a matter of our asking God to intervene miraculously in the course of nature, with God then deciding whether or not to oblige. What then *is*

6. Kendrick, pp. 78–9.

happening? We are all linked at a deep unconscious level in a universal network in which our thoughts, and even more our emotions, are all the time affecting others, as others are in turn affecting us. When, in prayer or meditation, we direct our thought to a particular individual, this is intensified. And so when a theist prays for someone, or when a Buddhist makes a loving-kindness meditation on behalf of someone, they are doing the same thing within different religious frameworks. In the case of bodily healing, another's mind affects the patient's mind, which in turn affects the patient's body. We know rather little about either the telepathic or the psychosomatic phases of the process. But that prayer or meditation does sometimes make a tangible difference is a matter of experience.

In this chapter I have been discussing the naturalistic, or humanist, or materialist position as a distinct theory in its own right, in contrast to religion understood generically. But when we turn from these logically distinct options to the states of mind of individual people, we find that the religious and naturalistic outlooks are often mixed together in a confused jumble. The naturalistic assumption operates for most of the time, although there are also moments for many when it is bypassed. We are struck by one of the 'signals of transcendence' that are everywhere around us, and we participate for a moment in a religious response to the universe. There are yet others who consciously adopt the naturalistic assumption but nevertheless leave open the possibility that some future experience may breach it. But the map that I have drawn, showing the religious and naturalistic poles, can nevertheless be useful, preventing our personal uncertainties and vaguenesses from obscuring the basic logical options.

2

NATURALISM AS BAD NEWS FOR THE MANY

HARD AND SOFT NATURALISM

Taking the naturalistic and religious positions generically, the basic difference as far as our human interests are concerned is that a naturalistic interpretation of the universe, *if true*, is very bad news for humanity as a whole, whilst a religious interpretation, *if true*, is (with exceptions to be noted presently) very good news for humanity as a whole. I am not proposing the obviously fallacious argument that therefore the religious interpretation must be true. I am concerned at the moment only to point out a dire implication of naturalism, because although this is obvious enough when pointed out, many naturalists do not seem to be, and indeed do not seem to want to be, aware of it.

It is however frankly acknowledged by the more realistic and hard-headed naturalistic thinkers. Thus Bertrand Russell, in a famous early essay whose message he reaffirmed much later in his life, wrote:

> That Man is the product of causes which had no prevision of the end they were achieving; that his origin, his growth, his hopes and fears, his loves and his beliefs, are but the outcome of accidental collocations of atoms; that no fire, no heroism, no intensity of thought and feeling, can preserve an individual life beyond the grave; that all the labours of the ages, all the devotion, all the inspiration, all the noonday brightness of human genius, are destined to extinction in the vast death of the solar system, and that the whole temple of Man's achievement must inevitably be buried beneath the debris of a universe in ruins – all these things, if not quite beyond dispute, are yet

> so nearly certain, that no philosophy that rejects them can hope to stand. Only within the scaffolding of these truths, only on the firm foundation of unyielding despair, can the soul's habitation henceforth be safely built.[1]

But cannot naturalistic thinkers reasonably take a much shorter view in which there are good grounds for a positive outlook on life? Can they not point to human love and goodness; the warmth of human community in family and society; the joys of artistic creation and the enjoyment of beauty; awe, wonder, excitement in response to art, literature and the natural world; the search for truth in the sciences and philosophy; the physical enjoyments of sex, food, sports, entertainment? The list could continue indefinitely.

The answer is 'yes of course' – all these things are real and of immense value. But, we have to ask, to whom are they available? And the answer is that too much of this realm of good experiences is available only to those who have been lucky in the lottery of life. For those who are fortunately situated, experiencing a sufficient level of material prosperity in a stable society, with adequate nutrition and medical care and the level of health usually associated with these, and who can enjoy the fruits of a fairly good education and a fairly rich cultural milieu, it can truly be said that life can be, should be, and (with too many tragic exceptions) is predominantly good. Of course even the fortunate go through bad episodes – illnesses, setbacks, broken relationships, bereavements, and so on. But, for the fortunate, these occur within the context of a predominantly contented life. It is the lack of that context that makes these afflictions unbearable to others. And so the optimistic aspect of a naturalistic worldview rings true to those who have been fortunate, but not to those who have been unfortunate in the circumstances of their birth and environment. Humanists or naturalists can only be regarded as realistic when they are ready to acknowledge this.

More about this in a moment. But as well as straightforward naturalistic humanists, there are also today religious thinkers who teach a spiritually positive outlook which is likewise only an option for a fortunate minority. They urge the non- or anti-realist view that such terms as God, Brahman, Dharmakaya, eternal life, do not refer to realities but express only our own hopes, fears or aspirations. Thus the theologian Don Cupitt holds that God is a personalized expression of our human ideal of love and goodness, and that in so far as we live out the requirements of this ideal, our life becomes instrinsically valuable

1. Bertrand Russell, 1918, pp. 47–8. Referring to this essay in a 1962 letter Russell said, 'My own outlook on the cosmos and on human life is substantially unchanged' (Bertrand Russell, 1969, pp. 172–3).

and hence positively satisfying. So this form of naturalism is life-affirming – in Nietzsche's phrase, a joyful wisdom. The philosopher D.Z. Phillips holds that it is possible from a religious point of view to accept the tragedies and horrors of life with serenity and resignation as the mysterious providence of a loving God, even though there is in fact no such being! The implication of this more religious form of naturalism is just as pessimistic as that of secular naturalism. And it is just as rare for its proponents to recognize this. Don Cupitt, for example, in his recent *Mysticism After Modernity*, is unable to face this implication of his position. He says, '[Hick] describes open non-realism as being elitist and unkind to all those humble folk who need to believe in a posthumous compensation for the wretchedness of this life.'[2] But the point that I had made (and make again here) is simply that naturalism, if true, is very bad news for humanity as a whole. Cupitt ignores this. His message is elitist in that it can only make sense to the fortunate among us. I do not suggest that such a message is therefore false; an elitist philosophy could be the truth about our human situation. But will its proponents please face and acknowledge its grim implications. For no form of naturalism can be other than bad news for humankind when we look beyond our own relatively fortunate circumstances.

NO HOPE FOR THE MANY

There are two main aspects to this. One is actual physical pain and mental and emotional suffering. Here the picture is extremely complex and any attempt to characterize it requires many caveats and qualifications. For example, the fact that for so many centuries people lived without our familiar modern amenities and comforts did not trouble them because they had no conception of electricity, refrigerators, washing machines, cars, aeroplanes, telephone, radio, TV, computers and so on; and likewise we are not troubled by the fact that future generations will no doubt enjoy all sorts of more advanced technology unknown to us. Again, given a basic material sufficiency, happiness is not generally increased by greater wealth. According to Robert Lane, 'almost all of the many studies of quality of life in advanced economies report that above the poverty level, say, for 80 per cent of the population, there is almost no relation between happiness or self-satisfaction and the level of income.'[3] But when we turn to the other 20 per cent below the poverty line the situation is very different. We are not now talking about a lack of relative luxuries but about lack of the calories, proteins and vitamins necessary for the body's growth and

2. Cupitt, p. 40.
3. Lane, p. 12.

health. Today, according to the United Nations' Food and Agriculture Organization, 20 per cent of the world's population, living mostly in Africa, Asia and South America, are chronically undernourished. A 1997 Unicef report showed that half the children in southern Asia and a third of the children in sub-Saharan Africa suffer from malnutrition, and that this is a factor in the deaths of some six million children every year.

But the dark end of the spectrum of human experience covers much more than desperate poverty. Vast numbers of people have experienced one or other or several of a range of conditions that relentlessly grind down the human spirit. These include living as slaves or serfs subject to the arbitrary will of an often unfeeling master; being helpless before the violence of marauding armies; being prey to debilitating disease due to bad diet, polluted water, lack of sanitation; being chronically anxious about one's own and one's family's survival. The twentieth century has included two world wars that have slaughtered tens of millions; brutal dictatorships; widely practised torture, the appalling Jewish Holocaust; Stalin's and Pol Pot's genocides; an uprooted and vulnerable refugee status for millions, and many other horrors. The total number of those killed since 1900 in war and genocide is estimated at about 187 million.[4] It may well be said that nearly all of this is humanity's own collective fault; for war, extreme poverty, exploitation and genocide are humanly performed or humanly permitted evils. As a race we have the know-how to achieve a balance – though on a simpler level than that of the present richest 20 or so per cent – between the world's population and its capacity to feed itself adequately. But whilst this is true, it does not alter the actual situation within which hundreds of millions have lived and are living today.

The second aspect is the lack of fulfilment of the human potential. Here again there are many aspects and many complexities. It has been estimated that the average life span of prehistoric humans was about eighteen years,[5] and in ancient Greece and Rome, some twenty to twenty-two years.[6] In the modern era, to take one particular country, in Britain in 1841 life expectancy was forty years for a man and forty-two for a woman; in 1993, seventy-four for a man and seventy-nine for a woman. The earlier averages were of course affected by very high infant and child mortality. Indeed it is probably true that until fairly recently the majority of people who have ever been born have died before reaching their teens. In such cases the human potential has been cut off very early in its development. But that potential has also remained very largely unfulfilled in millions who have been cut off in war in the full

4. Hobsbawm, p. 12.
5. Dublin, p. 394.
6. Lerner, p. 8.

tide of youth, and only very partially fulfilled in hundreds of millions of others who have even lived into old age.

For quite apart from the sometimes tragic brevity of so many lives, even those who have lived the longest can seldom be said to have arrived, before they die, at a fulfilment of the human potential. We human beings are for so much of the time selfish, narrow-minded, emotionally impoverished, unconcerned about others, often vicious and cruel. But according to the great religions there are wonderfully better possibilities concealed within us. We see the amazing extent of the human potential in the great individuals, the mahatmas or saints, the moral and spiritual leaders and inspirers, and the creative artists of all kinds within every culture. We see aspects of it in innumerable more ordinary, but in some ways extraordinary, men and women whom we encounter in everyday life. We see around us the different levels that the human spirit has reached and we know, from our own self-knowledge and observation and reading, that the generality of us have a very long way to go before we can be said to have become fully human. But if the naturalistic picture is correct, this can never happen. For according to naturalism, the evil that has afflicted so much of human life is final and irrevocable as the victims have ceased to exist.

In the end, the full humanity of each requires the full humanity of all. For we share a common nature and are bound together in a common human project. Religiously this is expressed in the idea of the divine creation of the human race as a single entity – Adam in the Jewish, Christian and Muslim scriptures; or the Hindu idea of the *atman* which we all are in the depths of our being, or again the idea of the universal buddha nature in which we all participate. Morally and politically, this has immense implications. It requires commitment to work for a just society both nationally and internationally: nationally between economic classes, internationally between the developed and the developing nations, and throughout the world between men and women. And yet hundreds of millions have already lived and died in unjust societies in an unjust world. And so in its implications for humanity as a whole, past and present, and in all likelihood future, the naturalistic interpretation of the universe comes as profoundly bad news.

Let me make it clear that I am not suggesting that all this is the fault of the humanists or naturalists! I am pointing out that, with the exception of tough-minded atheists, such as Bertrand Russell, they do not seem to be aware that they are announcing the worst possible news to humanity as a whole. They ought frankly to acknowledge that if they are right the human situation is irredeemably bleak and painful for vast numbers of people. For – if they are right – in the case of that innumerable multitude whose quality of life has been rendered predominantly negative by pain, anxiety, extreme deprivation, oppression, or whose lives have been cut off in childhood or youth, there is no chance of their ever participating in an eventual fulfilment of the human potential. There is no possibility of this vast century-upon-century tragedy being part of a much larger process which leads ultimately to limitless good.

But might it not be said that these evils afflicting the human race are equally bad news for a religious understanding of the universe? How could an all-powerful and all-loving God permit them? That is to pose the question in terms of the anthropomorphic conception of God that we rejected earlier. But we are moving in these chapters towards a different conception of the ultimately Real which sets the problems and possibilities of life in a significantly different light.

3

WINDOWS ON THE TRANSCENDENT

WINDOWS IN THE PHYSICAL SCIENCES

Although (as I argued in chapter 1) the science versus religion debate has been a deplorable mistake in that the dimension of reality which the religions affirm is not such that its existence or non-existence could ever be established by the physical sciences, there are nevertheless significant mysteries at the boundaries of science, 'signals of transcendence', which can open windows in our minds onto the Transcendent. Because these signals are always there we easily overlook them, and it takes a deliberate effort to focus upon them. But let us now make that effort.

We meet one such when we go outside on a cloudless night with the countless multitude of stars shining across the dome of the sky. We look up into the immensity of space, aware that many of the stars that we see are thousands of light years away, and that beyond them are billions more beyond our sight, the galaxies most distant from us being an unimaginable twelve billion or so light years away. It is presently calculated that our own galaxy contains about a hundred thousand million stars, and that the presently observable universe contains about a hundred thousand million other galaxies.[1] Very possibly among those billions of billions of stars in billions of galaxies some have planets on which, like our own, there is life and intelligence, philosophical questioning and spiritual yearning. But either way, whether our earth is unique in this respect or is one of many life-bearing planets, when the lid of cloud is lifted and we see into the vastness of space we cannot help

1. Hawking, p. 37.

being filled with a sense of wonder. This wonder is appropriate and should be cherished. For when we pause to think about it, the universe into which we look is to us a sheer mystery. We believe that it came into existence, at least in the form that we know, with the big bang of some fifteen billion years ago. But what brought it into existence? What caused the big bang? It is indeed a meaningless, because in principle unanswerable, question to ask why there is *something* rather than *nothing*. But it is not meaningless to ask why the something that exists began with the big bang and is this particular exploding universe that includes ourselves. Science has, and can have, no response to the enigma except the entirely proper one, within its own inherent limitations, that this is how we find things to be. This is equally true whether it turns out (depending on the amount of gravity-exerting matter in the universe) that the big bang was an absolute beginning or only one in a perhaps beginningless succession of expansions and contractions; or indeed whether the universe is, according to another recent theory, a self-contained space–time continuum without boundaries and thus without beginning or end.[2] Either way, what we are presented with is a sheer mystery. Given the big bang, or given an infinite series of big bangs, or given a spatio-temporally unbounded universe, the sciences are increasingly able to trace how its present state has come to be. But they cannot explain, even in principle, why there has been a big bang or a series of big bangs or why there is an unbounded universe. From inside our universe we cannot discover by the methods of the physical sciences why it exists with the structure that it has. This remains to us a sheer mystery. And a sheer mystery suggests that there is more to reality than our resources can uncover. A question mark hangs in the air, and no one is entitled to assert that the question has no answer, even if the answer is beyond our comprehension.

WINDOWS IN THE SOCIAL SCIENCES

As well as the physical sciences there are the psychological and social sciences, dealing with the realm of the mind and its expression in human (and non-human) behaviour and society. When these are pursued within the borders of a naturalistic, or physicalist, worldview it has to be assumed either that mental activity is identical with the electro-chemical activity of the brain (mind–brain identity, or central-state materialism); or is a temporary by-product of it (epiphenomenalism); or, according to a more recent idea, that some brain processes have ‘inner’ mental attributes (the dual attribute theory). But each of these options simply

2. Ibid., pp. 140–1.

presents its own reformulation of the mystery of consciousness. To say that my present thinking as I am now writing is continuously correlated with specific activity in the brain is entirely intelligible, and is indeed well established by extensive neurological research. But to say that my present thinking actually *is*, identically and without remainder, a series of electro-chemical events is to say something unintelligible. The mind–brain identity theory holds that my present mental image of a tree actually *is*, as distinguished from being correlated with or caused by, a series of electro-chemical events. But it is impossible to give this any testable meaning that could be either verified or falisfied. And it is no less mystery-making to grant, with epiphenomenalism, that self-consciousness is a non-physical reality, and thus of a different order from the physical, and then to say that it is somehow created by, or is a by-product of, electro-chemical events. This is not a scientific theory but a mythic picture; and as Stephen Toulmin has pointed out, 'the myths of the twentieth century . . . are not so much anthropomorphic as mechanomorphic'.[3] It is no less an appeal to mystery to say that brain events have dual attributes, with mental as well as physical properties. As D.M. Armstrong, himself a proponent of the mind–brain identity theory, has recently commented, 'Although the dual-attribute view is important it inherits the considerable difficulty and confusion which surrounds the philosophical theory of properties. There are many difficulties in giving a satisfactory account of what it is for a thing to have a property, and these difficulties transmit themselves to this sort of theory of the mind–body relationship.'[4] In yet another recent development within the materialist theory of mind, self-consciousness is defined as an aspect of the total functioning of the highly complex human animal. No doubt it is, but this does not tell us what consciousness *is*. Having started as science – tracing the development from primitive automatic responses to the use of language – the theory ends as pure metaphor. Thus Daniel Dennett, one of the most influential contemporary materialist philosophers, concludes that 'our languages permit us to review, recall, rehearse, redesign our own activities, turning our brains into echo chambers of sorts, in which otherwise evanescent processes can hang around and become objects in their own right. Those that persist the longest, acquiring influence as they persist, we call our conscious thoughts.'[5] This is an intriguing poetic image but no more. It does nothing to dissolve the mystery of consciousness. And outside the entirely proper limits of neurological research, that mystery remains in its baffling entirety. It is an aspect of our existence that opens up the possibility of a reality transcending

3. Toulmin, p. 24.
4. Armstrong, p. 491.
5. Dennett, p. 155.

the neutrons and positrons, the energy, mass and gravity that, according to the naturalistic assumption, constitute the entirety of existence.

In recognizing such mysteries, we are encountering what the sociologist Peter Berger has called signals of transcendence, indicating aspects of the universe that fall outside our naturalistic framework of thought. But to be prompted by such signals to a tentative religious response requires a readiness to allow one's naturalistic assumption to be temporarily suspended. This is always an individual and personal matter. For an event or situation that is to one individual a signal of transcendence can pass another by. To quote the Victorian poet Ella Wheeler Wilcox:

> One ship drives east and another drives west
> by the self-same gale that blows.
> 'Tis the set of the sail, and not the gale,
> that determines the way she goes.

For any hint of transcendence meets a blank wall in a mind which automatically interprets everything in naturalistic terms. It is, I believe, this intellectual barrier, rather than any moral or spiritual defect, that ensures that our present western epoch is an age of firmly entrenched scepticism concerning the supra-natural.

WINDOWS IN THE NATURAL WORLD

We encounter other signals of transcendence when we turn attention to our earth with its beauty – both the beauty of the natural world and humanly created beauty in music, painting, dance, sculpture, architecture and so on. We have to resort to metaphor and poetry when we speak of the grandeur of a mountain range or the numinous quality of such vast rock formations as the Grand Canyon; or cloudscapes spread across the sky in their processions of huge changing shapes; or the ocean stretching away to the horizon; or a scarlet sunrise or a slow majestic sunset; or again, flowers, stately trees, bird songs, forests, lakes, waterfalls, the whole ongoing cycle of animal and plant life . . . All of this can induce an awe, a responsiveness, a sense of wonder that is felt as a point of contact between our own spiritual nature and a greater spiritual reality within, around, and beyond us. Perhaps the best-known poetic expression of this is in Wordsworth's 'Lines Composed near Tintern Abbey':

> And I have felt
> A presence that disturbs me with the joy
> Of elevated thoughts; a sense sublime
> Of something far more deeply interfused,
> Whose dwelling is the light of setting suns,
> And the round ocean and the living air,
> And the blue sky, and in the mind of man:
> A motion and a spirit, that impels
> All thinking things, all objects of all thought,
> And rolls through all things.

But once again religious or naturalistic responses to nature depend alike upon the observer. Each is possible, but each stems from a different mental stance, arising from different presuppositions.

WINDOWS IN HUMAN LIFE

Yet other signals of transcendence come through our human neighbours. Love, not meaning here only sexual attraction, but going beyond this to a deep mutual commitment and caring for one another; or the sense of receiving a great gift and responsibility in the birth of a new life; or an encounter with the mysterious boundary when a loved one dies and yet continues to be loved; or co-operation and unity of spirit in a common cause, motivated by a common faith or ideology; or mutual support in the face of danger (in which even the madness of war can bring out qualities of heroism and altruism); or being part of a community in family, tribe, nation, the human race – all of these can evoke in a mind so disposed a sense of reality transcending our human concerns and yet impinging upon us through them, inscribing in our minds a great question mark that silently invites a response.

Even more powerful signals of transcendence come through goodness as embodied both in ordinary and in saintly people. In order to get away from the ecclesiastical associations of the word 'saint' I shall sometimes speak instead of mahatmas, great souls. A mahatma is a person who has undergone – usually very gradually – a transformation from natural self-centredness to a re-centring in the Transcendent, the Holy, the Divine, the Ultimate. The ego point of view has been very largely transcended and the individual has become 'transparent' to a greater reality that is now in varying degrees embodied, or incarnated, in him or her.

The saints are crucial for our understanding of the nature of reality, and I am going to say more about them later. Part V could in fact have been incorporated at this point, and if any readers are inclined to read it next they should feel free to do so.

As we have seen, humans have always tended to experience the natural in terms of the supra-natural, although of course that distinction would not have occurred to our early ancestors. They did not need any special pointers to the Transcendent because it was for them part of the normal fabric of life. But today most of us do need special pointers. And we can find them above all in the mahatmas, the great spirits of all traditions. It remains possible that the lives of those great spirits are based on delusion. But if we identify, and then discount, the pervasive naturalistic assumption of our culture, it is equally possible that the saints are not mistaken but are in fact more closely in touch with reality than the rest of us. In the end we are taking a cognitive and spiritual risk when we accept them as guides worthy to be followed, and equally so when we dismiss them as self-deceivers. The risk is, on the one hand, that of fooling ourselves by wishful thinking, and on the other hand, that of shutting out of our consciousness, at least for now, an immensely important fifth dimension of reality.

4

THE KEY TO UNDERSTANDING

PERCEPTION AS INTERPRETATION

The religious ambiguity of the universe, such that our experiencing it religiously or naturalistically depends upon our own response to it, is of a piece with ambiguity at all levels of meaning. At this point we enter the field of epistemology, which asks, 'How do we know – anything?' And – as Immanuel Kant showed in one of the most influential books of philosophy ever written, the *Critique of Pure Reason* – an answer to this question is also by implication an answer to the question 'What can we know?' For what we can know, and in what form we can know it, depends upon the scope and functioning of our own cognitive equipment.

The principle of critical realism, of which Kant laid the groundwork (although the term itself is a twentieth-century invention), is that awareness is not a simple and straightforward matter of the environment imprinting itself just as it is upon our consciousness. Kant argued that the innate structure of the mind determines what we can know. This principle applies far beyond sense perception, but for the moment we are looking at this basic level of awareness. One does not have to adopt Kant's entire complex theory to be convinced by his basic thesis that so far from being a passive receptor, the mind is continuously active in perception. And cognitive psychology has since shown in some detail how it is busy performing a complex, many-levelled operation of selecting, grouping, extrapolating, excluding, projecting, relating and imposing its own interpretive categories, a process that goes on unconsciously all the time with only the outcome appearing in consciousness.

The basic fact that the mind imposes order and meaning upon the data it receives is true at all levels of awareness, physical, moral, aesthetic and religious. I refer to these as levels or layers of meaning because the ethical and the aesthetic presuppose, and are mediated through, the physical, whilst the religious can presuppose and be mediated through each or all of the others, whereas the reverse does not hold. We shall be mainly interested here in the religious meaning both of limited situations and of the unlimited situation which we call the universe. But because the same epistemological structure runs through the entire hierarchy of forms of awareness, it will be useful first to look briefly at the other levels.

Our awareness of the material world requires physical receptors, the five senses which enable us to see, hear, feel, taste and smell. These reveal our environment to us, but only those selected aspects of it in relation to which we have to act and react. For in selecting, our senses exclude much more than they let in. They have developed to aid our survival as organisms occupying our particular evolutionary niche, and they accordingly function as meshes through which only a certain range of signals can pass. As Brian Magee puts it, 'If we think in terms of the metaphor of catching things in the network of experience, [the categories of thought] are the meshes of our net. Only what can be caught in them is available to us. Anything that passes through them untouched will not be picked up by us, and neither will whatever falls outside our nets altogether.'[1] For example, within the known electromagnetic spectrum extending from cosmic rays as short as four ten-thousand-millionths of an inch, to radio waves as long as eighteen miles, our senses only respond to those between sixteen and thirty-two millionths of an inch. We are likewise deaf to a vast range of acoustic stimuli, and insensitive to the great majority of chemical differences. We thus inhabit a humanly selected and simplified version of our environment. If the whole range of light waves affected us we would be unable to distinguish objects affecting our survival. If every sound wave registered in our consciousness, we would be so confused by the universal cacophony as to be unable to react to the sounds that we need to hear. And if, for example, instead of seeing water as the continuous shiny substance that we can drink, we perceived it as a cloud of electrons in rapid swirling motion, and the glass that holds it as a mass of brilliantly coloured crystals, themselves composed of particles in violent activity, we would soon die of thirst. We can only live in the

1. Magee, p. 182.

distinctively human environment registered by our sensors, and this differs in many ways from that of other mammals, insects, birds and fishes.

The senses having thus registered their minute selection of the mass of information flowing through and around us all the time, the mind then processes it, organizing it into our familiar environment. For example, we see three-dimensionally, although the light waves falling upon the eye only directly affect the (almost) flat surface of the retina. But the mind/brain immediately converts this information into our familiar three-dimensional experience by a continuous set of complex calculations based on a variety of clues, including the disparity between the images they receive, the angle of convergence of the two eyes, which are converted into an awareness of depth, and at greater distances by the position of images in the visual field (the higher the more distant). Although this is normally done habitually and unconsciously, our ability to see depth and judge distances is an acquired skill made possible by correlating touch with movement in space. And so peoples living in dense forests who never experience objects at a distance, when brought onto an open plain, have been found to see distant things at first as small instead of as distant. They have not had the experience of moving towards them and correlating their position towards the top of the visual field with the time and effort needed to walk towards them.[2] Again, in recognizing a building, we see it as three-dimensional, with depth and a back as well as the flat side actually visible to us. We are extrapolating in this way all the time, guided by the memory-deposits of our previous experience of moving about in a three-dimensional world.

Our awareness of the physical environment is thus an extremely complex process. It is also normally a successful process, otherwise the species would not have survived. For on this level the world has taught *homo sapiens*, on pain of death, to interpret correctly. If we failed to recognize the significance for us of the hard rock, or the steep cliff, or the predatory tiger, or the oncoming car, the world would eliminate us. And so at this level we have very little cognitive freedom. Each species has been programmed through the evolutionary process to interpret the signals of the physical environment correctly as they affect that particular life form. And although in the case of humanity there are some cultural differences, these do not affect the basic fact that we have very little cognitive freedom at this level of awareness. The physical environment forces itself upon our attention as vulnerable creatures occupying our particular place on the macro–micro scale.

2. Gregory, p. 162.

COGNITIVE FREEDOM . . .

However, our cognitive freedom increases in relation to the value-laden aspects of our environment. For we are not only animal organisms but also persons, and in a phrase of John Macmurray, personality is essentially inter-personality. We can only become persons through interaction with others. And at the personal level of awareness, situations often carry a practical meaning that transcends their purely material character. Suppose I am driving along a country lane and find a crashed car with its occupant severely injured and crying out for help. At the purely physical level of awareness this is a particular configuration of metal, plastic, oil, flesh, blood, and various sounds and smells. As such, it has no moral quality whatever. But as a moral being I am also aware of another level of significance. I am conscious of a claim upon me to try to help the injured person. An ethical meaning thus superimposes itself upon the physical meaning of the situation. In comparable circumstances people anywhere in the world are automatically aware of this, for a moral capacity appears to be part of our nature as social beings. As the Chinese philosopher Mencius wrote in the third century BCE, 'every man has a heart that pities others, for the heart of every man is moved by fear or horror, tenderness and mercy, if he suddenly sees a child about to fall into a well. And this is not because he wishes to make friends with the child's father or mother or to win praise from his countryfolk and friends, nor because the child's cries hurt him. This shows that . . . no man is without a heart for right and wrong.'[3] There are, it is true, a small number of individuals who for some reason – most probably a destructively distorting upbringing – seem to be completely amoral, devoid of any ethical sense. But the normal human being operates most of the time on the ethical, or social, as well as on the physical level of awareness.

And yet as well as feeling the moral claims of others upon us, we are also animal organisms genetically motivated to self-preservation and self-enhancement. We live in a continuing tension between the instinct to treat only ourselves, or a small kinship group with which we identify ourselves, as ends, and the ethical requirement to treat *all* persons equally as ends in themselves; and it is within this tension that we exercise our moral freedom. In this awareness of the ethical meaning of our life situations we exercise a much greater degree of cognitive freedom than in relation to the physical environment. We can let in or shut out the moral claims upon us created by the existence of other persons and the situations in which we interact with them. We do so in

3. Lyall, p. 48.

many different ways and degrees. A very common way is to deceive ourselves by avoiding becoming fully conscious of the claims of conscience. We reconceptualize the situation by marshalling contrary considerations, de-emphasizing and marginalizing unwelcome aspects, highlighting and giving greater weight to others, and generally setting the matter in a different and more acceptable light.

There is a psychologically brilliant picture of this in the second chapter of Jane Austen's *Sense and Sensibility*. Mr John Dashwood, a wealthy country squire, is a narrow-minded and selfish man with an even more narrow-minded and selfish wife. John Dashwood's father had, at his death, left behind a widow by his second marriage (John's mother having been the first wife) and her three children, who are thus John's stepmother and half-sisters. As the father was dying he asked his son to look after them. The widow herself has an income for life, but the daughters have nothing. At first Mr Dashwood intends to give them £1,000 each, this being what he can afford without any great sacrifice. However as he discusses the matter with his wife all sorts of problems emerge. So on second thoughts he decides that a small annuity might be better. But then, as his wife points out, the daughters might live long enough for the annuity to amount to more than the originally proposed £1,000. Eventually, after a long process of whittling down, it seems best not to give them any money at all, but rather to do such neighbourly kindnesses as helping them to move house and sending them occasional presents of fish and game and the like – this, he and his wife finally conclude, must be the sort of thing his father had in mind. And so John Dashwood gradually arrives at the selfish conclusion to which he was already half-consciously disposed.

This is a small-scale example of the familiar process of moral self-deception in which we all sometimes engage. The self-deception takes place on a much larger and more dangerous scale when Bosnians and Serbs in the former Yugoslavia, or Jews and Arabs in Israel–Palestine, or Catholics and Protestants in Northern Ireland, selectively forget aspects of their common history whilst vividly remembering others, with disastrous results for everyone. We see it again on a large scale when many Germans in the late 1930s, accepting the Nazi propaganda, began to see their Jewish fellow-citizens as sub-human enemies of civilization; or when most white South Africans in the apartheid era saw Blacks as inherently inferior, so that it was proper to repress and exploit them, falsifications which continue today in many other places as anti-Semitism and racial prejudice. Those who carry out policies of genocide and 'ethnic cleansing' generally seem to do so with a largely clear conscience because they are only obeying orders, or are exterminating dangerous social parasites, or wreaking a just vengeance, or are simply being realistic in a difficult and complex situation for which they are not responsible. So whilst a moral sense is innate, we nevertheless exercise a fateful degree of cognitive freedom on this social and distinctively human level of awareness.

The other side of the coin, however, is that without this dangerous freedom we would not be moral beings. Our ethical decisions, instead of expressing our own responsible choices, would be determined by an inner programming. To be human is to have a fateful cognitive freedom proportional to the scale of the moral claims and spiritual opportunities that life mediates to us.

. . . IN RELIGIOUS AWARENESS

We turn now to the religious awareness which (according to our big picture) is superimposed upon physical and moral awareness. Here our cognitive freedom is at its maximum. Although we seem to have an innate tendency to experience the natural in terms of the supra-natural, we are nevertheless under no compulsion to do so. This is why, in a culture dominated by the naturalistic assumption, it can seem so obvious to so many people that the supposed objects of worship and foci of religious meditation can only be figments of the imagination.

Our essential personal freedom is preserved by the epistemic distance – a distance not in space but in knowledge – between ourselves and the divine reality. We saw in the last chapter how a variety of signals can open a door to the Transcendent in receptive minds, and we shall see in later chapters some of the forms that this awareness takes, drawing us through that inner door. But let us first ask, 'Why this freedom?' Would we not be better off if the supra-natural were overwhelmingly evident to us?

If our big picture is basically correct, the ultimately Real can only enter our consciousness in the range of forms made possible by our own conceptual systems. Because we are persons, much the most common form is deity, a divine Thou with whom a relationship of devotion and mutual love is possible. In terms of the monotheistic traditions first, why should not the personal divine presence be unmistakably evident to us? The answer is that in order for us to exist as autonomous finite persons in God's presence, God must not be compulsorily evident to us. To make space for human freedom, God must be *deus absconditus*, a hidden God – hidden and yet readily found by those who are willing to exist in the divine presence, accepting the divine claim on the living of their lives. If we were from the beginning set 'face to face' with God we would never be able to make a free response to the Deity. There could be no question of freely loving and choosing to worship One whose very presence utterly overwhelms us. 'Only because of the intensity of His manifestation is He veiled, and only because of the sublimity of His Light is He hidden from view', says the Sufi Ibn 'Ata'Illah.[4] We must, as finite and imperfect creatures, have the freedom partially or wholly to shut God out of our lives as well as to welcome God into them.

In the case of non-theistic awareness of the ultimate, the same basic principle holds, although in a different form. According to T.S. Eliot in 'Burnt Norton', 'Humankind [in our 'fallen' or pre-enlightened state] cannot bear very much reality'. This is affirmed in the Buddhist *Bardo Thodol*, where it is said that at the moment of death the soul confronts the clear light of reality. Those few who are able to embrace, or be embraced by, the light are immediately united with the ultimately Real. But the great majority, who are not ready for this, have to continue further round the cycle of rebirths.[5] For generally, both in Buddhist and Hindu thought, enlightenment, liberation, awakening, whilst it may finally occur in a moment of time, only happens at the end of a long process of spiritual growth. It cannot be forced. The readiness has to come from within.

This is why religious awareness does not share the compulsory character of sense awareness. Our physical environment must force itself upon our attention if we are to survive within it. But our supra-natural environment, the fifth dimension of the universe, must *not* be forced upon our attention if we are to exist within it as free spiritual beings.

According to our big picture, this cognitive freedom does not express a divine plan or intention – for these are human constructs – but is simply an aspect of the spiritual dimension of the universe. To be a person is, amongst many other things, to be a (relatively) free agent in relation to those aspects of reality that lay us under a moral or spiritual claim.

But this vital cognitive freedom has the consequence not only that we are not compelled to be aware of our supra-natural environment, but also that when we are, this awareness can take not only appropriate but also intensely inappropriate and distorted forms. We can deceive ourselves religiously as well as morally, as we shall see in chapter 17.

4. Ibn 'Ata'Illah, p. 88.
5. Evans-Wentz, p. 89.

5

TURNING THE CRITICAL REALIST KEY

THE TRANSFORMATION OF INFORMATION

In the language of cybernetics 'information' does not mean, as in ordinary conversation, items of information embodied in propositions, such as that the London train leaves at 8.10, or that fighting has broken out in the Balkans. In the cybernetic sense, every impact of the environment upon us constitutes information,[1] and what is interesting about this, for our present purpose, is the way in which information is transformed or translated in the course of appropriating it.

We have already noted that light waves impacting the retina of the eye are transformed, through a complex process, into our conscious experience of seeing the world as we humans perceive it. Light waves are not themselves coloured, but their impact is transformed within us into the experience of colour vision. Sound waves, which are not themselves noises, are transformed by our receptive apparatus into the experience of hearing noise. In broadcasting, the sound waves that the speaker emits in a studio are transformed into radio waves, which are then translated back by our receiver into sound waves, which we translate into heard sounds. Likewise TV waves are transformed into lines and dots on the screen, which we then transform into the experience of seeing coloured pictures. Consciousness of our environment always involves a continuous transformation of information from one mode into another.

Different life forms, with their different sense organs and differently developed structures of consciousness, experience the world differently.

1. See Wiener, 1968.

For some (including we humans) the dominant sense, providing our normal framework of consciousness, is sight – a larger area of our brain is dedicated to processing visual than other stimuli. But for others (such as the mole) the dominant sense is smell, and for yet others (such as the bat) it is sound. Insects operate in terms of environmental features too small for large animals, such as the elephant, to be aware of them. The ant is not aware of the elephant, and the elephant is not aware of the ant, although both are part of the same vast network of life. And within this network the same virtual infinity of information is reduced in different ways by different selective mechanisms, and transformed into fields of consciousness with different structures and qualities.

That the world is perceived in different ways by differently constituted observers is thus well established. To take us a little nearer to the way in which the Transcendent is experienced by some as an all-powerful cosmic Person and by others as an infinite non-personal reality, consider the difference between, say, the table that we experience as a solid, hard, brown, partly shiny, enduring three-dimensional object, and the account of it given by the physicists as mostly empty space in which infinitesimal packages of discharging energy are moving about at a great pace. None of these have any of the properties of the table that we perceive – neither colour, weight, extension, density, nor even fixed position. Let us now add other, non-human observers – say angels, Proto-Centureans, Meta-Vulcans, Ultra-Betazoids – each species being equipped with different sensors and processing the input of those sensors through their own different conceptual systems. As a result, each perceives something different from what is perceived by the others, and also from the table that we perceive. Here is something very distantly analogous to the situation envisaged in our big picture, in which people formed by the different religious traditions become aware of the Transcendent in significantly different ways. The analogy, however, breaks down – as any analogy does when pressed far enough – because it cannot encompass the idea of ineffable, or transcategorial, reality.

The various God-figures and the various non-personal foci of religious meditation are, according to our big picture, different transformations of the impact upon us of the ultimately Real. But that reality, in itself beyond the range of conscious human experience, does not fit into the systems of concepts in terms of which we are able to think. It is what it is, but what it is cannot be described in human categories. We can only describe its 'impact' upon us, as this is filtered by our limited receptivity and translated in terms of our conceptual systems into one of the personal or non-personal 'objects' of religious experience.

'Impact' appears here in quotation marks because it is not being used in its literal or dictionary sense as one solid body colliding with and thus impacting another. I am using it as it functions within our big picture, according to which there is an aspect of us that is 'in tune' with the Transcendent. This aspect is referred to as the image of God within us; or as the divine spark spoken of by Plotinus, Pseudo-Dionysius, Eckhart, Ruusbroec, Suso, Tauler and many other Christian mystics; or as 'that of God in every man'; or as the *atman* which in our deepest nature we all are; or as our 'true self', the 'selfless self', or as the universal buddha nature within us. It is this aspect of our being that is affected by the ultimately Real to the extent that we are open to that reality. The forms that this awareness takes are human constructions created from material within the inherited imagery of a religious tradition and from each individual's life story and psychological make-up. If our tradition has conditioned us to think of the Transcendent in personal terms, and to practise I–Thou prayer and worship, we shall be conscious of a personal divine presence, or a divine call, claim, leading or revelation. And so Christian mystics have received visions and/or auditions, seeing and hearing the figure of Christ on the cross, or shining in heavenly glory, or of the Virgin Mary or one of the saints as mediators of God's presence. Within the neighbouring Islamic world, mystics have their own different visions. Al-Ghazali says of a certain stage of the inner path, 'The mystics in their waking state now behold angels and the spirits of the prophets; they hear these speaking to them and are instructed by them.'[2] Devout Hindus sometimes see visions of the gods. For example, one tells how, as a fourteen-year-old walking home one day from school, the lord Krishna met him coming out of a rice field, and embraced him. 'Since then', he says, 'I had no other thought but to serve only Krishna, and I became a sadhu.'[3] But if, on the other hand, our tradition has taught us to think of the Ultimate in non-personal terms and to practise a non-I–Thou type of meditation, our religious awareness will take one of the quite different forms described in eastern mystical literature. In the chapters on religious experience and on mysticism we shall look at examples of both types of awareness.

The critical realist principle – that there are realities external to us, but that we are never aware of them as they are in themselves, but always as they appear to us with our particular cognitive machinery and conceptual resources – is thus a vital clue to understanding what is happening in the different forms of religious experience.

2. Al-Ghazali, 1994, p. 64.
3. Klostermaier, p. 31.

CRITICAL REALISM

At this point it may be useful to clarify the distinction between non-realism, naive realism and critical realism. If we take as an example (to be described in chapter 13) Julian of Norwich's visions of Christ and her hearing him speak of the limitless divine love, the non-realist interpretation is that the entire experience was a self-induced hallucination – not in any sense a revelation, not an expression of the 'impact' of the Transcendent upon her. The naive realist interpretation – which was probably her own understanding of her experiences – is that the living Christ was personally present to her, producing the visions that she saw, and uttering in Middle English the words that she heard. But the critical realist interpretation, which I believe to be correct, is that she had become so open to the transcendent, within her and beyond her, that it flooded into her consciousness in the particular form provided by her Christian faith. She was aware of the goodness – from our human point of view – of the Real as the unconditional love of a personal God, expressed in the characteristic fourteenth-century form of the bodily agonies of Jesus on the cross. Her experience was thus a genuine contact with the Transcendent, but clothed in her case in a Christian rather than a Hindu, Buddhist, Islamic or other form. In different symbolic worlds, what was for Julian a divine love expressed in the voluntary sufferings of Christ is expressed in other modes. It is known, for example, in the figure of Vishnu who, in the *Bhagavad Gita*, is 'as a father with his son, a friend with his friend, a lover with his beloved'.[4] In Buddhism the ultimate Dharmakaya, in itself beyond human conceiving, is expressed in the infinite compassion of the Buddhas. And the ninety-nine names, or attributes, of Allah in the Qur'an include love, beneficence, mercy, forgiveness, forbearance, generosity, compassion. The mystics of Islam have accordingly been intensely conscious of the divine love. 'Love is affection without bounds,' says Rumi. 'Hence it is said that Love is truly God's attribute, while it is the attribute of His servants only in a derivative sense. . . Know that Love and Affection are Attributes of God.'[5]

In these and many other ways the impact of the transcendent reality upon us receives different 'faces' and voices as it is processed by our different religious mentalities.

Religious experience, then, occurs in many different forms, and the critical realist interpretation enables us to see how these may nevertheless be different authentic responses to the Real. But they may also not be. They may instead be human self-delusion. Or they may be

4. XI, 44; Bolle, p. 141.
5. Chittick, p. 196.

a mixture of both. And so a critical stance in relation to them is essential. We shall come to the important question of criteria of authenticity in chapter 18. But whether or not (or to what degree) authentic, the forms taken by religious experience are provided by the conceptual equipment of the experiencer. It was a brilliant insight of Thomas Aquinas that 'Cognita sunt in cognoscente secundum modum cognoscentis' – 'Things known are in the knower according to the mode of the knower.'[6] This fundamental epistemological principle has a wider application than Aquinas himself intended. For the mode of the knower has been differently formed within the various religious traditions, producing our different awarenesses of the divine. The fourteenth-century Sufi Al-Junayd expressed the same principle more poetically when he said, 'The colour of the water is that of its container'; and Al-'Arabi later added, 'If [one] knew Junayd's saying, "The water takes its colour from the vessel containing it", he would not interfere with other men's beliefs, but would perceive God in every form of belief.'[7] For the different traditions are the containers that give its recognizable colour (i.e. character) to human awareness of the Transcendent.

When we see the different religious cultures as diverse contexts in terms of which the universal presence of the Ultimate is differently appropriated, we cease to be perplexed by their apparently conflicting teachings. For it is possible to use very different sets of concepts and images, with very different communal and historical resonances, to speak about the benign (from our human point of view) character of the Ultimate, about the total claim and gift that its presence constitutes for our lives, and about the inner transformation from self-centredness towards a radically new orientation centred in the ultimately Real.

6. *Summa Theologiae*, II/II, 1, 2; p. 1057.
7. Nicholson, p. 88.

PART II

THE MEANING OF LIFE

6

THE RELIGIOUS MEANING OF LIFE

PRACTICAL MEANING

The notion of the meaning of life is initially very vague. In order to be useful it has to be specified further, and different people will quite reasonably do this in different ways. So I must say in what sense I shall be using the expression. First, I am not referring to semantic meaning, the meaning of words and sentences, but what for want of a better term I shall call practical meaning – a meaning which makes a direct difference to the ways in which, actually or potentially, we act and react in the world. The practical meaning for us of a thing, event or situation expresses itself in the dispositional state – the readiness to act in one way rather than others – which it evokes in us as a result of our identifying or misidentifying it as being that particular kind of thing, event or situation.

This 'dispositional' element in belief was first identified by John Locke in his *Essay Concerning Human Understanding* (1690). He pointed out that most of our beliefs are 'habitual' or stored rather than 'actual' or occurrent.[1] For example, as I walk around the house I believe that the floor beneath me is solid and able to bear my weight. But I do not go about consciously affirming this proposition in my mind. My believing it is shown by my confidently walking about the room rather than anxiously testing the floor with each step in case the next section should give way. And much the greater part of anyone's belief system is made up, not of occurrent, but of stored beliefs which consist in persisting behavioural dispositions. Minimally then, to believe any

1. Book IV, chapter 1, section 8.

proposition, *p*, is to be in a dispositional state to behave in relevant circumstances on the basis that *p* is true; and this holds whether or not I have also consciously formulated and assented to *p*.

It follows that we see from people's actions more reliably than from their words what they really believe. If someone says that he can walk on burning coals without being hurt, but when challenged always finds a reason not to try, we deduce that he does not really believe what he says he believes. It also follows that not only humans have beliefs. Belief is 'something that can be pre-intellectual, and can be displayed in the behaviour of animals'.[2] The difference is that at the human level we are able to crystallize our beliefs in language, and so to contemplate them, consciously assent to them, and criticize them. We are likewise able to pretend, even to ourselves, to have beliefs that we do not have, something that the other animals cannot do. Some of them can deceive others, but not (we presume) themselves.

The idea of practical meaning is linked with this dispositional aspect of belief. An object's meaning for us consists in the actual or potential difference that it makes to us, that is to say, in what we find it appropriate to do or avoid doing in relation to that object. To identify something as an *x*, or in other words to believe it to be an *x*, is to be in a dispositional state to behave in ways that (we think) are appropriate to its being an *x* rather than something else. As a trivial example, I believe that what I am holding is a tennis ball if it is true of me that I will treat it, in circumstances in which the issue arises, as a tennis ball rather than, say, as a cricket ball or a hand grenade.

Practical meaning is always both species- and culture-relative: a kitten might see the tennis ball as something to play with, and stone-age persons, transported here in a time-machine, would not have the concepts of tennis or tennis ball and would accordingly see the same object as something to be treated quite differently. So the basic epistemological truth discussed in chapter 4 comes into view again, namely that the perceiver contributes significantly to the character and meaning that things have for him or her.

Let us now move on from objects to situations. A situation is a complex of objects which has its own meaning over and above the sum of the individual meanings of its constituent elements. A situation is formed by our selective attention operating on a higher level than in object-awareness – higher in the logical sense that it presupposes object-awareness – and human life is ordinarily lived on this higher level of situational meaning. If, for example, I am reading a paper to a philosophical gathering, the meaning of the situation for those present

2. Bertrand Russell, 1948, p. 161.

is such that we all behave in ways appropriate to its being a session of an academic conference. I read my paper aloud and the audience politely listens whilst thinking up difficult questions to raise in the discussion period. But if the stone-age persons I imagined earlier suddenly materialized among us, they would not find the same meaning in this physical configuration. For them it would constitute a very different situation because they would not have such concepts as conference, university, academic paper, philosophy, and so on, that are constituents of our cultural world.

I want in due course to move from limited situations like this to the unlimited situation of our existence in the universe. But first I want to stress again the basic fact of the perceiver's contribution to all our awareness of meaning. During the two centuries since Kant this has become increasingly widely accepted. Its significance for the epistemology of religion was first suggested to me by Wittgenstein's disciple, John Wisdom, in his lectures in Cambridge shortly after Wittgenstein's death in 1951 – although neither Wisdom nor Wittgenstein would necessarily have approved of the use that I want to make of it. In the *Philosophical Investigations* (Part II, section xi) Wittgenstein discusses what he called 'seeing as', as when you see an ambiguous picture first in one way and then in another. He used as an example the well-known duck–rabbit picture, which can be seen as a duck's head facing left or as a rabbit's head facing right. It seems natural to expand the concept of 'seeing as' into that of 'experiencing as', using all our senses together. John Wisdom took this further. Attending his lectures was a strange experience. Bored stiff, one would listen to his apparently formless and unprepared meanderings for weeks on end, and then suddenly he would say something so excitingly illuminating that one had to keep coming back for more. For example, he once spoke of doing metaphysics as being like seeing the pattern in a puzzle picture, like when one suddenly sees a face in what had been an apparently random scattering of lines and dots. As was typical with Wisdom's lectures, this was a tantalizingly suggestive throw-out remark. To me it was a clue to the nature of religious awareness and hence of the religious understanding of the meaning of life.

RELIGIOUS MEANING

The way in which we inhabit the universe – not necessarily from day to day but in the overall tenor of our lives – is a reflection of the character that we believe and hence experience it to have. And so the meaning-of-life question is, 'What is the nature of this universe in which, and as part of which, we find ourselves?' Above all, is its ultimate nature, so far as we humans are concerned, benign, hostile, or indifferent? I say 'so far as we humans are concerned' because we are minute fragments of the universe, and it seems very unlikely that we have the conceptual equipment to comprehend the nature of reality as a whole. We may however be able to comprehend its nature is as it affects us. And, as John Stuart Mill said, 'If to know authentically in what order of things, under what government of the universe it is our destiny to live, were not useful, it is difficult to imagine what could be considered so. Whether a person is in a pleasant or in an unpleasant place, a palace or a prison, it cannot be otherwise than useful to him to know where he is.'[3]

Each of the great world religions offers a comprehensive conception of the universe, and in so far as such pictures are believed and are built into our dispositional structure, they automatically affect the way in which the believer lives. They determine the overall meaning of life for us. We are of course talking here of genuine beliefs, beliefs on which we are prepared to act – what Cardinal Newman called real, as distinguished from notional, assents.[4]

As a relatively trivial example of our dispositional state affecting the way in which we experience our environment, consider the following imagined situation. I am in a strange building, and walking by mistake into a large room I find that a militant secret society is meeting there. Many of the members are armed, and as they take me for a fellow member I think it expedient to acquiesce in the role. Plans are being discussed for the violent overthrow of the constitution. The whole situation is alarming in the extreme. Its meaning for me is such that I am extremely apprehensive. Then I suddenly become aware in the dim light above us of a gallery in which there are silently operating cameras, and I realize that I have walked by accident onto the set of a film. This realization consists in a changed awareness of my immediate situation. Until now I had automatically experienced it as 'real life' and as demanding considerable circumspection on my part. Now I experience it as having a quite different significance. But at ground level there is no change in the course of events; the meeting of the secret society proceeds just as before. However my new awareness of the more comprehensive situation alters my experience of the more immediate one. It now has a new meaning for me such that I am in a very different dispositional state in relation to it. For example, if one of the 'conspirators' noticed my arrival and threateningly pointed his gun at me, I might act as though terrified but would not actually be so.

3. Mill, p. 69.
4. Newman, chapter 4.

This is not an adequate analogy for our religious situation because the cameras and their operators in the balcony are more of the same kind of reality as the set and the actors on the floor. But it may nevertheless help to make intelligible the suggestion that I am making. This is that the understanding of our lives as taking place in the presence of, and as grounded in, the Divine, the Transcendent, the ultimately Real, can make a profound difference to our sense of the meaning of our life now.

COSMIC OPTIMISM

'Cosmic optimism' is not a term that figures in the distinctive vocabulary of any of the world faiths. It is however a generalization of their distinctive affirmations about the Transcendent in its relation to human beings. The great monotheisms affirm that 'as the heavens are high above the earth, so great is [the God of Israel's] steadfast love towards those who fear him';[5] or that the heavenly Father of the New Testament is a limitlessly loving God; or that the Allah self-revealed in the Qur'an is ever gracious and merciful. Most Hindus are also, either ultimately or penultimately, theists; and the *Bhagavad Gita* says of Vishnu that he is 'the great Lord of the universe and friend of all beings'.[6] But turning to the non-theistic faiths, advaitic Hinduism affirms that in our deepest nature we already are the infinite reality of Brahman, but have yet to become what we truly are. Again, in a more totally non-theistic faith, in Buddhism it is affirmed that our true nature is one with the universal buddha nature of the universe, and again we have to become what in a sense we already are. In both cases they teach that we can, whether suddenly or gradually, whether on earth or in heaven, whether in this life or through many lives, receive or achieve the salvific transformation into a new relationship to, or a newly discovered identity with, that ultimate reality.

Each tradition draws a radical distinction between the state from which we desire to be saved or released, or out of which we need to awaken, and the limitlessly better state to which it shows a way. There is a deeply pessimistic view of our present predicament, combined with a highly optimistic view of what is ultimately open to us. The pessimism understands ordinary human life to be fallen into sin and guilt, or lived in disobedience and alienation from God, or caught in the unreality of spiritual blindness (*avidya*) and the consequent round of anxious suffering existence (*samsara*). But there is also the affirmation of a limitlessly better possibility available to us because the Ultimate is, from

5. Psalm 103:11.
6. V, 22; Bolle, p. 69.

our human point of view, benign. By divine grace or divine mercy, or by a gradual transcending of the ego point of view and a realization of our own deepest nature, we can attain or receive our highest good. And in so far as this limitlessly better state is said to be available to everyone, the message of each of the great religions constitutes good news for humankind.

I mean by the cosmic optimism of the world faiths then, that in each case, if their conception of the nature of the universe is basically correct, we can be glad to be part of it and can rejoice in and be thankful for our present human existence. For the meaning of life is such that we can have an ultimate trust and confidence, even – at least in principle – in life's darkest moments of suffering and sorrow.

However we need at this point to draw a distinction like that drawn by Wilfred Cantwell Smith between what he calls faith and what he calls the cumulative traditions.[7] I do not in fact think that 'faith' is the best term for what he is referring to, namely the actual response to God, or to the Transcendent, that informs a person's life. I shall speak instead of life responses to the Transcendent, distinguishing this from religion in the external and institutional sense in which it is studied by anthropologists, sociologists, politicians and historians. The distinction becomes evident when we note that it makes no difference for these disciplines whether or not God exists or whether or not there is, more broadly, a higher and ultimate spiritual reality. It is sufficient that individuals and communities have believed that there is. In other words, the 'scientific' or 'objective' study of religion is the non-religious study of religion. This is an entirely legitimate, indeed a fascinating and extremely valuable, enterprise. But if we discount our pervasive naturalistic assumption, the religious interpretation of religion is no less legitimate. The two are only rivals when the methodological naturalism of the sciences is elevated into a dogma. Religion as observed by the social sciences then becomes the entire subject. It thus actually bypasses religion as participated in by religious people.

There is however generally a wide gap between the meaning of life as taught by our religion and the immediate concrete meanings in terms of which we live our daily lives. It does not follow from the fact that our religion teaches a form of cosmic optimism that we, as believers, are always in a cheerful and optimistic frame of mind! Nor does the belief that human existence is ultimately good mean that our present self-centred, unredeemed, illusion-bound existence is good, even though there is a great deal of good within it. Pain and suffering, starvation and disease, war and genocide, repression and exploitation are real, and

7. Smith, 1978.

they effectively blot out the ultimate goodness of life for very many people for much or even most of their lives. That human existence is good means that it is a process or project leading to a limitlessly good future. But although the religions explicitly teach this, probably the majority of men and women of each faith live their daily lives devoid of any such thought. Belief in the goodness of the Transcendent from our human point of view remains, for most people most of the time, a notional rather than a real belief, although it is one that may come vividly to life in some moment of crisis.

Further, the teachings of the great traditions contain elements that conflict with belief in a wholly good outcome of the human project, so that the 'cosmic optimism' thesis has to be qualified. It has been believed within the monotheistic faiths, and strongly so in the medieval period, that the large majority of the human race are destined to an everlasting hell, either because they are outside the church, or because they are infidels, or pagans. Furthermore, within each tradition wicked individuals who die unrepentant have been believed to be consigned to eternal damnation, so that for them no redemption is possible. Today, within each religion, there is a large fundamentalist wing that retains this medieval view. But we have to recognize that any teaching of the exclusion of a proportion of men and women from the fulfilment of the human project is a form of cosmic pessimism, and also that there is such a strand within each of the great monotheisms.

When we speak of the ultimate goodness of the universe from our human point of view, we are talking about the total character of a reality which far exceeds what we can presently see and the physical sciences can ever discover. For it is clear from the evils that afflict humanity, and from the equally evident fact that the human potential is seldom fulfilled in this present life, that if the creative process is ever to reach its completion it must continue beyond this life, more about which in chapter 26. Thus the faith that, in the words of Julian of Norwich, 'all shall be well, and all shall be well, and all manner of thing shall be well' presupposes a structure of reality which makes this possible.

The great traditions and their sub-traditions have developed different pictures of this structure, and of the final fulfilment, as heaven, paradise, union with God, the beatific vision; or an absorption into Brahman in which separate ego existence has been transcended; or nirvana, or the universal realization of the buddha nature of all things. But it is important to note that the idea of a good outcome of the life process does not require that any one of these specific conceptions will turn out to be accurate. Indeed thoughtful people within each tradition have always been aware that the scriptural accounts of heaven/paradise are painted in a poetic imagery that points beyond our present imaginations; or in the eastern faiths, that the final unity that is sought is, once again, not thinkable in earthly terms.

There are then, two closely related conditions that qualify a religion to be a form of what I am calling cosmic optimism. One is that it conceives of the ultimately Real as benign from our human point of view; the other, that it conceives a structure of the universe that is consonant with this.

Let us now look briefly at the great world religions to see to what extent they fulfil these conditions.

7

COSMIC OPTIMISM IN THE EAST

IN HINDUISM

The term 'Hindu' was invented by foreigners – initially probably in the time of the Persian emperor Darius, who invaded India in the mid-first millennium BCE – to refer to the people of the Indus valley in north-west India, so that in effect it simply meant 'Indian'. However, the concept of Hindu*ism*, as a religion, is a modern western creation which has been exported to India and become generally accepted on the sub-continent. Some use the term to cover all forms of religion originating there, including Buddhism, Jainism and Sikhism, but most restrict it to those forms that revere the scriptures known as the Vedas; and I shall use the word in this latter sense.

However, even in this more focused sense, Hinduism is bewilderingly varied. It includes an immense collection of Sanskrit scriptures, above all the Upanishads; a wealth of sacred rituals, sacrifices and ceremonies dealing with every aspect and stage of life; the caste structure of traditional Indian society; multitudes of holy men, ancient and modern – rishis, acharyas, gurus, mahatmas, swamis, yogis; a wide variety of often competing philosophies; the worship of innumerable deities; a vast, rich, colourful and dramatic mythology which has moulded the imagination of millions, overlapping and intermingling with the philosophical speculations of the Upanishads and their interpreters. A recent writer has aptly likened Hinduism to an ancient banyan tree: 'From widespread branches [a banyan] sends down aerial roots, many of which in time grow thick and strong to resemble individual tree-trunks, so that an ancient banyan looks like an interconnected collection of trees and branches in which the same life-sap flows . . . Like the tree, Hinduism is an ancient collection of roots and branches, many indistinguishable one from the other, microscosmically polycentric, macrocosmically one, sharing the same regenerative life-sap, with a temporal foliage which covers most of recorded human history.'[1]

In early Vedic times the gods were very numerous, coalescing or dividing or changing their character over the centuries in ways that only mythological thinking permits. They did not disappear when the idea developed of the one ultimate, ineffable or formless reality, Brahman. On the contrary, they were now seen as manifestations of Brahman. Indeed even within the early Vedas it was said that 'the Real (*sat*) is one – sages name it variously'.[2]

The Hindu *bhakti* tradition of fervent devotion to a personal deity was eventually dominated by the two great figures of Shiva, whose cosmic dance constitutes the ongoing life of the universe, and Vishnu, with Rama and Krishna as *avatars* or incarnations of Vishnu. And most practising Hindus today are either Shaivites or Vaishnavites, depending usually on where in India they were born. But these two great deities are not seen by educated Hindus as rival claimants to ultimacy. Neither is the goddess joined with them and known under various names and forms – Kali, Durga, Lakshmi, etc. These, together with the innumerable lesser gods, are all seen as many forms of access to the ultimate reality of Brahman.

It is an almost universal theme of Hinduism that we are immersed in *samsara*, the beginningless and endless round of rebirths through which we live out our karma, the causal effect of our own mental and physical actions. The given circumstances of life, our genetic make-up, including our sex, our basic dispositions, our family, our caste (in India) and some of the major events in our lives, are thought to result from our previous lives. The great aim is to escape from this round of *samsara*, and thus from a return to another life of striving and suffering. Indeed, in spite of its many joys and pleasures, ordinary human life as a totality is seen as defective, unsatisfactory, lacking the great good that we sometimes glimpse. This is a virtually pan-Indian outlook, expressed in Buddhism as well as Hinduism. And our deepest longing must be to transcend this process of *samsara*. This is in fact possible, for within the constraints of karma we have a vital freedom to move spiritually upwards or downwards. Our karmic inheritance is like the keys of a piano. These determine what possibilities are available, but leave the pianist free to

1. Lipner, p. 5.
2. *Rig-Veda* I, 164, 46.

make his or her own music with them. And so life is to be treated as an opportunity for progress – particularly since, whilst there are many other spheres of existence, it is only in human embodiment that this progress can occur. Further, there are ways of overcoming bad karma. In the devotional (*bhakti*) traditions it is believed that divine grace may release us from its grip. Again there is sometimes the idea of a transfer of merit to lessen another's accumulated karmic debt. Yet again, the burial and commemorative rites for the dead are extremely important, partly because it is believed that, if properly performed, they may release the departed from any bad karma.

Within Hinduism then, our existence is seen, both in this life and beyond it, as a journey. The sacred texts describe this journey only for males; for like the other ancient texts (Hebrew, Christian, Muslim and Buddhist, as well as Hindu) they reflect the patriarchal societies of their time. But for men the four ideal stages are those of the student, the householder, the ascetic, and finally the mendicant renouncer. On the larger time-scale our existence is a journey through many lives, in which our souls (*jivas*) are gradually moving towards their final liberation. As we read in the *Gita*, 'the man of discipline (*yogi*) makes a serious effort. He becomes pure. After a number of births, perfected, he reaches the highest goal.'[3] Within the samsaric process *jivas* arise, are embodied many times, eventually attaining liberation, and although the process itself is beginningless and endless, the progress of a given *jiva* within it does eventually come to an end.

This end, the highest goal, is differently conceived within the non-theistic and the theistic strands of Hinduism. According to Shankara (about 700 CE) our surface personality, or conscious ego, is only a fleeting material individuation of the universal *atman*, which is ultimately identical with the eternal Brahman. And so liberation, both in this life and beyond it, consists in realizing our identity with Brahman. On the other hand, according to the theistic philosopher Ramanuja (eleventh century CE), the material universe, including our human selves, constitutes the 'body' of God, and the ultimate state lies within the divine life, though such a single-sentence summary cannot do justice to his complex and fascinating philosophy. But the point at the moment is that the ultimate state, whether it be identity with the infinite being–consciousness–bliss of Brahman, or loving communion with the infinite Person, is utterly desirable. Further, this desirable state can begin to be experienced now. One who has attained freedom in this life, and is thus a liberated soul (*jivanmukta*), has transcended the ego point of view and lives as a source of light to others. Well-known modern

3. VI, 45; Bolle, p. 81.

examples of such figures include Sri Ramakrishna (who died in 1886), Ramana Maharshi (who died in 1950), Paramahansa Yogananda (who died in 1952) and, according to many, Sai Baba (now living near Bangalore).

However we need to remember that there are many different degrees of appropriation of any religious tradition and that a great deal of religious belief remains, for most of the time, 'notional' rather than 'real'. As Julius Lipner says, whilst many 'look on *moksha* [spiritual liberation] in one form or another as a desirable goal', nevertheless 'a great many Hindus do not actively expect or even seek some post-mortem "salvation" or liberation. If at all, this is a distant ideal. Religiously, they are more concerned just to stay afloat as they continue life's journey over the hazardous waters of *samsara*. Health, recovery from illness, contentment, economic security, consolation in distress, offspring, success in various ventures, protection from various dangers, possibly a happy rebirth – these are the things that occupy their religious attention.'[4] And indeed is this not, with appropriate variations, the outlook of ordinary religious believers within each of the great traditions?

Nevertheless, to the degree that someone really believes that the universe is as pictured in Hindu thought, he or she experiences it accordingly and is, however falteringly, in an appropriate dispositional state. This involves living out one's place in the whole vast scheme of things with its many levels of existence inhabited by many gods and goddesses. We are called to be faithful to our station and its duties as we proceed through life after life. Concretely this has involved, for millions of people through many centuries, a great variety of moral obligations and ritual observances, with their family duties and prohibitions determined by their caste and stage of life.

It is also the case that within the Hindu picture of the universe there are many hells as well as many heavens. But these are not in the same category as the heaven and hell of the western monotheisms. They are levels of existence on which *jivas* (souls) spend limited periods of time. But the ultimate state, whether conceived as a union with Brahman in which individual egoity has been entirely transcended, or as individual life within the life of God, is eternal and finally awaits us all.

How universal is Hinduism's offer of *moksha*, liberation from the ills of samsaric existence? There have been those who held that the traditional Hindu wisdom applies only to Indians because only an Indian has a place within the caste system. But the more philosophical forms of Hinduism have spread far and wide in the west, particularly

4. Lipner, p. 324.

since the impact of Swami Vivekenanda at the World Parliament of Religions in Chicago in 1893. And so today, as well as the temple and family religious observances of those who have migrated from India to Europe and North America, many Europeans and North Americans have also been influenced by Hindu ideas and methods of meditation. For them the message of the Upanishads has a universal relevance.

IN BUDDHISM

Like Hinduism, Buddhism is not the single uniform entity that our modern western reifying name would suggest. It is a history of experience and thought launched in northern India some twenty-five centuries ago by Gautama, the (or rather a) Buddha, and developing ever since within different cultures to form a distinctive family of traditions. In its early centuries the Buddhist movement reflected the pervasive 'Hindu' outlook of India, although it also reacted against some central aspects of it. Thus the Buddha's *anatta* (no substantial self) teaching rejected the idea of an eternal unchanging personal core, and the Buddhist movement rejected the hierarchical caste system of India. When it moved north early in the common era, the Mahayana Buddhism of China, Tibet, Korea and Japan took forms which are in some ways different from the southern Theravada Buddhism of Sri Lanka and South-East Asia. Very roughly, the more world-denying ethos of India gave way in China to a more world-affirming outlook, the two eventually coalescing, it can be argued, in the startling discovery that *samsara* and nirvana are identical: that is to say, earthly life in its full concrete particularity is already nirvana for those who have been liberated from the ego point of view.

The terms enlightenment, liberation, awakening, nirvana and so on have both psychological and metaphysical connotations. Some westerners, usually in reaction against the anthropomorphic picture of God as a limitlessly magnified person, have responded eagerly to Buddhism, seeing it as essentially a technique for attaining inner peace and serenity without involving any belief in the Transcendent. This particular western appropriation of Buddhism parallels the contemporary non- or anti-realist versions of Christianity mentioned earlier (pp. 21–2), according to which God is not a transcendent (as well as immanent) reality but an imaginary personification of our human ideals. But, as will become evident, it is impossible to sustain such a picture from the Pali scriptures or from the understanding of most of those who have been deeply embedded from birth within the Buddhist tradition.

The Buddha taught the evanescent character of the world as a universal interdependent process of ceaseless change (*pratitya samutpada*) in which each event in some degree conditions and is conditioned by every other in an unbounded interactive web. Everything is compounded of elements with only a fleeting momentary existence, and the appearance of solid enduring entities, including the human self, is in the end illusory. Indeed, it is the deep realization of this that can free us from the self-centredness that makes our experience of life so often one of anxious craving, sorrow and joylessness, in Buddhist terms *dukkha*.

The Pali *nibbana* (or in Sanskrit *nirvana*) means literally, blowing out, as in the blowing out of a flame. This is not, however, a simple ceasing to exist, but the blowing out or destruction of illusion and its fruits. The Buddha taught that 'the destruction of lust, the destruction of hatred, the destruction of illusion, friend, is called Nibbana'.[5] This is not only an individual psychological state, but a reflection within a particular momentary occasion of the ultimate universal reality variously referred to as nirvana, the *dharmakaya*, *sunyata*, the buddha nature of the universe. Thus nirvana is described in the Pali scriptures as 'the unborn . . . unageing . . . undecaying . . . undying . . . stainless'.[6] In a famous passage the Buddha teaches, 'Monks, there is a not-born, a not-become, a not-made, a not-compounded. Monks, if that unborn, not-become, not-made, not-compounded were not, there would be apparent no escape from this here that is born, become, made, compounded.'[7] Accordingly, the contemporary leading Theravadin scholar, Narada Mahathera, speaks of nirvana as 'the permanent, immortal, supramundane state which cannot be expressed by mundane terms'.[8] And Takeuchi Yoshinori, of the Kyoto school of Zen philosophy, endorses Friedrich Heiler's words, 'Nirvana is the equivalent of what Western mysticism understands as the "Being of beings", the supreme and one reality, the absolute, the divine . . . Nirvana is the infinite, the eternal, the uncreated, the quality-free, the ineffable, the one and only, the highest, the supreme good, the best, the good pure and simple.'[9] Again, Edward Conze, a western authority on Buddhism, says that 'it is assumed first of all [in Buddhism] that there is an ultimate reality, and secondly that there is a point in ourselves at which we touch that ultimate reality. The ultimate reality, also called Dharma, or Nirvana, is defined as that which stands completely outside the sensory world of illusion and ignorance, a world

5. *Samyutta Nikaya* IV, 250; Woodward, 1956, p. 170.
6. *Majjhima Nikaya* I, 163; Horner, 1954, pp. 206–7.
7. *Udana* 80, 3; Woodward, 1948, pp. 97–8.
8. Narada, pp. 24–5.
9. Takeuchi Yoshinori, pp. 8–9.

inextricably interwoven with craving and greed. To get somehow to that ultimate reality is the supremely worthwhile goal of the Buddhist life. The Buddhist idea of ultimate reality is very much akin to the philosophical notion of the "Absolute", and not easily distinguished from the notion of God among the more mystical theologians, like Dionysius Areopagita and Eckart.'[10]

However, the focus of Buddhist attention is always upon the present life, and indeed upon the present moment. The Dharma is wholly practical, a way to liberation. Gautama said, 'As the great ocean is saturated by only one taste, the taste of salt, so this teaching and system is saturated by only one taste, the taste of salvation [i.e. liberation].'[11] Metaphysical speculations about the ultimate structure of the universe are accordingly discouraged as a dangerous distraction from the demanding and all-absorbing work of seeking enlightenment.

But it is important to realize that this warning against philosophizing as a substitute for the spiritual quest occurs within the context of the belief, continuously either affirmed or assumed, that the ongoing karmic structure of which we are a temporary expression continues through many lives until enlightenment/liberation/awakening is at last achieved. Thus it is taken for granted that the structure of the universe enables human existence to move, on a vast time-scale, towards a limitlessly good fulfilment.

Normative Buddhism, then, offers a picture of the universe as structured towards the ultimate 'nirvanization' of all life. Different schools of thought hold either that enlightenment is possible in this life for all who seek it with all their heart and mind, or in this life only for those who have already approached it through many previous lives; that it occurs suddenly, that it occurs in stages; that it liberates us *from* the material world, and that it liberates us *for* the material world. There is thus immense variety within the Buddhist tradition.

Given this worldview, what is its correlative dispositional response? How are Buddhists taught to pursue enlightenment/liberation/awakening/nirvana? The Buddha taught a practical way of release from the pervasive anxiety and insecurity of ordinary human life as we encounter pain, sorrow, grief, despair, frustration, sickness, ageing and death. Life has for us this *dukkha* quality, he taught, because we habitually experience the world as centring upon ourselves. I experience everything in its relation to *me*, as welcome or unwelcome, propitious or threatening, as satisfying or frustrating my desires; and this way of experiencing creates a basic angst which is sometimes conscious and sometimes unconscious. Liberation is accordingly achieved by

10. Conze, pp. 110–11.
11. *Vinaya Pitaka, Cullavagga* IX, 238; Horner, 1963, p. 335.

transcending the ego point of view to participate in a more universal perspective.

There is an interesting analogy between the role of the universal point of view in Buddhism and the Kantian ethic. According to Kant, morally right action is action which is best, not in the private interests of the agent, but from a universal and impartial point of view in which every individual is valued equally as an end in him- or herself. This is achieved, according to Kant, by applying a universalization criterion: Would the principle on which I am proposing to act (for example, that it is acceptable to cheat on my income-tax return) be acceptable if everyone acted on it? We can say that Buddhism teaches the inner spiritual attitude of which the Kantian ethic teaches (in an overly schematic form) the practical application.

The way to this is the 'Noble Eightfold Path', which is both ethical and spiritual. Ethically it consists in developing a universal compassion (*karuna*) and loving-kindness (*metta*). There are practical steps to this. We are enjoined to practise:

- right speech – not lying or slandering or maliciously gossiping;
- right action – not stealing or acting dishonestly, not taking life, not indulging in illegitimate sex;
- right livelihood – not earning one's living in ways that harm others, such as by dealing in armaments or harmful drugs.

Spiritually, the way to enlightenment is that of prolonged meditation, producing a realization of the insubstantial and fleeting nature of the self and so leading to an eventual detachment from the ego point of view. This is a transcendence both *from* egoity and *to* (and here there is a variety of terms) – enlightenment, liberation, awakening, nirvana, *sunyata* ('emptiness'), conscious participation in the universal buddha nature.

All who have an inkling of this state will seek it in this present life. For 'Above, beyond Nibbana's bliss, is naught';[12] and again 'He that doth crush the great "I am" conceit – this, even this, is happiness supreme.'[13] And in the *Dhammapada*, a collection of the Buddha's sayings which constitutes the Theravada bible, there is a continual stress upon the blessedness of approaching the nirvanic state now:

> Happily do we live without hate among the hateful . . . happily do we live without yearning among those who yearn . . . happily the peaceful live, giving up victory and defeat . . . there is no bliss higher

12. *Therigatha* 476; Davids, p. 169.
13. *Udana* II, 1; Woodward, 1948, p. 13.

> than Nibbana . . . Nibbana, bliss supreme . . . Nibbana is the highest bliss . . . the taste of the joy of the Dhamma.[14]

Here Buddhism's cosmic optimism reaches down into the present moment.

14. Narada, chapter 15.

8

AND IN THE WEST

IN JUDAISM

Judaism is the religion of the Jewish people. Its cosmic optimism – not a term within traditional Jewish discourse – consists in a special covenant relationship between the people and their God, and a faith in the people's future welfare and ultimate fulfilment within the divine kingdom.

The focus has always been on this present life as lived in the presence of God. On the one hand, the God of Israel has been active on earth, delivering his chosen people from slavery in Egypt, leading them to a promised land, and sustaining and disciplining them throughout their long history. On the other hand, in his fuller development, their God is also lord of the whole universe, beyond human comprehension. For 'my thoughts are not your thoughts, neither are your ways my ways, says the Lord',[1] and 'a thousand years in thy sight are but as yesterday when it is past'.[2] And yet again, this transcendent God is close to his people in loving compassion: 'For as the heavens are high above the earth, so great is his steadfast love toward those who fear him; as far as the east is from the west, so far does he remove our transgressions from us. As a father pities his children, so the Lord pities those who fear him. For he knows our frame; he remembers that we are dust.'[3]

Until towards the end of the biblical period this divine presence was thought of as assuring the continuity and fulfilment of the people rather than the individual. Individuals descended at death into the darkness of a bloodless wraith-like existence in Sheol. But during the last two

1. Isaiah 55:8.
2. Psalm 90:4.
3. Psalm 103:11–13.

centuries BCE the realization began to crystallize that the fulfilment of God's purpose for his people must include the restoration of the righteous dead, and the notion of the world to come (*olam ha-ba*) became part of Jewish thinking.

At first, in the period preceding and including New Testament times, this meant the bodily resurrection of the dead. Around the middle of the second century BCE it was prophesied that on the great day 'many of those who sleep in the dust of the earth shall awake, some to everlasting life, and some to shame and everlasting contempt'.[4] In the New Testament period, belief in the future resurrection had become orthodox among the Pharisees although not among the more conservative Sadducees. Later, as the Jewish Diaspora (its dispersion beyond Palestine) became part of the Greco-Roman world, the very different idea of the immortality of the soul entered Jewish thinking alongside the older belief in resurrection. We perhaps see a mingling of the two in St Paul's concept of the spiritual body (*soma pneumaticon*) in I Corinthians 15:44.

Since biblical times Judaism has been the Judaism of the rabbis. Many of them held the two strands of thought – bodily resurrection and immortality of the soul – together in the picture of a disembodied existence until reunion with the body at the final judgement. During the medieval centuries there were debates about the rewards and punishments to be expected, and the rabbinical imagination created torments in hell as lurid as those of medieval Christendom. But among the more philosophical rabbis there was a trend away from material conceptions of heaven towards the idea of the immortality of the soul. The great Jewish thinker Maimonides, for instance, said that 'in the world to come the body and the flesh do not exist but only the souls of the righteous alone'.[5] There were also debates about the fate of non-Jews, eventually settled in the talmudic conclusion that 'the righteous of all nations have their place in the world to come'.[6] But such eschatological questions have long since ceased to be central either in the exegetical work or the spiritual teachings of the rabbis. On the whole they are content to leave the world to come as something about which it is unprofitable to speculate.

The Jewish kabbalistic mysticism which flourished in the medieval period included elaborate theories about the life, or indeed lives, to come. Themes familiar in other mystical traditions appeared in Jewish versions: the pre-existence of souls, their descent into matter, and their eventual return to the divine source through a long process involving several reincarnations (*gilgulim*). Kabbalism has however faded out in

4. Daniel 12:1–2.
5. *Code of Repentance*, 3:6.
6. *Sanhedrin*, p. 13.

the modern period. Since the European Enlightenment of the seventeenth and eighteenth centuries the conception of a larger existence, of which this life is only a part, has greatly weakened within western consciousness, including western Jewish consciousness. Further, since 1948 Jewish faith has found in the State of Israel a compelling earthly focus that marginalizes ideas of a world to come. Orthodox Judaism retains the traditional resurrection belief within its liturgical life and faith, and Reform Judaism retains a belief in the immortality of the soul, but these ideas probably have about the same rather slight hold on the minds of most educated Jews today as do equivalent ideas on the minds of most educated Christians. Nevertheless, as a contemporary Reform rabbi writes, 'Without the promise of Messianic redemption, resurrection, and the eventual vindication of the righteous in Paradise, Jews will face great difficulties reconciling the belief in a providential God who watches over his chosen people with the terrible events of modern Jewish history. If there is no eschatological unfolding of a Divine drama in which Jewish people will ultimately triumph, what hope can there be for the Righteous of Israel?'[7] For whilst Jewish thinkers revolt against any minimizing of the appalling evil and horror of the Shoah (or Holocaust) by the thought of the victims' survival in the world to come, it remains true for Judaism as for other faiths that we cannot in the end, as thinking beings, be reconciled to life in a world in which such things happen without invoking some conception of further life beyond this one. Putting it as a general proposition, rather than from a specifically Jewish point of view, we can only affirm the goodness of the universe, having in mind not only the fortunate few but the entire human race, if life continues beyond its present earthly phase to some kind of ultimate fulfilment. That there will be such a fulfilment is integral to traditional Jewish teaching.

IN CHRISTIANITY

The phrase 'good news' in a religious context comes from Christianity. After his forty days of solitude in the wilderness, 'Jesus came into Galilee, preaching the gospel [*euangelion* = good news] of God, and saying, "The time is fulfilled, and the kingdom of God is at hand."'[8] And the Christian message has been proclaimed, first throughout the Roman Empire, and later throughout the world, as good news for all humanity. It must however be added that during much of the medieval period, and in the theology of the Protestant Reformation, and also within the large contemporary Christian fundamentalist movement, this

7. Cohn-Sherbok, 1987, p. 34.
8. Mark 1:14–15.

news has a dark and threatening side to it. But I shall nevertheless declare my own Christian standpoint by treating the good news aspect as central and normative.

In Jesus' teaching, so far as this can be discerned from the four gospels – today believed to have been written between forty and seventy years after his death – there is a very clear affirmation, expressed in parable after parable, of both the love and justice of God. God is our heavenly father, whose attitude is like that of the father in the parable of the prodigal son in Luke 15. But at the same time, God is a stern judge separating the good from the evil, as depicted in the parables of the worthy and unworthy servants, and of the sheep and the goats, in Matthew 25. Jesus' teaching is, in fact, strongly ethical and practical, addressed to ordinary sinful men and women, and included the fact that there are consequences in the world to come of what we do in our daily lives now. St Paul expressed this karmic principle when he said that 'whatever a man sows, that he will also reap'.[9] In Matthew 25 the criterion of judgement turns upon doing God's will, not upon religious professions: 'Not everyone who says to me "Lord, Lord", shall enter the kingdom of heaven, but he who does the will of my father who is in heaven.'[10] Although Jesus apparently saw himself as 'sent only to the lost sheep of the house of Israel',[11] there are several points within the gospels at which he thinks beyond this, particularly the parable of the good Samaritan, and the incidents with the woman of Samaria and the healing of the Roman centurion's servant, which ends with the saying that 'many will come from east and west and sit at table with Abraham, Isaac, and Jacob in the kingdom of heaven'.[12] It therefore seems reasonable to suppose that if Jesus had lived longer, and the question had arisen of whether the good news of God's kingdom was for the rest of humanity well as for his fellow Jews, he would have given the affirmative answer later given by St Paul.

The first generation of Christians expected the early return of Jesus in messianic glory to judge the world on God's behalf and establish divine rule on earth. Whether this expectation goes back to Jesus himself is disputed among New Testament scholars. A number of sayings attributed to him clearly teach such an expectation, for example, 'there are some standing here who will not taste death before they see that the kingdom of God has come with power'.[13] But questions have been raised about the authenticity of these sayings (as indeed about many others), and we are left in a degree of uncertainty. But there is no uncertainty about the expectations of the dominant wing of the early church, led by St Paul. Writing around 50 CE, Paul was

9. Galatians 6:7.
10. Matthew 7:21.
11. Matthew 15:24.
12. Matthew 8:11.
13. Mark 9:1.

emphatic that although some of the Christian community had already died, 'we who are alive, who are left until the coming of the Lord, shall not precede those who have fallen asleep [i.e. died]';[14] and later he says, 'Brethren, the appointed time has grown very short.'[15] But as the century progressed and the end was continually delayed, Jesus' second coming receded into the indefinite future and the church settled down within the realities of earthly history. It survived sporadic but sometimes very severe bouts of persecution to become progressively established from 313 CE, thanks to the emperor Constantine, as the religion of the Roman Empire and so of Europe, both western and eastern. Within this transition from a Jewish eschatological sect to a world religion, Jesus, already recognized retrospectively within the church as the expected messiah, was exalted to a divine status and eventually, in the fourth century, was declared to be the incarnation of the second Person of a Divine Trinity.[16]

It seems clear that Jesus himself believed in the reality of the divine kingdom, whether as already present in himself, or as a future transformed earthly reality, or as lying beyond this life and this world, or as all of these. It is also clear that he declared a future retribution for presents acts of cruelty, injustice and inhumanity. But it is a matter of dispute whether he believed that this consisted in an eternal and therefore infinite punishment. Nearly all the sayings cited to support this interpretation refer to a real but not necessarily endless retribution beyond this life; and even where the word *aeonios* (translated as 'eternal') is used, it can also mean for the period of this *aeon* or age. I believe that a good case can in fact be made that Jesus did not specify the eternity of hell.[17] Further, there are strong moral and religious arguments against that idea. First, no finite human sin could justly deserve an infinite punishment, and second, such retribution could never serve a good purpose – compatible with the limitless love of God – because, being endless, it could never lead to the eventual restoration of the sinner. Nevertheless, the church has throughout most of its history confidently affirmed an eternal hell, and many have shared St Augustine's belief that the majority of human beings will be consigned to it.[18] And so it has to be acknowledged that this side of Christian teaching has compromised its character as good news for all humanity.

In the early centuries, and through the medieval era and the Reformation period down to the seventeenth and eighteenth centuries,

14. I Thessalonians 4:15.
15. I Corinthians 7:29. See also Romans 13:11–12; II Corinthians 4:14 and 5:1–10; Philippians 1:19–26.
16. On this historic transition, see for example my *The Metaphor of God Incarnate*, chapters 3–4.
17. Hick, 1994, chapter 13.
18. St Augustine, p. 395.

the ideas of heaven and hell stirred hopes and fears which affected the living of peoples' lives. Positively, the idea of heaven linked the living with the dead. The thought of the departed in heaven, and the prospect of a future reunion, alleviated grief and inspired the religious imagination with the picture of a vast mysterious but glorious reality above us in which we may one day participate. Negatively however, the idea of hell has served as a powerful instrument of social control by reinforcing the authority of the church. Its dogmatic theology has been used to justify the torture of heretics (forcing them to recant and thereby escape eternal damnation), and has led Christians to see those outside the church as needing to be converted to the true faith, thus providing the colonizing ambitions of western merchant venturers with a religious validation.

But despite the fact that until comparatively recently the Christian imagination included this black hole of eternal damnation, the dominant theme has always been the gracious love of God. The same has been true to an even greater extent of the Christian mystics, and of the teaching of many of the local clergy. Within the major Catholic and Protestant forms of Christianity since the European Enlightenment, the doctrine of hell has been progressively abandoned, or reduced to the idea of annihilation rather than endless torment. Even when it has not been rescinded it has generally been allowed to fade into the background, ceasing to play any vital role in the minds of most Christians.

Given this Christian worldview, what is the appropriate practical response? How should one seek the kingdom of God?

Here again there are many different levels of spiritual aspiration, which I shall however compress into two. These are the ecclesiastical and the mystical (or in the terms of William James, the institutional and the personal), the latter normally including but going far beyond the former. In the Catholic and Orthodox traditions the ecclesiastical response to the Christian message is basically sacramental. In the Eucharist one feeds on the mystical body and blood of Christ, thus receiving divine grace and being incorporated anew into the life of the Second Person of the Holy Trinity. Within the Reformed branch of Christianity, grace is mediated as much, or more, through the Bible, received as the Word of God and preached in the churches. And in our own time Catholic and Reformed (more than Orthodox and Pentecostal) Christians have come, at least in a significant minority, to see an authentic response to God as requiring a dedication, individually, nationally and globally, to social justice and the preservation of endangered Mother Earth.

We shall be looking later at mystical Christianity. Suffice to say at the moment that, whilst generally using to the full the sacramental life of the church, this has involved a more focused and more intensely dedicated search for self-transcendence into 'unity' with God.

And so we can affirm that Christianity, despite the internal inconsistencies embedded in its history, is at its heart a form of cosmic optimism, offering good news to a needy humanity.

IN ISLAM

As a form of cosmic optimism (although 'cosmic optimism' is, once again, not an Islamic term), Islam exhibits essentially the same structure as the other Abrahamic faiths, Judaism and Christianity. That is to say, there is an affirmation that the Ultimate is gracious and kindly towards humanity, and that God's good purpose for all who obey God will be fulfilled in the life of paradise. And, as in the case of the other two closely related monotheisms, there is the threat of hell for evil-doers. Indeed, the reality of a life beyond death, and of encounter with a gracious but just God, is generally more powerful today within Islam than within Judaism or Christianity, both of which have been strongly influenced by the European Enlightenment.

Each surah, or chapter, of the Qur'an begins, 'In the name of God, *rahman hahim* ['most benevolent, ever merciful'],[19] and the ninety-nine qur'anic names of God include: The Protector; The Forgiver; The Bestower; The Provider; The Forbearing One; The All-Forgiving; The Generous One; The Loving; The Protecting Friend; The Giver of Life; The Source of All Goodness; The Pardoner; The Compassionate; and The Guide to the Right Path.[20] That God is merciful when we go astray is a constant refrain of the Qur'an; for example, 'Surely God forgives all sins. He is all-forgiving and all-merciful';[21] 'Beg your Lord to forgive you, and turn to Him. Indeed my Lord is compassionate and loving.'[22] Islam has a generally optimistic understanding of human nature. As Frederick Denny says, 'If the Bible, and especially the New Testament, harps on how unholy mankind are, the Qur'an (and Islamic literature in general) hastens almost in every verse to remind humans of their marvelous possibilities as *homines religiosi*.'[23]

In Islam it is not particular sins but the complete rejection of God that leads to hell. This is not necessarily a rejection of the qur'anic revelation – since many peoples have not received this – but of God's revelations through any of the long succession of prophets, for 'Never

19. My quotations from the Qur'an are from the Ahmed Ali translation.
20. Friedlander, 1978.
21. Qur'an 39:53.
22. Qur'an 11:90.
23. Denny, p. 72.

has there been a community to which an admonisher was not sent.'[24] It follows from the unity of God and the unity of mankind that divine revelation is also unitary, although manifested at different times and places and in different scriptures: 'So has God, all-mighty and all-wise, been revealing to you and to others before you . . . He has laid down for you the same way of life and belief which he had commended to Noah, and which We have enjoined to you, and which We have bequeathed to Abraham, Moses and Jesus . . . Say [to the Jews and Christians]: "I believe in whatever Scripture God has revealed, and I am commanded to act with equivalence among you. God is our Lord and your Lord. To us our actions, to you your deeds. There is no dispute between you and us. God will gather us all together, and to Him is our returning" . . . God is gracious to His creatures, and bestows favours on whosoever He will. He is all-powerful and all-mighty.'[25] Again, 'Surely the believers and the Jews, Nazareans [i.e. Christians], and the Sabians, whoever believes in God and the Last Day, and whosoever does right, shall have his reward with his Lord, and will neither have fear nor regret.'[26] And when the Muslims invaded India, some – but by no means all – of them recognized Zoroastrians, Hindus, Buddhists and Jains as also 'People of the Book', who were therefore allowed to retain their religion and culture. For behind the Arabic Qur'an revealed through the prophet Muhammad, there lies the 'cosmic Qur'an', the heavenly Book, *al-Qur'an al-takwini*.[27] This is the eternal Word of God that is expressed in different human situations through different prophets and different revelatory scriptures.

Islam, as a framework for life, has been a rock of stability and a source of trust for hundreds of millions of people, mostly living in what is now called the Third World and often in conditions of poverty and hardship. The stability comes from obedience to divine law, which prescribes a whole way of life, at the same time expecting God's compassion when one fails. Trust in God brings men and women through life's calamities, accepted as the mysterious divine will. Thus, at the death of a loved one, a Muslim will recite the qur'anic verse 'Everything is from God and returns to God', a Stoic-like outlook that is paralleled in the Calvinist strand of Christianity.

Islam opens out into a joyful love of God and a celebration of God's love in many of the Sufis, the mystics of Islam. God is seen as our loving Friend. The thirteenth-century Ibn 'Ata'Illah says,

24. Qur'an 35:24.
25. Qur'an 42: 3, 13, 15, 19.
26. Qur'an 2:61.
27. Nasr, p. 192.

> If you were to be united with Him
> only after the extinction of your vices
> and the effacement of your pretensions,
> you would never be united with Him!
> Instead, when He wants to unite you to Himself,
> He covers your attribute with His Attribute
> and hides your quality with His Quality.
> And thus He unites you to Himself
> By virtue of that which comes from Him to you,
> Not by virtue of what goes from you to Him.[28]

One of the greatest of the Sufis, the thirteenth-century Jalaluldin Rumi, says that 'Love makes the millwheel of the heavens spin, not water; 'Love makes the moon go forward, not feet.'[29] Again:

> Love (*mahabbat*), and ardent love (*'ishq*) also, is an Attribute of God; Fear is an attribute of the slave to lust and appetite. Love hath five hundred wings, and every wing reaches from above the empyrean to beneath the earth. The timorous ascetic runs on foot; the lovers of God fly more quickly than lightning. May Divine Favour free thee from this wayfaring! None but the royal falcon hath found the way to the King.[30]

As in the New Testament, the Day of Judgement and the reality of heaven and hell are almost palpable. That to believe in God includes believing in the Last Day is a theme running throughout the Qur'an. Surah 56, for example, begins with this vision:

> When what is to happen comes to pass . . .
> Degrading some and exalting others;
> When the earth is shaken up convulsively,
> The mountains bruised and crushed,
> Turned to dust, floating in the air . . .
> Those of the right hand – how happy will be those of the right hand!
> Then the foremost, how pre-excellent,
> Who will be honoured
> In gardens of tranquility . . .
> On couches wrought of gold,
> Reclining face to face.
> Youths of never ending bloom will pass round to them
> Cups and decanters, beakers of sparkling wine,
> Unheady, uninebriating;
> And such fruits as they fancy,
> Bird meats that they relish.

28. Ibn 'Ata'Illah, p. 79.
29. Rumi, 1983, p. 160.
30. Rumi, 1995, p. 102.

And companions [houris] with big beautiful eyes
Like pearls within their shells,
As recompense for all they have done . . .
But those of the left hand – how unhappy those of the left hand -
Will be in the scorching wind and boiling water,
Under the shadow of thick black smoke.[31]

However, as with the very material pictures of heaven and hell in the New Testament – with the evil being thrown into the lake of fire that burns with sulpha, and the good entering the heavenly city whose walls are jasper, the city of pure gold, its twelve gates made of pearls, and so on (Revelation 21) – later believers have by no means always taken these pictures literally. Thus the eleventh-century Abdullah Ansari says, 'O God, if I devote but a moment to you, how then could I fancy houris and mansions in Paradise?'[32]

Nor is the idea entirely absent that hell might in the end be empty. Rumi tells a story – much of his teaching is in story form – about an evil-doer who is 'sent to the fiery prison . . . [avenging angels] pricking him with their spears, and saying "O dog, begone to thy kennel." Then the prisoner will cry, "O Lord, I am a hundred, yea, a hundred times as wicked as Thou sayest. But in mercy Thou veilest my sins . . . I fix my hopes on Thy mercy alone . . . I sue for free pardon from Thy unbought justice. O lord, who art gracious without thought of consequence, I set my face towards that free grace of Thine . . . Seeing Thou gavest me my being first of all; Thou gavest me the garment of existence unasked, wherefore I firmly trust in Thy free grace."' And the story ends, 'When he thus enumerates his sins and faults, God at last will grant him pardon as a free gift, saying, "O angels, bring him back to me, since the eyes of his heart were set on hope. Without care for consequences I set him free, and draw the pen through the record of his sins!"'[33]

To summarize, the message of Islam is good news for all in the sense that all – and not only Muslims – can freely live so as to enter paradise. And whilst in the main stream of the tradition it is assumed that in fact many forfeit this, there is also a profound sense of the unfathomable mercy of God.

31. Qur'an 56:1–6, 8–24, 41–3.
32. Ansari, p. 187.
33. Rumi, 1979, pp. 244–5.

PART III

THE GODS AND ABSOLUTES AS MANIFESTATIONS OF THE REAL

9

THE REAL EXPERIENCED AS GOD

THE PLURALIST HYPOTHESIS

We now encounter what is known as religious pluralism, this being the name that has been given to the idea that the great world religions are different human responses to the same ultimate transcendent reality. That reality is in itself beyond the scope of our human conceptual systems. But nevertheless it is universally present as the very ground of our being. And in collaboration with the religious aspect of human nature it has produced both the personal and non-personal foci of religious worship and meditation – the gods and absolutes – which exist at the interface between the Real and the human mind.

This means that the different world religions – each with its own sacred scriptures, spiritual practices, forms of religious experience, belief systems, founder or great exemplars, communal memories, cultural expression in ways of life, laws and customs, art forms and so on – taken together as complex historical totalities, constitute different human responses to the ultimate transcendent reality to which they all, in their different ways, bear witness.

So far as their belief systems are concerned, these are structured on various levels, from their basic conceptions of the Ultimate down through middle-level speculations about the afterlife – eternal heaven or hell versus reincarnation – to such cultural matters as marriage customs and forms of family life. The differences at each level are real, but it is important to realize that at the middle level they consist of different legitimate human speculations open, at least in principle, to critical discussion, and that at the cultural level they are aspects of our different ways of being human, open again to mutual criticism and influencing.

What does all this mean for the status of the great spiritual figures who founded or contributed to the founding of the world religions? It means that they were men – always men, in the cultures of their times – who were exceptionally open to the Transcendent, experiencing it with extraordinary vividness in ways made possible by their existing religious contexts. Such immensely powerful moments of God-consciousness, or of Transcendence-consciousness, are what we mean by revelation. These primary revelations were so overwhelming that the lives and words of the founders communicated the reality of the Divine or the Transcendent to others, setting in motion major new currents within the stream of human religious experience. The founders are always to be revered, but were men of their own times, so that we have to bring their central message into our own time rather than try to conform ourselves to the culture of theirs.

Each religious community, at least since the axial age, has assumed that its own experienced God (Jahweh, Vishnu, Shiva, Holy Trinity, Allah, etc.) or its own non-personal Absolute (Brahman, Tao, Dharmakaya, etc.) is itself the ultimately Real. However, according to the pluralistic hypothesis, none of these is the Real in itself, although all are authentic manifestations of it to humanity. The descriptions of ultimate reality embodied in the theologies and philosophies of the different traditions speak literally (or analogically) about their own God or Absolute, and thereby speak mythologically about the Real in itself. And mythological religious truth is instrumental truth, consisting in its capacity to evoke and develop appropriate human responses to the Ultimate.

In the west this conception has always been more at home within the mystical than the ecclesiastical–doctrinal thought-world. There are historical reasons for this. Medieval Christendom was a cohesive religious culture in which the only known 'others' were the hated and despised Jews within and the hated and feared Muslims without. Christian writers (until Nicholas of Cusa in the fifteenth century) were not usually concerned to take serious account of realms of religious life and experience beyond their own borders. The Indian sub-continent, on the other hand, was always a multi-faith region, with the Shaivites and the Vaishnavites within what is today called Hinduism, and the Jains, Parsis, Buddhists, and later the Muslims, Christians and Sikhs all coexisting, sometimes as hostile, and even violently hostile, but most of the time as friendly, neighbours. And so the pluralistic idea has a more familiar and accepted status in India and further east. But the most explicit teaching of pluralism as religious truth comes from the region between east and west, namely Iran (Persia). It was here that the nineteenth-century prophet Bahá'u'lláh taught that the ultimate divine reality is in itself beyond the grasp of the human mind, but has nevertheless been imaged and responded to in different historically and culturally conditioned ways by the founders of the different faith-traditions. The Bahá'í religion which he founded continues to teach this message in many countries today.

PSEUDO-DIONYSIUS

The natural starting point in the west is Pseudo-Dionysius.[1] Although his name is scarcely known beyond those interested in the history of Christian mysticism, and although in a sense he never existed, Dionysius has in fact been one of the most influential of Christian writers. Thomas Aquinas, for example, quotes him some 1700 times.[2] Probably a Syrian monk, and probably writing around 500 CE, this anonymous author was for centuries believed to have been Dionysius, or Denys, the Areopagite, whose conversion by St Paul is mentioned in Acts 17:34. Such authorial concealment was by no means unique in the medieval period. Other Christian writers sometimes made use of New Testament names, and the *Zohar*, which has been as influential within Jewish as Pseudo-Dionysius within Christian mysticism, and which purports to be by a revered second-century CE Palestinian rabbi, was almost certainly written by Moses de Leon in Spain in the thirteenth century. Other Jewish writers of the thirteenth and fourteenth centuries likewise produced works which they attributed to ancient authorities. If Pseudo-Dionysius' writings had been in the form of a printed book, not only would they have borne a false name on the title page, but the deception would have gone further, for the texts themselves are ostensively addressed by Dionysius the Elder to Timothy, a fellow elder in the apostolic church. And as one who had supposedly been close to St Paul, Denys (to use the more reader-friendly name) was accorded an almost apostolic authority which greatly eased the absorption of his Neoplatonism into the stream of Christian thought. He writes with a self-confidence that suggests that he must have lived in a theologically open-minded community, and probably occupied a position of leadership. But it is one of the ironies of the history of western thought that an implausible literary deception – implausible in that Denys's

1. My quotations from Pseudo-Dionysius are from *The Complete Works*, translated by Colm Luibheid from the Greek text in the Migne edition. In the citations *DN* = *The Divine Names*, *MT* = *The Mystical Theology*, *CH* = *The Celestial Hierarchy*, *EH* = *The Ecclesiastical Hierarchy* and *L* = the *Letters*.
2. Pelikan, 1987, p. 21.

ideas show an overwhelmingly strong Neoplatonic influence of which Paul's canonical letters have no trace – should have had such far-reaching effects.

Denys is famous for his insistence upon the absolute and unqualified ineffability of God. He is as emphatic as it is possible to be that God is utterly transcendent, totally ineffable, indescribable and incapable of being conceptualized by the human mind. This is the central theme of *The Mystical Theology*. The title means the secret or hidden theology, for Denys held that the higher truth, with which he was concerned, was for a spiritual and intellectual elite: 'See to it', he says, 'that none of this comes to the hearing of the uninformed.'[3] As he says elsewhere, 'Not everyone is sacred, and, as scripture says, knowledge is not for everyone.'[4] (The Jewish *Zohar* was likewise originally intended only for a spiritual elite.)

God, according to Denys, is 'indescribable',[5] 'beyond all being and knowledge',[6] and, in the culminating fifth chapter of *The Mystical Theology*, he says in every way he can think of that God is transcategorial, beyond and outside all our categories of thought: [The supreme Cause] is not soul or mind, nor does it possess imagination, conviction, speech, or understanding . . . It cannot be spoken of and it cannot be grasped by understanding. It is not number or order, greatness or smallness, equality or inequality, similarity or dissimilarity. It is not immovable, moving, or at rest . . . It does not live nor is it life. It is not a substance, nor is it eternity or time. It cannot be grasped by the understanding . . . It is neither one nor oneness, divinity nor goodness. Nor is it spirit, in the sense in which we understand that term. It is not sonship or fatherhood and it is nothing known to us or to any other being . . . There is no speaking of it, nor name nor knowledge of it. Darkness and light, error and truth – it is none of these. It is beyond assertion and denial.'[7] And there are dozens of other statements by Denys to the same effect. One more will suffice: 'Beings are surpassed by the infinity beyond being, intelligences by that oneness which is beyond intelligence. Indeed the inscrutable One is out of the reach of every rational process. Nor can any words come up to the inexpressible Good, this One, this Source of all unity, this supra-existent Being. Mind beyond mind, word beyond speech, it is gathered up by no discourse, by no intuition, by no name. It is and it is as no other being is.'[8]

However, as we saw in the case of the Hindu concept of Brahman, those who assert the totally transcategorial nature of ultimate reality (as so many of the great thinkers of each tradition have done) also want, for the purposes of the religious life, to make positive statements about

3. *MT* 1000A.
4. *CH* 140B.
5. *MT* 1033C.
6. *MT* 97B.
7. *MT* 1045D–1048B.
8. *DN* 588B.

it. For otherwise it could not be directly worshipped. And so our basic question is whether, or to what extent, it is possible to have it both ways by using positive religious language and yet acknowledging an ultimate ineffability.

Pseudo-Denys was fully conscious of the problem: 'How then can we speak of the divine names? How can we do this if the Transcendent surpasses all discourse and knowledge, if it abides beyond the reach of mind and of being, if it encompasses and circumscribes, embraces and anticipates all things while itself eluding their grasp and escaping from any perception, imagination, opinion, name, discourse, apprehension, or understanding?'[9]

His response can be summarized in seven propositions:

1. God, whom he frequently refers to in non-personal terms as the One, the Source, the Transcendent, the Transcendent One, the Godhead, is ultimately transcategorial, beyond the range of all human concepts: 'There is no speaking of it, nor name nor knowledge of it.'[10] This is also a key element in the modern pluralist hypothesis.
2. Nevertheless, the ineffable God is self-revealed in the Bible: God is the 'Source which has told us about itself in the holy words of scripture'.[11] Taken straightforwardly, this directly contradicts the total ineffability that Denys has affirmed. A way round the contradiction is however prepared in the next proposition, according to which the biblical revelation is to be understood in a symbolic or metaphorical sense.
3. In the Bible 'the Deity has benevolently taught us that understanding and direct contemplation of itself is inaccessible to beings, since it actually surpasses being'.[12] Thus the biblical discourse operates, perforce, within the borders of the humanly thinkable and sayable, whilst the Transcendent, the Ultimate, the One, lies beyond those borders. What the scriptures reveal is accordingly cast throughout in human terms, which are adapted to varying levels of human comprehension, so that 'the things of God are revealed to each mind in proportion to its capacities'.[13] But even at the highest level of understanding the scriptural revelation cannot give knowledge of the ultimate One in itself, which remains 'above and beyond speech, mind, or being itself'.[14] Hence 'the Transcendent [which is beyond being] is clothed in terms of being . . . We use whatever appropriate symbols we can for the things of God.'[15] And so in *The Celestial Hierarchy* Denys repeatedly emphasizes the symbolic character of

9. *DN* 593A–B.
10. *MT* 1045D.
11. *DN* 589B.
12. *DN* 588C.
13. *DN* 588A.
14. Ibid.
15. *DN* 592B–C.

the scriptural revelation. He says that 'the Word of God makes use of poetic imagery',[16] and he speaks of 'what scripture has revealed to us in symbolic and uplifting fashion',[17] and of how the divine Light makes truth known to us 'by way of representative symbols'.[18]

Again, 'this divine ray can enlighten us only by being upliftingly concealed in a variety of sacred veils which the Providence of the Father adapts to our nature as human beings'.[19] Although the Pseudo-Areopagite does not himself use the term, Denys Turner is surely right in holding that for him the language of revelation is metaphorical. Although, 'like most Platonists, he lacks an adequate appreciation of the logic of metaphors . . . it is perfectly clear that he treats these affirmations and their corresponding denials in the way which is appropriate to metaphorical utterances'.[20] This view is supported by the way in which the biblical imagery that Pseudo-Denys discusses ranges indiscriminately from the sublime to the ridiculous. God is spoken of not only in such liturgically and devotionally familiar terms as lord, king, almighty, good, loving, etc., but also in some very earthly and sometimes off-putting ways. Denys points out, for example, that in the Bible, 'God is clothed in feminine adornments or in the armor of barbarians. He is given the attributes of an artisan, be he potter or refiner. He is put on horses, on chariots, on thrones. Well-laid feasts are put on for him. He is represented as drinking, as inebriated, as sleeping, as someone hung-over . . .'[21] Such language not only invites but positively requires a metaphorical interpretation. That first-order religious language about the Ultimate is metaphorical, or mythological, is likewise part of the pluralist hypothesis.

4. In addition to scripture, and in addition to the daily liturgical life of the church which was always for Denys the context of the mystic quest, the world itself provides further symbols and metaphors of God: 'And so it is that as Cause of all and as transcending all, he is rightly nameless and yet has the names of everything that is.'[22] Again, 'we know [God] from the arrangement of everything, because everything is, in a sense, projected out from him, and this order possesses certain images and semblances of his divine paradigms'.[23]
5. These 'images and semblances' are drawn from the 'good' aspects of the world, an apparently arbitrary restriction which however makes sense within the Neoplatonist picture. For this conceived of the universe as a vast divine emanation, an overflowing of the infinitely rich and fecund divine life away from the ultimate One in a

16. *CH* 137A–B.
17. *CH* 121A.
18. *CH* 121B.
19. *CH* 121B–C.
20. Turner, p. 35.
21. *L* 9, 1105A–B.
22. *DN* 596C.
23. *DN* 896D.

descending cascade of being in which higher and lower forms of existence, from archangels down to inanimate rocks, embody greater and lesser degrees of reality according to their closeness to or distance from the Source. To exist at all, however, even at the most lowly level, is still to participate to some degree in the divine reality. Thus everything that exists is, as such, good, and evil only has a privative reality as the loss of the character proper to something. (To use an example from Augustine, who definitively grafted this Neoplatonic idea into Christianity, blindness is not a 'thing' in its own right, but a lack of proper function in something inherently good, namely the eye.[24]) As Denys says, in true Neoplatonic vein, 'Everything in some way partakes of the providence flowing out of this transcendent Deity which is the originator of all that is. Indeed nothing could exist without some share in the being and source of everything. Even things which have no life participate in this, for it is the transcendent Deity which is the existence of every being.'[25] So, whilst everything has some degree of reality-goodness, it was appropriate for Denys to take images from the higher levels of being.

Denys does however change the Neoplatonist picture by seeing the hierarchically ordered creation, not as an impersonal overflow of superabundant being, but in a more personal way as an overflow of divine love, *eros*. For him, creation is, in Denys Turner's vivid phrase, 'the divine *eros* in volcanic eruption'.[26] And yet Dionysius also wanted, in a way which he never spells out, to maintain the orthodox doctrine of creation *ex nihilo*. He says that 'with one causal gesture God bestows being on everything'.[27] These two notions, on the one hand an instantaneous creation of everything out of nothing, and on the other hand the universe as an emanation of the overflowing divine love, are not obviously compatible, and whilst they may possibly be reconcilable, as Turner suggests,[28] Dionysius himself does not offer any reconciliation.

Further, in this Neoplatonist picture we spiritual creatures are 'sparks of divinity' fallen into the gross material world. In the mystical life we are gradually freeing ourselves from material entanglements to ascend back into the unity of the One. In Denys's system this return consists in the purifying of human spirits as they move upwards towards God. You are, he says, 'with your understanding laid aside, to strive upward as much as you can

24. For a critical discussion of this privative conception of evil, see Hick, 1985, chapter 3.
25. *CH* 177C–D.
26. Turner, p. 29.
27. *DN* 869B.
28. Turner, pp. 31–2.

toward union with him who is beyond all being and knowledge. By an undivided and absolute abandonment of yourself and everything, shedding all and freed from all, you will be uplifted to the ray of the divine shadow which is above everything that is'[29] – and that phrase 'the ray of the divine shadow' is typical of Denys's frequent use of deliberately paradoxical language.

After it had become clear, thanks to the enquiring minds of Erasmus and others in the fifteenth and sixteenth centuries, that Denys was not after all an author from the apostolic period but an anonymous later writer, and therefore not exempt from criticism, some dismissed his writings as too Neoplatonist to be authentically Christian. Martin Luther, for example, declared that 'Dionysius is most pernicious; he platonizes more than he Christianizes';[30] but others have been concerned to defend his orthodoxy. Both judgements presuppose a decision concerning what constitutes authentic Christianity. We have learned in our own time to see Christianity as an enormously complex phenomenon within which many different and changing strands of thought, culture, life style, moral outlook and practice have coexisted within an institutional history which began as one (or perhaps even then as two, the Petrine and Pauline camps), then divided visibly into two in the eleventh-century Schism, and then into three in the Reformation of the sixteenth century, that third division itself quickly fragmenting further into a number of larger and smaller strands. In the early period, before Christianity had become the state religion of the Roman Empire, there was a freedom of theological speculation which was however curtailed during the reign of the emperor Constantine (272–337) in the interests of a uniform faith for a united empire: the crucial Council of Nicea (325) was summoned by Constantine precisely to fulfil this agenda. Jaroslav Pelikan, for example, says that the council was convened 'for the purpose of restoring concord to church and empire'.[31] During the following ten centuries, normative Christianity was defined by the ruling political-ecclesiastical powers in Rome and Constantinople. But any decision that one particular strand of Christian self-understanding is authentic, and another inauthentic, can only express a locally dominant point of view within this long and diverse history. The notion of heresy, which hung as a threat over so many of the Christian mystics, presupposes an all-powerful church which dictates what is to be regarded as unquestionably true. And so the Catholic

29. *MT* 997B–1000A.
30. Quoted by Bernard McGinn, 1991, p. 158, from Luther's *Babylonian Captivity of the Church* (*Weimarer Ausgabe*, 6, 562).
31. Pelikan, 1985, p. 52.

Inquisition of the thirteenth to fifteenth centuries, and the Reformed church in Calvin's sixteenth-century Geneva, punished, and even executed, theological deviants. Happily the church no longer has that degree of secular power or, except among some ecclesiastical leaders and some doctrinally fundamentalist theologians, that degree of dogmatic certainty. And so today theological speculation is able to flourish again in a rich variety of ways as it did in the early centuries. (It cannot however flourish today, alas, within the Roman communion under the repressive rule of the present Pope and his theological watchdog, Cardinal Ratzinger.)

6. Denys, then, endorses on its own level the positive language of scripture, tradition and liturgy. For on this level its metaphorical character presents no obstacle. Its function is to lead us towards an eventual unitive awareness beyond thought and reasoning: 'By itself it [the Good] generously reveals a firm, transcendent beam, granting enlightenments proportionate to each being, and thereby draws sacred minds upward to its permitted contemplation, to participation and to the state of becoming like it.'[32] Again he speaks, in a sentence quoted above, of 'what scripture has revealed to us in symbolic and uplifting fashion',[33] and says that the divine Word 'uses scriptural passages in an uplifting fashion as a way, provided for us from the first, to uplift our mind in a manner suitable to our nature'.[34] That this is the religious function of metaphor and myth is also part of the pluralist hypothesis.
7. The final unitive state lies beyond this life 'when we are incorruptible and immortal . . . And there we shall be, our minds away from passion and from earth, and we shall have a conceptual gift of light from him and, somehow, in a way we cannot know, we shall be united with him and, our understanding carried away, blessedly happy, we shall be struck by his blazing light.'[35]

DIONYSIUS' DILEMMA

To attribute to God the positive characteristics derived from scripture and nature is traditionally called positive (or cataphatic) theology. Negative (or apophatic) theology, on the other hand, holds that we cannot say what God is but only what God is not – for example that God is not 'word or power or mind or life or being'.[36] At first sight Denys's theology is both cataphatic and apophatic. In fact, however, it is more radical than either. For he sees the assertions and denials as cancelling out and thus as pointing beyond themselves to the truly

32. *DN* 588C–D.
33. *CH* 121A.
34. *CH* 137B.
35. *DN* 1:4, *L* 52–3.
36. *DN* 593C.

ineffable. The detail of his discussion is complex and fascinating. But for our present purpose it is sufficient to say that for every legitimate positive statement about God there is an equally legitimate negative statement to cancel it, and together they point beyond themselves to that for which we have no language, either positive or negative. In a key passage Denys says, 'Since it is the Cause of all beings, we should posit and ascribe to it all the affirmations we make in regard to beings, and, more appropriately, we should negate all these affirmations, since it surpasses all being. Now we should not conclude that the negations are simply the opposites of the affirmations, but rather that the cause of all is considerably prior to this, beyond privations, beyond every denial, beyond every assertion.'[37] Again, 'It is beyond assertion and denial. We make assertions and denials of what is next to it, but never of it, for it is both beyond every assertion, being the perfect and unique cause of all things, and, by virtue of its preeminently simple and absolute nature, free of every limitation, beyond every limitation; it is also beyond every denial.'[38]

The situation then, for Denys, is this. The ultimate reality that we call God is, in itself, beyond all the distinctions in terms of which we could make either assertions or denials about it. It lies outside all our categories of thought. It does nevertheless somehow affect us, both as the ultimate ground of the universe and as the inspirer of holy scripture. These furnish us with a rich symbolic or metaphorical language which can aid us on our spiritual journey towards ultimate union with the Transcendent.

In holding that the ineffable One 'has told us about itself in the holy words of scripture',[39] Denys was clearly in danger, depending on how this is understood, of cancelling the divine ineffability. And the danger became a reality in his acceptance of the central Christian doctrines, not as symbolic or metaphorical but (apparently) as literal truths. For a system of ideas which includes both the absolute ineffability of the ultimately real, and also a set of specifically Christian beliefs about that reality, is clearly fatally inconsistent. Either the ultimate One is totally ineffable, and all doctrines about it, including the doctrines of the Trinity and incarnation, are symbolic or metaphorical; or these doctrines are true of the ultimate One in itself, which is then not ineffable. But as a monk whose daily life was centred in the Eucharist and nourished by the scriptures, Denys lived within the all-encompassing thought-world of the church, whose hierarchical structure he believed mirrored the hierarchy of the heavenly beings. *The Mystical Theology* begins with an invocation to the Trinity and, as it

37. *MT* 1000B.
38. *MT* 1048A–B.
39. *DN* 589B.

proceeds, the dogmatic pillars of this thought-world are tacitly exempted from the erasing effect of ineffability. Denys is thus able to affirm that 'the Godhead is . . . one in three persons',[40] and at a number of other places he treats the trinitarian doctrine as a 'given'. Again, the incarnation is assumed without question to be a literal, although mysterious, fact. He says that 'the most evident idea in theology, namely, the sacred incarnation of Jesus for our sakes, is something which cannot be enclosed in words nor grasped by any mind, not even by the leaders among the front ranks of angels. That he undertook to be a man is, for us, entirely mysterious. We have no way of understanding how, in a fashion at variance with nature, he was formed from a virgin's blood.'[41] Denys was thus deeply implicated in the contradiction that, on the one hand, the transcendent Godhead lies beyond both being and knowledge and yet, on the other hand, that we know that it is self-revealed in the church's scriptures and that it is a divine Trinity, one person of whom became incarnate as Jesus of Nazareth.

Should we conclude that the contradiction, although logically self-evident, was invisible within Denys's medieval thought-world? Or can we conceive it to be his too-daring-to-utter speculation that the basic structures of the Christian dogmatic system, and not only its more obviously metaphorical details, point beyond themselves to an utterly transcendent reality that eludes all positive dogmas? This possibility is consistent with the fact that although Denys refers a number of times to the Trinity and the incarnation he has, for an orthodox theologian, remarkably little to say about them. The orthodoxy of his Christology was indeed suspected in the sixth century and had to be defended by his admirers. This may suggest that he was not particularly interested, or therefore careful, in his formulations in this area. Again, as Jaroslav Pelikan says, 'Dionysius manifests relatively little interest in the dogma of the Trinity as such'.[42] And although he quite often speaks of the ultimate Transcendent as the divine Trinity who has acted self-revealingly in the scriptures, he also sometimes speaks of the transcendent Godhead as beyond even divinity: 'There is the transcendent unity of God and the fruitfulness of God, and as we prepare to sing this truth we use the names Trinity and Unity for that which is in fact beyond every name, calling it the transcendent being above every being. But no unity or trinity, no number or oneness, no fruitfulness, indeed, nothing that is or is known can proclaim that hiddenness beyond every mind and reason of the transcendent Godhead which transcends every being.'[43] Again he speaks of the Trinity as a

40. *CH* 212C.
41. *DN* 648A.
42. Pelikan, 1987, p. 19.
43. *DN* 981A.

manifestation of the supreme deity: the scriptures, he says, 'describe it [God] as a Trinity, for with transcendent fecundity it is manifested as "three persons"'.[44] All this hints at the distinction between the unknowable Godhead and the known and worshipped God – a central theme of the pluralist hypothesis. McGinn finds such a distinction adumbrated by Denys in 'the fundamental distinction between God hidden and God revealed',[45] which he points to in the first chapter of *The Divine Names* where Denys speaks of the 'hidden transcendent God' which 'surpasses being',[46] and in the second *Letter*, where Denys says that 'he who surpasses everything also surpasses the source of divinity (*thearchia*)',[47] the Thearchy being the creative power which has produced the world. It is however unclear how strongly Denys intends this distinction, and we would probably not be justified in claiming his deliberate authority for it. Nor can we automatically assume that his writings are completely consistent. He would have been a very exceptional thinker if this were the case.

At any rate, Denys's affirmation of the transcategorial nature of ultimate reality, of the metaphorical character of human language about that reality, and of the practical function of that language in promoting spiritual growth, even though they may not cohere with everything else in his writings, express the basic elements of modern religious pluralism. They can readily be extended in a way that was not an option for the Pseudo-Areopagite, living as he did within a Christendom that was assumed to constitute the entire civilized world. For the distinction between, on the one hand, the transcendent and ineffable Godhead and, on the other, the personal God of the Bible, opens up a whole new realm of possibilities. It suggests that the known objects of devotion, or foci of meditation, within other religious traditions may stand in the same relation as does the biblical God to the ultimate transcendent reality. It might then be the case that not only Christianity, but also each of the other great world religions, has its own system of symbols, metaphors, myths, spiritual practices, forms of religious experience, historical exemplars and traditions, life styles and supporting communities, within which men and women are enabled gradually to transcend the ego-self and move towards union with the ultimately real.

MEISTER ECKHART AND OTHERS

An explicit drawing of the distinction between the unknowable Godhead and the known God of the Bible had to wait until the German mystic Meister Eckhart (1260–c. 1328), who was himself profoundly

44. *DN* 592A.
45. McGinn, 1991, p. 163.
46. *DN* 588C.
47. *L2*, 1068A.

influenced by Pseudo-Denys. 'God and the Godhead', he says, 'are as different from each other as heaven and earth'.[48] However he does not say a great deal more than this. He quotes Pseudo-Dionysius as speaking of 'the unknown God above all gods'[49] and he suggests that whereas the God of the Bible is personal and triune, and acts within human history, this cannot be said of the Godhead: 'God acts. The Godhead does not.'[50] Eckhart even accepts the implication that the known God of the Bible and of Christian experience exists only in relation to the worshipping community. 'For before there were creatures', he says, 'God was not god, but, rather, he was what he was. When creatures came to be and took on creaturely being, then God was no longer God as he is in himself, but god as he is with creatures.'[51] Or as he says elsewhere, 'before there were any creatures God was not "God"', i.e. not the humanly known god.[52] Thus Eckhart's distinction between Godhead (*Gottheit, deitas*) and God (*Gott, deus*), opens the door to the distinction between the Real and its plurality of manifestations, although it did not take Eckhart himself through that door. Probably the nearest that Christian thought came to this, prior to the twentieth century, was in Nicholas of Cusa (1401–64), with his affirmation that 'there is only one religion in the variety of rites'.[53]

Much more briefly, having concentrated on Pseudo-Denys because of his immense influence within Christian mysticism, we must note that mystical Judaism and mystical Islam also draw a distinction between God in God's ultimate ineffable being and God as humanly known and worshipped.

The Jewish mystics distinguished between *Eyn Sof* (the Infinite) and the revealed god of the scriptures. David Blumenthal says that 'in Zoharic and Lurianic Kabbala, the Eyn Sof is the unknowable, infinite, remotest aspect of God'.[54] And Gershom Scholem says, 'It has been argued that the difference between *deus absconditus*, God in Himself, and God in His appearance, is unknown in Kabbalism. This seems to me a wrong interpretation of the facts. On the contrary, the dualism embedded in these two aspects of the one God, both of which are, theologically speaking, possible ways of aiming at the divinity, has deeply preoccupied the Jewish mystics.'[55]

In Islam there is the distinction, among the mystics, between the ultimate reality, *al-Haqq*, and the revealed God of the Qur'an. Thus Al-'Arabi says, 'God is absolute or restricted as He pleases; and the God of religious beliefs is subject to limitations, for He is the God contained in the heart of His servant. But the absolute God is not contained in

48. Sermon 27; Eckhart, 1941, p. 225.
49. Sermon 1; ibid., p. 100.
50. Sermon 27; ibid., p. 226.
51. Sermon 28; ibid., p. 228.
52. Sermon 52; Eckhart, 1981, p. 200.
53. Nicholas of Cusa, p. 7.
54. Blumenthal, 1978, p. 180.
55. Scholem, 1980, p. 148.

anything.' Again, 'The Essence, as being beyond all these relationships, is not a divinity . . . it is we who make Him a divinity by being that through which He knows Himself as Divine. Thus, He is not known [as 'Allah'] until we are known.'[56]

And so the pluralist hypothesis, which is not itself a religious doctrine but a philosophical theory about the relation between the religions, and the status of their deities and absolutes, can appeal to significant concurring elements within each of the great monotheisms.

56. Al-'Arabi, p. 92.

10

THE REAL EXPERIENCED AS THE ABSOLUTE

IN HINDUISM

As we saw earlier, 'Hinduism' refers to the many and varied strands of Indian religious life and thought which have in common a reverence for the ancient Vedic scriptures. We are concerned now with the non-theistic advaita (non-dualist) Vedanta philosophy represented above all by the great medieval thinker Shankara.

The central focus is Brahman, that which is alone ultimately real as the eternal, unchanging, ultimate ground and being of everything. Shankara drew the momentous distinction between *nirguna* and *saguna* Brahman. The former is Brahman without attributes, formless or ineffable, transcategorial. It is what is is, but what it is lies outside our human conceptual repertoire. *Saguna* Brahman, on the other hand, is that same reality as humanly thought and experienced, namely as Ishwara, personal deity, known in different forms as Brahma, Vishnu, Shiva and very many more. These are regarded as different, generally regional, manifestations of the divine.

Nirguna and *saguna* Brahman (to adopt these terms into our English vocabulary) are not two different 'things', but are the same ultimate reality – that reality as it is in itself, and as it has been given concrete form within the realm of human thought and imagination. In the words of the fascinating Hindu text that I have already quoted, 'Thou art formless: thy only form is our knowledge of thee.'[1] If, then, there were no human beings, there would be no *saguna* Brahman, since this exists only in relation to human consciousness, but there would still be the

1. *Yogava'sistha* 1.28; Pansikar, p. 144.

eternal reality of *nirguna* Brahman. The *nirguna/saguna* distinction is analogous to the Kantian distinction between noumenon and phenomenon when applied to religion.

The perennial problem, however, for all who speak of the ineffable or *nirguna* aspect of the Real is, as we have seen, that they usually also want to attribute at least some positive qualities to it. No religious tradition has been able to resist this temptation. Thus in the last quotation Brahman is addressed as 'Thou'. And in Vedantic thought generally Brahman is referred to as *satchitananda* – *sat* (being, reality), *chit* (consciousness), and *ananda* (bliss, happiness). This characterization of *nirguna* Brahman unintentionally undermines the basic principle that Brahman is totally 'formless' or transcategorial. And as we saw in the last chapter, many western mystics likewise affirm the absolute ineffability of God and yet also, in their religious life, use the positive theological language of their tradition. This is in order, but only if we distinguish between God as ultimate reality, beyond the range of our human conceptualities, and God as impinging upon and conceptualized by us in our human terms. It is the latter who is described in our theologies and worshipped in our temples and churches.

Thus Hindu religious thought includes both an affirmation of the transcategorial nature of ultimate reality and also an acknowledgement of the validity of different limited forms of awareness of that reality. The implication of this for understanding religious diversity was evident to the Hindu mystics and poets known as the Alvars (sages or saints) in southern India in and around the tenth century CE. Part of one of their great texts, the *Bhagavata Purana* (chapter 22), written in the ninth or tenth century, as translated/interpreted by Swami Prabhavananda, reads: 'Truth has many aspects. Infinite truth has infinite expressions. Though the sages speak in divers ways, they express one and the same Truth. Ignorant is he who says, "What I say and know is true: others are wrong." It is because of this attitude of the ignorant that there have been doubts and misunderstandings about God. This attitude it is that causes dispute among men. But all doubts vanish when one gains self-control and attains tranquillity by realizing the heart of Truth. Thereupon dispute, too, is at an end.'[2] And in northern India around the fifteenth century, Kabir, revered by Hindus and Muslims alike, looked beyond the Hindu/Muslim division, and beyond the caste distinctions of his society:

> O servant, where dost thou seek me?
> Lo! I am beside thee.

2. Prabhavananda, pp. 270–1. For a more literal translation see Ganesh Vasudeo Tagare, *The Bhagavata Purana*, Part V, Delhi: Motilal Banarsidass, 1978, pp. 2050–1.

I am neither in temple nor in mosque:
  I am neither in Kaaba nor in Kailash:
Neither am I in rites and ceremonies,
  nor in Yoga and renunciation.
If thou art a true seeker, thou shalt at once see Me;
  thou shalt meet Me in a moment of time.
Kabir says, 'O Sadhu! God is the breath or all breath.'

It is needless to ask of a saint the caste to which he belongs;
For the priest, the warrior, the tradesman, and all the
  thirty-six castes, alike are seeking God.
It is but folly to ask what the caste of a saint may be;
The barber has sought God, the washerwoman,
  and the carpenter –
Even Raidas was a seeker after God.
The Rishi Swapacha was a tanner by caste.
Hindus and Moslems alike have achieved that End,
  where remains no mark of distinction.[3]

Some of Kabir's poems were later included in the Sikh scriptures, the *Adi Granth*, compiled in the seventeenth century, because they are so fully consonant with the spirit of the early Gurus. It is told that when Guru Nanak (1469–1539) returned from a period of silence in the jungle to initiate the Sikh faith he announced, 'There is no Hindu and there is no Mussalman.'[4] In the *Adi Granth* we read:

Some call on the Lord, 'Ram, Ram!' Some cry, 'Khuda!'
Some bow to Him as Gosain, some as Allah:
He is called the Ground of Grounds and also the Bountiful,
The Mountain of Mercies, the Merciful . . .
The Hindus bathe in holy waters for His sake;
The Moslems make the pilgrimage to Mecca.
The Hindus worship in temples, the Moslems go down
  on their mats.
There are those who read the Vedas and those others,
  Christians, Jews, Moslems, who read the Semitic scriptures.
Some wear blue, some white robes,
Some call themselves Moslems, some Hindus:
Some aspire to Bahishat, some to Swarga,
The paradises of the Moslems and Hindus.
But Nanak saith: He that knoweth the will of the Lord
He will find out the Lord's secrets![5]

3. Kabir, pp. 45–6. There is doubt as to whether some of the material that Tagore translated is indeed directly Kabir's. It does however come from traditional Kabiri songs and must reflect Kabir's teaching.
4. Harbans Singh, p. 97.
5. Rag Ramkali, 885; Trilochan Singh, pp. 193–4.

Behind this there lies the pan-Indian distinction between God in God's-self and God in relation to the creation. For Sikhism shared the assumption that 'God exists in two modes – in the *nirguna* mode as the supreme impersonal reality, and in the *saguna* mode as personal God who is the Creator and to whom men turn for prayer and succour'.[6] In more specifically Sikh terms, '*Nirankar* or *Ekam-kar* is the . . . Transcendent and Absolute, whilst *Omkar* is the ground of the Creation'.[7]

Further, for Nanak and many others who shared his pluralistic outlook, whilst the absolutely Real in itself is beyond human conceiving, it is nevertheless humanly pictured and responded to in different ways within the different religious traditions. This outlook has been pervasive in varying degrees within Hindu thought, and in the twentieth century it became politically powerful in the thought of Mahatma Gandhi who said, in the spirit of Kabir, 'Hindus, Mussalmans, Christians, Parsis, Jews are convenient labels. But when I tear them down, I do not know which is which. We are all children of the same God.'[8]

IN BUDDHISM

Within Buddhism, in its Mahayana or northern development, a distinction developed analgous to that between *nirguna* and *saguna* Brahman. Within the Trikaya (three bodies) doctrine, the Dharmakaya (dharma body) is, to quote Schumann's exposition, 'the absolute reality, besides which there is no other reality'.[9] Like almost everything else within so long, widely spread, and internally diverse a tradition as Buddhism, the concept underwent development. But centrally, the Dharmakaya is the 'transcendent truth or reality of all beings and appearances: the indestructible, timeless Absolute, the one essence in and behind all that was, or is, and will be'.[10] It is variously referred to as reality (*dharmata*), core of reality (*dharmadhatu*), 'thusness' (*tathata*), emptiness (*sunyata*), buddha nature (*buddhata*). And this ultimate reality is 'formless', empty of every humanly conceivable quality, totally ineffable, transcategorial.

The ineffable Dharmakaya is however concretely expressed in the transcendent Buddha figures of the Sambhogakaya ('body of bliss'), some of whom are known to humanity by name as the objects of Buddhist cults. Thus Amida is the focus of the (mainly Japanese) Pure Land tradition, which is a virtually theistic form of Buddhism. Here Amida is analogous to the Ishwara of advaitic Hinduism.

6. Sohan Singh, pp. 141–2.
7. Trilochan Singh, p. 53.
8. *Harijan*, 18 April 1936.
9. Schumann, p. 103.
10. Ibid., p. 102.

These 'heavenly' Buddhas sometimes become incarnate on earth as the human Buddhas (Enlightened Ones), constituting the Nirmanakaya ('manifest body'). We are at present within the era of Gautama Buddha, who lived in northern India during the axial age. The next Buddha, waiting to become incarnate on earth at some time in the future, is Maitreya, the Kind One.

Another key Buddhist term is *sunyata*, emptiness or void. This concept was particularly developed in the Madhyamika philosophy, the central philosophy of Mahayana Buddhism, occupying (as T.R.V. Murti has shown) a place analogous to that of Kant's philosophy in western thought.[11] For 'The great contribution that Buddhist thought made to Indian philosophy', Murti says, 'was the discovery of the subjective – the doctrine of appearance.'[12] This parallels the Kantian teaching that the experienced, or phenomenal, world is the appearance to distinctively human consciousness of the unexperienceable world-as-it-is-in-itself. On the one hand, according to the Madhyamika, 'the Real is non-dual – free from all empirical predicates and relation. It is Sunya, devoid of every kind of determination.'[13] That is to say, it is empty of everything that the human mind projects in its activity of awareness. 'To say that reality is "empty" means that it goes beyond definability, and cannot be qualified as this or that.'[14] But in our unenlightened state we are aware of it only in terms of our own human concepts. 'The implication of the Madhyamika method is that the real is overlaid with the undergrowth of our notions and views. Most of them are *a priori*; this is avidya (ignorance), which, in this system is equated with the ideal construction screening the real.'[15] Accordingly, 'God is a personal manifestation, the individualisation, of the Absolute. As this is a free phenomenalisation, there is no conceivable limit to the number, form and occasion of these manifestations.'[16] Thus the foci of worship and meditation within the different great religions are different phenomenal forms of the Real.

This distinction between the Ultimate in itself and the Ultimate as manifested in human thought and experience is clearly expressed by the great Pure Land thinker Shinran (1173–1262 CE), who quotes the earlier T'an-luan: 'Among Buddhas and bodhisattvas there are two aspects of dharmakaya: dharmakaya-as-suchness and dharmakaya-as-compassion. Dharmakaya-as-compassion arises out of dharmakaya-as-suchness and dharmakaya-as-suchness emerges into [human consciousness through]

11. Murti, 1980.
12. Ibid., p. 57.
13. Ibid., p. 228.
14. Suzuki, 1982, p. 103.
15. Murti, p. 212.
16. Ibid., p. 226.

dharmakaya-as-compassion. These two aspects of dharmakaya differ but are not separate; they are one but not identical.'[17] They are the ultimate reality in itself and in its impact on humanity.

In the east then, as well as in the west, the mystical strand of religion supports the basic elements of the pluralist hypothesis.

17. Shinran, p. 5.

PART IV

RELIGIOUS EXPERIENCE AND MYSTICISM

11

ALTERED STATES OF CONSCIOUSNESS

This fourth part deals with an enormously varied field. The material could have been arranged in several different ways and presented in several equally appropriate orders. But this order seems as suitable as any other.

SOME DISTINCTIONS

First, some philosophical distinctions. By experience I mean modifications of consciousness. So long as we are conscious, we are experiencing. And the basic distinction is between experience *of* something other than one's own mental state, and experience that is simply the reflexive awareness of that mental state. When I look through the window at the oak tree in the garden I am having a visual experience of the oak tree. But when I am doing mental arithmetic, adding up some numbers 'in my head', I am not experiencing anything 'out there' but am being aware of what I am doing in my own mind. The difference is that the counting operation exists only in my consciousness, whilst the tree exists in the garden. In each case there is a modification of my consciousness, but the latter constitutes an experience of something beyond me, the former an experience which terminates within my own mind. And the big question concerning religious, including mystical, experience is whether it is experience of reality beyond us or only an internally generated modification of one's own consciousness.

Since religious experience consists of *any* modification of consciousness structured by religious concepts, it is not necessarily experience of a transcendent reality. We will come later to the criterion by which we make this discrimination. But presuming upon that for the moment – and it will turn out to be a fairly non-controversial criterion – let us be clear that religious experience, simply as such, can express not only an openness, but also a closedness, to the Divine, and a closedness that is all the more dangerous for being expressed religiously. In terms of the universal metaphor of light, religious experience is sometimes a window open to the divine radiance, but sometimes a reflection of our own hatred, greed, spite, ignorance, fear or self-assertion. In traditional religious terms, it can be demonic as well as divine. And so whilst the experiential aspect of religion is vital and central to it, it is also central to its destructive aberrations.

ALTERED STATES

Ordinary human consciousness has developed in the struggle to survive and flourish within the physical world and the social group. As we saw in chapter 4, it is normally restricted to those aspects of the environment that are relevant to our practical needs. But there is ample evidence that the mind is capable of transcending these limitations. As William James said, 'Our normal waking consciousness . . . is but one special type of consciousness, whilst all about it, parted from it by the filmiest of screens, there lie potential forms of consciousness entirely different.'[1] The filtering function of the brain and nervous system, and of our own conceptual frameworks, protects our individuality by screening out the virtual infinity of information flowing around us all the time. For a finite consciousness is constituted by boundaries maintained by a grid that excludes all except a minute aspect of reality. From this point of view, the mind/brain functions as a kind of reducing valve, evolved to keep out far more information than it lets in.[2]

In altered states of consciousness this filtering mechanism is partially suspended, releasing a flood of information not normally available to us. Drugs which act directly on the brain to inhibit its normal screening function have for this reason long been used for religious purposes. Worship in ancient India used *soma*, the juice of a plant – precisely what plant is not certain – probably mixed with water and milk, some of which was offered as a libation to the god of the cult and the rest drunk by the priest and worshippers, no doubt with mind-changing effects. The ancient Aztecs used Mexican mushrooms and mescalin derived from the peyote cactus, and many other cultures have likewise used a

1. William James, p. 374.
2. Philosophers who have argued along these lines include Henri Bergson (in *Matter and Memory*), C.D. Broad (in *Religion, Philosophy and Psychical Research*), and H.H. Price (in *Philosophical Interactions with Parapsychology*).

variety of plants with psychedelic properties. These enhance other less dramatic but no less effective means that have also long been used throughout the world to induce altered states of consciousness. A controlled reduction of breathing can increase the concentration of carbon dioxide in the blood; fasting and sensory deprivation in dark caves and cells can disorientate normal consciousness, as can prolonged loss of sleep and bodily mortifications. Music and dancing – and I am not referring here to the ecstasy-driven rave dancing of today's young – can powerfully evoke a sense of transcendence, as can paintings, stained-glass windows, images, icons and of course architecture – great cathedrals with their spires pointing to the heavens, and great mosques with their beautiful symmetry symbolizing the perfect unity of God. These factors are carefully orchestrated in the rich liturgies of, for example, Catholic, Orthodox and high Anglican services, their numinous atmosphere enhanced by uplifting music, splashes of golden, purple and green vestments, candles, incense, tinkling bells, archaic language and solemn hieratic processions. Such aesthetic symphonies evoke, and are designed to evoke, a sense of the sacred and a response of worship.

DRUGS AND ALTERED STATES

I am assuming as something generally agreed that every mental event is correlated with a brain event, whether located in a specific part of the brain or involving a wider area. And I am assuming, in accordance with common experience, both that brain influences mind and that mind influences brain. On the one hand, when the nervous system, which extends from the brain throughout the body, is affected by the impacts of the environment, the brain, as the central mass of the system, undergoes changes which produce the modifications of consciousness that constitute our awareness of the world around us. More dramatically, it has been found in brain surgery that stimulation of particular parts of the temporal lobe can cause intense fear, of other parts despair, and of yet other parts a feeling of disgust, and such brain-mapping is advancing all the time.[3] So there is indisputable evidence that changes in the state of the brain are directly reflected in changes in consciousness. It is equally evident that events in consciousness bring about brain events. This happens whenever we exercise volition in thinking, speaking or purposefully moving our bodies. As I think about the sentence that I am constructing, this thinking automatically produces its correlative brain state. When I will to raise my right hand

3. For an up to date account, see Carter, 1998.

this produces an appropriate brain event, which sends messages along the nerves, causing my hand to rise. *How* this mutual influencing occurs we do not know, for consciousness itself remains a complete and utter mystery to us. But this mysterious two-way causality is a reality, and it applies to religious and mystical as much as to all other forms of experience.

We are concerned at the moment with the psychedelic, or mind-altering, drugs. We have already noted that peyote, containing mescalin, and the sacred mushroom, containing psilocybin and psilocyn, have been widely used in religious ceremonies. And the same is true of hemp (hashish, marijuana, cannabis, bhang, ganja). In recent times more complex synthetized drugs, such as LSD (lysergic acid diethylamide), have also become available and, although not used in religious contexts, produce effects that can be compared with religious experiences.

Most of the systematic studies of psychedelic drugs were made in the 1950s and 1960s before their use became illegal in the United States and Europe, and it is to this period that we look both for laboratory observations and for published accounts of freelance experiments. It was in 1968 that Carlos Castenada published his best-selling account of extraordinary experiences under the powerful influence of peyote, as a disciple of the (real or possibly fictional) Mexican Yaqui Indian shaman, Don Juan Matus. Earlier than that, in 1953, Aldous Huxley had written a classic description of his own experience after taking mescalin, and his short book is still a valuable document. It mainly illustrates the enormous capacity of the drug to intensify perception. At one point, for example, he noticed a garden chair: 'That chair – shall I ever forget it? Where the shadows fell on the canvas upholstery, stripes of a deep but glowing indigo alternated with stripes of an incandescence so intensely bright that it was hard to believe that they could be made of anything but blue fire. For what seemed an immensely long time I gazed without knowing, even wishing to know, what it was that confronted me . . . It was inexpressibly wonderful, wonderful to the point, almost, of being terrifying'. He adds, 'suddenly I had an inkling of what it must feel like to be mad.'[4] It seems very possible that some of the great painters – such as Van Gogh, Renoir and Monet – have seen the world with something of this enhanced intensity which they have then tried to capture on their canvasses. Indeed another 1950s mescalin experimenter, Raymond Mortimer, reported that 'the room looked like a rich Impressionist picture, so sensitive was I to the gradations in tonal value and reflected colour'.[5]

4. Huxley, pp. 43–4.
5. Zaehner, p. 210.

SELF-TRANSCENDENCE

More important for our present purpose is the capacity of drugs to induce ego-transcendence. The ego and its concerns cease to matter as the experiencer is aware of being part of a more universal reality, sometimes observing the little ego-self apparently from beyond it. Reporting his own experiences under LSD, Ray Jordan records several different kinds of ego-transcendence. One is reminiscent of the experience of advaitic mystics: 'I have realized that quite literally everything is Self, everything in the whole field of experience – both what is usually known as self and all that usually is not self (people, objects, sky, earth, etc.). This Self which is everything is not the same as the ego-self. It is not that I, Ray Jordan, am everything, but that there is a more fundamental self which is everything, including Ray Jordan.' In another kind of experience he 'has retained the usual ego-self – the "I" or "me" of everyday life – but has extended the boundaries of its identity. Certain people and objects physically separate from me have become quite literally me.' In yet another kind, reminiscent of an aspect of Buddhist experience, 'I have remained more or less the self I usually am, but I have become intensely aware of the relative nature of this self in relation to others. I have perceived that the self is not an independent entity completely separable from other selves. "I" and "other" have become correlative existences, neither of which could be isolated but both of which continually interact interdependently.' And analogous to another type of Buddhist experience, 'Distinguishable from all the above changes there has also occurred a complete disappearance of self in any and every sense – whether that of the ego-self, universal Self, or other selves. Consciousness has continued, and perhaps more clearly than ever, with all the activities of body, mind, feeling, other humans, cars, sun, sky, earth, etc., continuing on in a complex, boundless flow neither chaotic nor orderly. At such a moment reality (or Reality) simply is being as it is, and this "beingness" has been of the deepest significance, beyond both chaos and particular patterns.'[6] In yet another kind of experience, in which psychedelic drugs are used communally, individual selfish concerns disappear, releasing warm mutual affection throughout the group. This also may perhaps be an echo of the Buddhist discovery that self-transcendence naturally expresses itself in compassion for all life.

Since ego-transcendence of some kind is sought in almost all forms of religion, we have to ask whether this goal can be reached through drugs without the long practice and discipline taught by the religions.

6. Jordan, pp. 284–5.

The conclusion that seems to me most likely is that the self-transcendence induced by drugs can, in favourable circumstances, show experiencers something of their own spiritual nature. It can reveal to them that in another dimension of their being they are not the separate self-enclosed ego of our ordinary competitive existence, but are part of a greater reality, awareness of which is a joy that overflows in love. Whether this experience is understood in religious terms depends upon the cultural background of the experiencer. The same is true of mystical experiences that are not drug-induced. For according to our big picture, human awareness of the Transcendent takes many forms, not all of which are structured by religious concepts. If there is a divine reality, always and everywhere invisibly present to us, history shows that whilst it has normally been experienced in religious terms, it may also be experienced, particularly within a non-religious culture, without the use of religious concepts. Here, for example, is the ego-transcending experience of the atheist Marxist Arthur Koestler.

During the Spanish civil war in the 1930s Koestler was in Spain on the government (i.e. anti-Franco) side, and was at one point captured and imprisoned, with a real possibility of being taken out any day and shot as a spy. He tells how he was standing at the recessed window of cell No. 40, trying to distract himself by remembering geometrical proofs, and scratching mathematical formulae on the wall with a piece of iron-spring from his wire mattress. Such proofs had always enchanted him by their intellectual beauty and purity. Now he suddenly saw why: they were precise statements about the infinite.

> The infinite is a mystical mass shrouded in a haze; and yet it was possible to gain some knowledge of it without losing oneself in treacly ambiguities. The significance of this swept over me like a wave. The wave had originated in an articulate verbal insight; but this evaporated at once, leaving in its wake only a wordless essence, a fragrance of eternity, a quiver of the arrow in the blue. I must have stood there for some minutes, entranced, with a wordless awareness that 'this is perfect – perfect'; until I noticed some slight mental discomfort nagging at the back of my mind – some trivial circumstance that marred the perfection of the moment. Then I remembered the nature of that irrelevant annoyance: I was, of course, in prison and might be shot. But this was immediately answered by a feeling whose verbal translation would be: 'So what? Is that all? Have you got nothing more serious to worry about?', an answer so spontaneous, fresh and amused as if the intruding annoyance had been the loss of a collar-stud. Then I was floating on my back in a river of peace, under bridges of silence. It came from nowhere and

> flowed nowhere. Then there was no river and no I. The I had ceased to exist . . .

Commenting on his experience he says, 'The I ceases to exist because it has, by a kind of mental osmosis, established communication with, and been dissolved in, the universal pool. It is this process of dissolution and limitless expansion which is sensed as the "oceanic feeling", as the draining of all tension, the absolute catharsis, the peace that passeth all understanding.'[7] Koestler himself assumed – in accordance with his naturalistic worldview – that, however wonderful, this was a purely psychological phenomenon. But an experient's own understanding of his or her experience is no more automatically correct in the case of a naturalistic than of a religious construal of it. It is possible that in the moment when 'there was no I' he was accessing what Zen refers to as the selfless self.

But there is also a dark side to self-transcendence. I am not thinking here only of frenzied orgiastic rites in the ancient world in which human sacrifices were offered to the gods, but also of the self-transcendence experienced by religious and ideological devotees in the modern world. In the great Nuremberg rallies of the 1930s and 1940s, when 'a delirious mass of Nazi fanatics gathered in the huge stadium on the last night of the party rally',[8] thirty thousand arms were raised in the Nazi salute amid triumphant banners and stirring martial music as young men and women were lifted out of themselves into a common dedication to Race, Nation and Fuhrer. Self-transcendence can open us to the divine, but it can also open into a world of demonic chauvinism, communal self-assertion, and contemptuous hatred of outsiders.

THE INFLUENCE OF SET AND SETTING

Huxley insists upon something that the psychologists who have investigated the effects of drugs also constantly emphasize, namely that the quality of the experience, as wonderful or terrifying, depends upon the state of mind of the user and the context of the use. As Huxley puts it, mescalin can open doors both to heaven and to hell. He concludes, 'It is faith, or loving confidence, which guarantees that visionary experience shall be blissful . . . Negative emotions – the fear which is the absence of confidence, the hatred, anger or malice which exclude love – are the guarantee that visionary experience, if and when it comes, shall be appalling.'[9] The psychiatrist Charles Tart, speaking of 'bad trips', says that 'in many d-ASCs [drug-altered states of consciousness],

7. Paffard, pp. 73–4.
8. Shirer, p. 383.
9. Huxley, p. 109.

defenses against unacceptable personal impulses become partially or wholly ineffective, so that the person feels flooded with traumatic material he cannot handle'.[10] And he cites a range of evidence that the effects of marijuana (cannabis), and even of the much stronger LSD, depend to a large extent on the prior state of mind of the user, concluding that 'psychological factors are the main components of the d-ASC associated with marijuana use'.[11] Ray Jordan reports the conclusion of a number of investigators that the effects of LSD and mescalin 'are dependent not only upon dosage, but on the intention of the subject as he submits himself to the experience, the kind of preparation he has had prior to the taking of the material, the setting of the session'.[12] This is borne out again in the case of mescalin by the fact that a number of others who experimented with the same drug in the 1950s sometimes reported results very different from Huxley's. R.C. Zaehner collected some of their accounts. Rosalind Heywood, for example, had fascinatingly beautiful moments of the extraordinary intensity of perception that Huxley experienced, but at other moments 'I seemed to be caught like a wasp in the sordid brown treacle of a man's anger. I saw a wild black figure chopping off heads, because it was so funny to see them fall. Worst of all, I came upon the "lost", squatting, grey-veiled, among grey rocks, "at the bottom", unable to communicate, alone beyond despair.'[13] Raymond Mortimer shared the extraordinary intensity of perception that seems to be a common feature of the experience, but also found that 'the drug eventually produced the most horrifying experience I have ever known'.[14] Zaehner himself, on the other hand, responded quite differently. Although at one stage he saw strange movements and pulsations in the pictures he was looking at, the main result of the drug in his case was uncontrollable laughter, at everything and nothing. He says that 'in Huxley's terminology "self-transcendence" of a sort did take place, but transcendence into a world of farcial meaninglessness'.[15]

It seems clear then, that mescalin does radically change one's perception of the physical world but that, beyond this, its effects depend to a great extent upon the state of mind of the user. The fact that drugs can open a variety of doors, but do not determine which door we open, is a key to the difference between drug experiences simply as such, and as an aid to religious awareness. The psychologist Walter Pahnke reports that 'our evidence has suggested that careful preparation and expectation play an important part, not only in the type of experience attained but in later fruits for life. Positive mystical experience with psychedelic drugs is by no means automatic. It would seem that the

10. Tart, p. 225.
11. Ibid., p. 153.
12. Jordan, p. 288.
13. Zaehner, p. 209.
14. Ibid., p. 211.
15. Ibid., p. 226.

"drug effect" is a delicate combination of psychological set and setting in which the drug itself is the trigger or facilitating agent – i.e. in which the drug is a *necessary* but not *sufficient* condition. Perhaps the hardest "work" comes after the experience, which in itself may only provide the motivation for future efforts to integrate and appreciate what has been learned. Unless such an experience is integrated into the on-going life of the individual, only a memory remains rather than the growth of an unfolding renewal process which may be awakened by the mystical experience.'[16] From the point of view of our big picture, whilst drugs can affect the brain in such a way as to induce ego-transcendence, this *in itself* has no religious significance. Whether or not, and to what degree, ego-transcendence opens the consciousness to the universal presence of the Real depends upon the spiritual state of the experiencer. A genuine contact with the Holy, the Divine, the Real – whether or not structured by religious concepts – is life-transforming in the ways that we see clearly in the mahatmas or saints.

The importance of mind-set, and (as we shall see presently) of social setting, depends upon the fact that as well as brain states influencing mental states, the reverse is also true; mental states produce their corresponding brain states. It has, for example, been found experimentally that in Zen and in some forms of yogic meditation, the alpha rhythm of the brain increases.[17] Indeed we know from feedback experiments in psychological laboratories that it is possible for the conscious mind to learn to influence the autonomic nervous system responsible for such functions as the rate of heartbeat, blood pressure and body temperature.[18] There is therefore no a priori reason to doubt the claims of some yogic practitioners to be able to do this by extraordinary mental concentration.

But as well as the outlook and expectations of the drug user, the setting in which the use takes place – which of course in turn affects that outlook and expectation – is equally important. An example of drugs being used with conscious intention and skilled techniques to open worshippers to the divine presence is described by the anthropologist J.S. Slotkin in his fascinating study of the Menomini Indians of Wisconsin, in whose religious life peyote played a central part. Their peyote-eating rite was 'a means of supplicating the Great Spirit to give the Peyotists and their families enough power to "live well" in this world, and to achieve heavenly bliss after death'.[19] They believed that 'by eating peyote under the proper ritual conditions a person can incorporate some of the Great Spirit's power . . . The preconditions are physical and spiritual purification. Physical purification is achieved by

16. Pahnke, p. 273.
17. Ornstein, p. 216.
18. Ibid., p. 224.
19. Slotkin, p. 582.

bathing and dressing in clean clothes; spiritual, by putting aside evil thoughts and adopting a humble and receptive attitude towards the Great Spirit.'[20] Slotkin says, 'The Peyotists are supposed to have a feeling of brotherly love for one another. This is expressed during the rite by means of elaborate forms of courtesy, respect, and honoring, as well as gift giving. Such brotherhood also extended to Peyotists of other tribes. There is much intertribal visiting when a meeting is held.'[21] The rites were conducted in a solemn way, controlled throughout by a spiritual purpose. 'As for the condition of the Indians during the ceremony, they were neither stupified nor drunk. Each individual was sufficiently aware of what was going on to be able to sing or drum when his turn came. The participants were never out of rhythm or fumbled their words; they were all quiet, courteous, and considerate of one another; and none acted in an unseemly manner.'[22] According to Slotkin, the Indians did not value the purely visual effects that so impressed Aldous Huxley. These were merely an incidental distraction from communion with the Great Spirit. And indeed Huxley himself says, 'I am not so foolish as to equate what happens under the influence of mescalin or of any other drug, prepared or in the future preparable, with the realization of the end and ultimate purpose of life: Enlightenment, the Beatific Vision.'[23]

We shall look later at the long-term significance of religious and mystical experience. But the only significance of altered states of consciousness simply as such, apart from their considerable curiosity value, is that, as Zaehner says, the experience 'always leaves one with an impression of greater reality than anything supplied by ordinary sense perception'.[24] In terms of our big picture, we must conclude that altered states of consciousness *can* be a contact with the Transcendent. But they can also be a nightmarish encounter with repressed imaginings, fears, anxieties, hatreds, guilts and denials, producing the sometimes dangerous delusions of drunkenness and the disturbing and hellish experiences of the drug-induced 'bad trip'. Further, drug use can be, and indeed usually is, a temporary retreat from the stresses, strains and pressures of ordinary life, which when over-indulged can be morally disabling, producing an apathetic disengagement from the world. Aldous Huxley listed as one of the features of the mescalin experience that 'the mescalin taker sees no reason for doing anything in particular and finds most of the causes for which, at ordinary times, he was prepared to act and suffer, profoundly uninteresting'.[25] Raymond Mortimer likewise reported that 'thought and memory remained; emotion entirely vanished. I remembered without pleasure or pain; I

20. Ibid., p. 568.
21. Ibid., p. 571.
22. Ibid., p. 570.
23. Huxley, pp. 58–9.
24. Zaehner, p. 70.
25. Huxley, pp. 20–1.

looked forward without desire or fear . . . I thought without the faintest affection of the persons to whom I was most attached; I could muster no resentment against persons who had treated me badly.'[26]

Much more could be said about both the positive and negative forms of drug-induced experiences, but the time has come to move on to the more normative kinds of religious and mystical experience which do not depend upon chemical aids.

26. Zaehner, p. 210.

12

RELIGIOUS EXPERIENCE

PRELIMINARY DISTINCTIONS

According to the definition adopted in the last chapter, for us to experience is for our consciousness to undergo modifications. By distinctively *religious* experience I mean modifications of consciousness structured by religious concepts. And by religious concepts I mean, for our present purpose, concepts of transcendent non-physical reality or realities – such as gods, demons, angels, Dharma, Tao, Brahman, heaven, hell, eternal life. These are religious concepts in that their primary or literal use is in religious discourse. But they can also be fused with non-religious concepts, such as when we speak of totem animals, sacred places, sacramental acts, inspired shamans, prophets, divine incarnations and other holy persons. Here we conscript such concepts as animal, mountain, tree, river, sun, moon, the stars, human beings, water, bread, wine, clothes – in principle virtually anything – for a religious use.

I take 'religious' and 'mystical' experience to be two terms for the same range of phenomena, which extends from a mild sense – momentary or enduring – of a divine or holy presence to the most powerful visions, auditions and experiences of unity with a greater and higher reality. Like all other forms of experience, this involves the interpretive activity of the mind. However we are not referring here to intellectual interpretation, as when a reader interprets a text or a detective interprets the clues. The situation is not that the religious and the non-religious person have the same conscious experience but interpret it differently, as some philosophers have held.[1] Rather, interpretation occurs in the genesis of the experience itself.[2] This is why religious and non-religious minds can respond to this mysterious universe in different ways. To one it mediates a more than spatial transcendence, to the other not. We can however distinguish between experiences mediated through physical situations that are capable of being experienced either religiously or non-religiously, and those others that are not externally mediated and can only occur with the use of religious concepts. It is these latter that are often called mystical.

As an example of religiously ambiguous situations, recall the well-known lines that I quoted earlier in which Wordsworth expresses his sense of 'a presence . . . whose dwelling is the light of setting suns, and the round ocean and the living air, and the blue sky, and in the mind of man: a motion and a spirit, that impels all thinking things, all objects of all thought, and rolls through all things'. Many others must have been where Wordsworth sat, on the bank of the river Wye a few miles above Tintern Abbey, without the scene stirring within them any such sense of transcendence. So we can say that, in itself, the scene on the Wye is religiously ambiguous – capable of being experienced both religiously and non-religiously.

As an example of the kind of experience that is inherently structured by religious concepts, if someone sees a vision of Jesus Christ as pictured in Christian art, saying, 'I am the way, the truth, and the life. Follow me,' this is by definition a religious experience. There could not be two people, both experiencing this vision and hearing these words, one of whom regards it as a religious and the other as a non-religious experience. For according to our definition, it *is* a religious experience. But it could be that one of them regards it as a veridical and the other as non-veridical or delusory experience. To regard it as veridical is to respond either as a naive realist, believing that Jesus Christ was personally present, uttering those words; or as a critical realist, accepting the experience as a cognitive response, expressed in a distinctively Christian form, to the impact of the Transcendent. To regard it as delusory is to believe that there is no transcendent reality, or that if there is, that reality was not manifested in this particular experience. Of course the same distinctions apply to religious or mystical experience within the other traditions.

THE SENSE OF PRESENCE

Most of us can probably remember a much more common and less powerful experience than Wordsworth's when, in the presence of a

1. For example, Ninian Smart, 1965.
2. As argued, for example, by Steven Katz, 1978.

magnificent sunset or sunrise, or a scene of mountains or a lake, or of the sea stretching out to the horizon, or in a peaceful forest or garden or some other setting, we have had the fleeting sense of an all-embracing mystery, or have experienced what the great nineteenth-century theologian Schleiermacher called 'the feeling of absolute dependence' – dependence upon a greater unseen reality. This can be described as a vaguely religious experience, structured by a very general religious concept. The triggering circumstances can be very varied, resulting in a 'feeling' or 'sense' of the Transcendent, for example, when in the presence of sheer human goodness in relatives, friends, neighbours, strangers; or when seeing or hearing about an act of unselfish bravery done on behalf of others; or on being struck by something that someone says or that one reads; or on being present at the birth of a new life; or on encountering the mystery that we face in the death of a loved one; or when being aware of transcendence in the delicate beauty of a flower, a butterfly, a snow flake, a sea shell, or the majesty of a mountain, a lake, a sunrise, the starry night . . . or again, less vaguely, when reading the Bible or the Qur'an or the *Bhagavad Gita* or some other sacred scripture and being opened to the divine presence to which it witnesses. The proper function of common worship is to be an enabling context of religious experience. When and to the extent that it is this, it constitutes a transforming awareness of the Transcendent. All of these are among the innumerable different settings in which the inbuilt religious propensity of our nature is evoked. And when evoked it leads to what we can only call faith or trust. But faith or trust in what? For some, trust in a personal God, for others, trust in the ultimate structure of reality, but in each case freeing us, at least momentarily, from the burdens of the self-enclosed ego.

SOME EXAMPLES

In surveying the wide field of religious experience, relatively recent cases are in many ways preferable to those described in holy scriptures and other religious classics, as it is easier to gauge the social and cultural milieu of those culturally closer to ourselves. I shall take some from a range of autobiographical writings, and others from the reports collected by the Religious Experience Research Unit, founded in 1961 by the then Linacre Professor of Zoology at Oxford University, Sir Alister Hardy.[3] The Oxford Unit, like the National Opinion Research Center in the United States, discovered from its questionnaires and the responses to its advertisements that approximately one-third of people

3. These reports have been made available in several publications: Beardsworth 1977, Robinson 1977 and 1978, Hardy 1979, Cohen and Phipps 1979, Hay 1982 and 1990, and Maxwell and Tschudin 1990.

of all kinds seem to have had 'religious or other transcendent experiences' at least once in their lives,[4] and that quite often the remembered moment has been permanently significant to them.

We can begin with the sense of the presence of God or, better, the sense of being in God's presence. Here the pre-conscious interpretative activity is not necessarily triggered by any particular event or person or circumstance, but by life as a whole, by the universe around us. For some – a fortunate few – this forms the background of consciousness during large stretches of their lives. The experience is sometimes highly 'ramified',[5] with distinctive features drawn from a particular theological system, and sometimes less so, being formed in terms of the more general idea of the divine, the holy, the sacred, the numinous. Many people (including myself) have occasionally, but alas only briefly, enjoyed this sense of existing within a transcendent holy presence in which we know it to be profoundly good to exist and in which the unknown future holds no possible threat.

As we shall see in chapter 17, plenty of lunatics and fanatics have experienced vivid forms of religious experience that have sometimes led them to perform the most terrible deeds, and such individuals have unfortunately become better known than the generality of people reporting religious experiences. But within that much larger generality, complete sanity seems to be the norm. Hay summarizes, 'People reporting such experiences are more likely than other people to be in a good state of psychological well-being',[6] or again, 'People reporting religious experience are on the whole better balanced mentally, happier, and more socially responsible than others.'[7]

The transformation of perception in religious and mystical experience, when unconnected with drugs, tends to be gentle, affecting the *meaning* of the environment, which is now experienced in religious terms. The eighteenth-century theologian Jonathan Edwards describes such a transformation thus: 'The appearance of everything was altered; there seemed to be, as it were, a calm, sweet cast, or appearance of divine glory, in almost everything. God's excellency, his wisdom, his purity and love, seemed to appear in everything; in the sun, moon and stars; in the clouds and blue sky; in the grass, flowers, and trees; in the water and all nature.'[8] Again, George Fox, the founder of Quakerism, recorded in his journal that 'all things were new; and all the creation gave another smell unto me than before, beyond what words can utter'.[9]

4. Hay, 1990, pp. 65, 79.
5. This useful idea was introduced into the discussion of mystical experience in Ninian Smart, 1965.
6. Hay, 1990, p. 89.
7. Ibid., p. 103.
8. William James, p. 248.
9. Fox, p. 17.

Such transformations of perception, and losing oneself in a larger reality, are often structured in non-theistic or pan-theistic terms. For example, 'The phenomenon invariably occurs out of doors . . . It is generally prefaced by a general feeling of "gladness to be alive". I am never aware of how long this feeling persists but after a period I am conscious of an awakening of my senses. Everything becomes suddenly more clearly defined, sights, sounds and smells take on a whole new meaning. I become aware of the goodness of everything. Then, as though a light were switched off, everything becomes still, and I actually feel as though I were part of the scene around me.'[10] In another case: 'I was walking across a field turning my head to admire the Western sky and looking at a line of pine trees appearing as black velvet against a pink backdrop, turning to duck egg blue/green overhead, as the sun set. Then it happened. It was as if a switch marked "ego" was suddenly switched off. Consciousness expanded to include, *be*, the previously observed. "I" was the sunset and there was no "I" experiencing "it". No more the observer and observed. At the same time – eternity was "born". There was no past, no future, just an eternal now . . . then I returned completely to normal consciousness finding myself still walking across the field, in time, with a memory.'[11] Or again, in his autobiography Forrest Reid tells of 'hours when I could pass *into* nature, and feel the grass growing, and float with the clouds through the transparent air; when I could hear the low breathing of the earth, when the colour and the smell of it were so close to me that I seemed to lose consciousness of any separate existence'.[12] Innumerable other comparable reports could be cited.

It may be that these various reports of ego-transcendence are (like those sometimes induced by drugs) describing something akin to the transforming awareness of the interconnectedness of all things in a living universe, with freedom from the angst of the ever-grasping ego, that occurs in Zen Buddhist *satori* (awakening, enlightenment). For one aspect of the nirvanic experience is the inner peace and joy of the awakened mind as it experiences the world without the distortions of ego-centredness. D.T. Suzuki, who more than anyone else introduced Zen to the west, says, 'Zen . . . opens a man's mind to the greatest mystery as it is daily and hourly performed . . . it makes us live in the world as if walking in the Garden of Eden . . . I do not know why – and there is no need of explaining – but when the sun rises the whole world dances with joy and everybody's heart is filled with bliss.'[13] I once asked a *roshi* (Zen Master), in his room in the Japanese monastery of which he was the abbot, the foolish and impossible question, 'What was it like

10. Hardy, p. 35.
11. Hay, 1990, p. 50.
12. Paffard, p. 38
13. Suzuki, 1964, pp. 45, 75.

when you first experienced *satori*?' (For he had made it clear that *satori* occurs many times, not just once.) Struggling to help me by conveying at least something of an experience that is indescribable, he gestured through the window to the trees and bushes and birds outside and said, 'I became part of all this.' It is clear, from him and from others, that this was only the hint of a hint. But a loss of the sense of ego in becoming one with the living universe may be a link between western 'nature mysticism' and Zen 'enlightenment'. However it is of the essence of the nirvanic experience that it does not terminate in the natural world. For to transcend the ego in becoming one with the universal process is at the same time to become one with the eternal buddha nature of all things. In *satori*, according to Buddhist teaching, a human moment in time coincides with the eternal present of the ultimate reality, Nirvana, the Dharmakaya, *Sunyata*. As the Zen philosopher Masao Abe says in a quotation captured by Thomas Merton, 'The realizer does not stand outside the reality, but may be said to be at least a part of that reality. So I said that he is a self-realization of reality as such. This realization – that one is the self-realization of ultimate reality as such – is *his* realization.'[14]

The reports analysed by the Oxford Religious Experience Unit cover many different kinds of experience, but a striking proportion of them are experiences of being 'surprised by joy'. Leslie Weatherhead's account of his vividly remembered experience as a young student has often been quoted. It happened on a murky winter afternoon 'in the corner of that dingy, third-class compartment with the feeble lights of inverted gas mantles overhead and the Vauxhall Station platform outside with milk cans standing there':

> For a few seconds only, I suppose . . . the whole compartment was filled with light. This is the only way I know in which to describe the moment, for there was nothing to *see* at all. I felt caught up in some tremendous sense of being within a loving, triumphant and shining purpose. I never felt more humble. I never felt more exalted. A most curious, but overwhelming sense possessed me and filled me with ecstasy. I felt that all was well for mankind – how poor the words seem! The 'well' is so poverty stricken. All men were shining and glorious beings who in the end would enter incredible joy. Beauty, music, joy, love immeasurable and a glory unspeakable, all this they would inherit . . . In a few moments the glory departed – all but one curious, lingering feeling. I loved everybody in that compartment. It sounds silly now, and indeed I blush to write it, but at that moment I think I would have died for any one of the people in that compartment.[15]

14. Merton, p. 17.
15. Hardy, p. 53.

The experience confirmed Weatherhead in his vocation to become a Methodist minister.

This particular experience was structured by the theistic faith of a Christian theological student. But as a reminder that there are other quite different forms of equally vivid religious experience, here is the great nineteenth-century Indian mystic Ramakrishna's account of a moment at a Hindu shrine: 'It was as if houses, doors, temples and everything else vanished altogether; as if there was nothing anywhere! And what I saw was an infinite shoreless sea of light; a sea that was consciousness. However far and in whatever direction I looked, I saw shining waves, one after another, coming towards me.'[16] A dramatic and often cited experience is recorded by the American psychologist Richard Bucke, a Professor of Mental and Nervous Diseases, and superintendent of a mental asylum, in Ontario in the 1880s. When aged thirty-six he had spent an evening with friends reading and discussing Wordsworth, Whitman and other 'Romantic' poets, and was driving home in an English city in a hansom cab. He describes his experience in the third person:

> All at once, without warning of any kind, he found himself wrapped around as it were by a flame-colored cloud. For an instant he thought of fire, some sudden conflagration in the great city; the next, he knew that the light was within himself. Directly afterwards came upon him a sense of exultation, of immense joyousness accompanied or immediately followed by an intellectual illumination quite impossible to describe. Into his brain streamed one momentary lightning-flash of the Brahmic Splendor which has ever since lightened his life; upon his heart fell one drop of Brahmic Bliss, leaving thenceforward for always an aftertaste of heaven. Among other things he did not come to believe, he saw and knew that the Cosmos is not dead matter but a living Presence, that the soul of man is immortal, that the universe is so built and ordered that without any peradventure all things work together for the good of each and all, that the foundation principle of the world is what we call love and that the happiness of everyone is in the long run absolutely certain.[17]

From a critical realist point of view we note that this momentary openness to the Transcendent was clothed in the universal symbol of light, and is articulated by Bucke in the quasi-Hindu terms then current among many of Whitman's readers.

Although without any reference to Hinduism, the poet Alfred Lord Tennyson described an experience that could be duplicated by some advaitic meditators: 'individuality itself seemed to dissolve and fade

16. Isherwood, p. 65.
17. Bucke, pp. 9–10.

away into boundless being, and this not a confused state but the clearest, the surest of the surest, utterly beyond words – where death was an almost laughable impossibility – the loss of personality (if so it were) seeming no extinction, but the only true life'.[18] This experience of transcending the ego to become one with the Ultimate will be critically examined more fully in chapters 15 and 16. But before that let us look at yet another range of religious experience, the phenomena of visions and voices, in a case study of the English mystic Julian of Norwich.

18. Paffard, p. 58; for other examples see pp. 79, 80, 88.

13

VISIONS – A CASE STUDY OF JULIAN OF NORWICH

THE EMERGENCE OF WOMEN VISIONARIES

For the most part, Christian mystics prior to the fourteenth century did not report extraordinary experiences, but wrote biblical commentaries designed to elicit the deeper meaning of the sacred texts. This was an intellectual exercise, producing mystical theology. But from the late fourteenth century, visions and voices and other ecstatic experiences increasingly abound, and women made a major contribution to this development. Women, who had seldom figured before in the history of Christian mysticism, now have a prominent place – Bridget of Sweden, Catherine of Siena, Catherine of Bologna and Catherine of Genoa in Italy, Julian of Norwich and Margery Kempe in England, Margaret and Christina Ebner in the Rhineland, Collette of Corbie and Joan of Arc in France, Hadewijch of Antwerp, and Margaret of Porete, who was burned at the stake. Why, after so many centuries largely (though not of course entirely) devoid of them, did visionary experiences now burst forth around the Christian world and why was it women mystics who led the way? For whilst there were famous male mystics in this period – including Ramon Lull, Meister Eckhart, John Tauler, Ruusbroec, Walter Hilton, Richard Rolle, and the authors (presumably male) of the *Cloud of Unknowing* and the *Theologia Germanica* – these wrote mystical and devotional theology rather than accounts of mystical experiences. The partial exceptions are Suso, Rulman Merswin, and the Friends of God, a movement that began in Strasbourg and spread into the Rhenish provinces, Switzerland and

Bavaria. But still the majority of the well-known visionaries of that period were women.

It seems to have required a woman's eye to see that, as Grace Jantzen says, 'Though it is rarely noted in the histories of medieval mysticism, one of its most striking features is that until the emergence of the phenomenon of visionary women . . . almost all the main figures are male.'[1] And she offers an explanation of this. She points out that it would have been regarded by the male-dominated church as out of the question for such supposedly intellectually feeble creatures as women to presume to produce commentaries on the holy scriptures. As she says, 'women were not usually allowed access to books or to the education necessary to appreciate them. They were not encouraged to write. Hence the scholarship involved in poring over the biblical texts and discerning their mystical meaning was not available to women.'[2] And so the women mystics 'did not begin, as many men did, from a study of scriptural texts and an effort to ascertain the mystical meaning of scripture . . . the source of their spirituality was experiential more than intellectual'.[3] She suggests that there had probably always been women of deep spirituality who, if they had been men, would have been recognized by the church as mystics, but to whom the ecclesiastical culture denied any adequate means of expression. But around the fourteenth century these women found themselves having visions embodying their spiritual insights.

Why at this particular time rather than earlier or later? There is no assured answer, but during the thirteenth and into the fourteenth century women were playing an increasing part in business, running shops, buying and selling, hiring and firing, and it may be that generally women were becoming increasingly ready to take a lead. At any rate, as visionary mystics they were now freed to express themselves, though in a way that put them in the perilous position of reporting a direct access to God which was a potential threat to the absolute authority of the church. As Jantzen says, 'By those who accepted it as authentic, the authority claimed by the visionary could not possibly be gainsaid; and it cut straight across all the usual channels like education and ecclesiastical position, rendering them totally unnecessary.'[4] And so we find that many of the female mystics met with strong suspicion and were sometimes in danger of being condemned as heretics or witches.

JULIAN HERSELF

The fact that mystics sometimes gained status by virtue of their claimed direct access to God has tempted some writers to conclude that

1. Jantzen, 1995, p. 108.
2. Ibid., p. 108.
3. Ibid., pp. 58–9.
4. Ibid., p. 169.

mysticism is essentially a strategy of the weak and marginalized to obtain power.[5] This is an example of the naturalistic assumption overruling the evidence. For many well-known mystics have not gained social or ecclesiastical status – none, for example, of the English mystics, Richard Rolle, Margery Kempe, Walter Hilton, John Woolman, Gertrude More, Augustine Baker, Henry Vaughan, the author of *The Cloud of Unknowing*, or, as we shall see, Julian of Norwich, though her distinctive contribution to theology was implicitly heretical by traditionally orthodox standards, as I shall show. Although not by any means every heresy has been an advance in Christian understanding, almost every advance in Christian understanding has been heretical or heterodox – until, that is, it was eventually adopted by the church. And today Julian's heresies are widely accepted even by Christians who have never heard of her. Fortunately, at the time she seems to have escaped the notice of the hierarchy. Her heresies come in the Long Text, written some twenty years after the Short Text, and judging from the paucity of surviving manuscripts neither version seems to have circulated at all widely in her lifetime.

She is variously referred to as Mother Julian, Dame Julian and Lady Julian. 'Mother' sounds to me too ecclesiastical, for she was not a nun. 'Dame' sounds today too domestic, for she was a solitary contemplative. So personally, I prefer 'Lady', although this must not carry with it the idea that she was of noble family, for we know nothing about her family. Some also speak of her as Juliana, but in fact she was named after the church of St Julian in Norwich to which her anchoress's cell, or anchorhold, was attached. This was probably not just a single cell, but a small bungalow with room for a servant as well as the anchoress herself. Such an existence would be supported mainly by gifts from those who came to consult her and by donations and bequests by pious lay people, unless of course the anchoress herself had private means. So Julian will have lived very simply, but probably not in ascetic poverty. The building would have a window or grille opening onto the outer world, or perhaps into a small consulting room, through which she would converse with people who came to her for advice. She had a reputation as a spiritual adviser – Margery Kempe of King's Lynn, for example, had heard of her and went to consult her. Margery's account of the visit confirms the consistency and integrity of Julian's outlook. She went to tell Julian of her own revelations. 'My reason for telling the anchoress was to find out whether I was deceived, for the good anchoress was an expert in such things and could give sound advice.' Julian advised her 'to fulfil the promptings of my soul as long as they

5. For example, J. M. Lewis, 1989.

didn't conflict with the worship of God or the well-being of my fellow Christians; for if they did then they sprang from the workings of an evil spirit and not a good one. The Holy Spirit never prompts us to act unkindly; if he did he would be acting contrary to his own nature, for he is pure love.'[6]

In her service to the community Julian was probably a combination of spiritual director, psychotherapist, and wise woman giving practical advice about all sorts of personal and family problems, and it would also be important to people to know that she was praying for them and for the whole community.

There would be a door through which the servant could go out to do the shopping. There might also be a small enclosed garden, or possibly graveyard, where the anchoress could get some fresh air. And there would be a slit or squint in the inner wall through which she could hear and perhaps see the services in the church. But, with these qualifications, she lived a strictly solitary life, and having once become enclosed in a solemn ceremony based on the burial service, she was regarded as having died to the world. Possibly no one but her maid will have seen her, except through a grille, once she had entered her anchorhold.

THE HISTORICAL SETTING

Julian tells us that the mystical experience she describes began on 8 May 1373, and that she was then thirty-and-a-half-years-old, so she was born in 1342. She was alive in 1413, according to the Introduction to the Short Text by someone other than herself, when she would be seventy-one, quite a respectable age at that time. How much longer she lived we do not know. An anchoress Julian is mentioned in wills of 1415, 1416 and even 1443. Her successors in the anchorhold probably took the same name, but the 1415 and 1416 references could perfectly well be to our Julian, though not the 1443 one. Her grave is unknown, and the Julian shrine in Norwich which can be visited today is only a hopeful reconstruction. That we can learn so little about Julian herself is consonant with her own attitude to her revelations. They did not indicate to her that she was anyone special. She says, for example, 'I am sure that there are many who never had revelations or visions, but only the common teaching of Holy Church, who love God better than I,'[7] and concerning her own revelation, 'I pray you all for God's sake, and I counsel you for your own profit, that you disregard the wretch to whom it was shown . . . and that you contemplate upon God, who out

6. Kempe, p. 48.
7. Julian of Norwich, p. 191, LT9.

of his courteous love and his endless goodness was willing to show it generally, to the comfort of us all.'[8]

It seems likely that Lady Julian wrote the Short Text of her *Shewings*, describing her experience, soon after it occurred, and then some twenty years later, after long reflection, the Long Text. This contains an essentially identical account of the experience itself, together with a wealth of theological ideas arising from it. She describes herself as 'a simple unlettered creature'.[9] This may only have meant that she had not been taught Latin, the language of the learned, though some believe that in fact she did read Latin and was familiar with the Vulgate as well as with Augustine and a number of other writers. At any rate, unless she dictated her book, she was highly literate, and in fact she produces a strong, confident, vivid, compact, highly effective English, which some place on a level with that of her contemporary, Geoffrey Chaucer. But there are many unanswered, or only speculatively answered, questions. Did she write the Short Text as an anchoress, or did she become one as a result of her mystical experience? Did she come from a relatively wealthy family, in which education would be possible? Was she a widow? Had she been a nun?[10] Did her disclaimer of learning just represent an, at that time, standard female modesty, whilst in fact she was well read in Latin? There were libraries in Norwich both at the Benedictine priory and at the house of Augustinian friars close to St Julian's church. And although a woman would probably not have had access to them, possibly her confessor or some other cleric may have borrowed books for her. My own guesses, which are no more than this, are that she probably came from a relatively well-off family; that she did have some serious education; that she either read Latin or had been in circles in which theological ideas were freely discussed; that because of the number of people who were present with her at the time of her mystical experience – not only a priest but the unnamed 'those who were with me'[11] – she became an anchoress as a result of it rather than before it, and that it was during the years of prayer and reflection in her anchorhold that she came to see more deeply into the significance of her experience and to write the Long Text. But, fortunately, none of these unresolved issues affect in the least the significance of her book.

A brief word about the social and religious world around Lady Julian. Socially it was a time of turmoil, tragedy and terror. In the background the Hundred Years War was raging; the Black Death had

8. Ibid., p. 191, LT8.
9. Ibid., p. 177, LT2.
10. Dean W. R. Inge thought that she 'was probably a Benedictine nun of Carrow, near Norwich, and then lived for the greater part of her life in an anchorage in the churchyard of St. Julian at Norwich'; Inge, p. 201.
11. Julian of Norwich, p. 163, ST21.

struck, hitting Norwich in 1349 and killing, it is estimated, a third of the population; there was a severe famine in 1369, provoking widespread disorder and violence, including Wat Tyler's rebellion and its bloody suppression. And in the church there was much corruption and naked power-seeking. There was the Great Schism of 1377, with the scandal of two rival Popes. The bishop of Norwich, Henry Despenser, who seems to have been about as unchristian as bishops can get, led a failed crusade on the part of Pope Urban VI against Pope Clement, and was subsequently a prime mover in the persecution of the Lollards, for whose execution he obtained the king's express authorization. The killing field in Norwich, known as the Lollard Pit, was only just out of sight of Julian's anchorhold. She would undoubtedly have been acutely aware, through the people who consulted her, of all the horrors going on around her.

But in spite of – or, some have suggested, because of – the widespread ecclesiastical corruption and the widespread violence, this was a time of the flowering of Christian mysticism. In England, Richard Rolle, Walter Hilton, and the author of *The Cloud of Unknowing*, were rough contemporaries of Julian, as were Ruusbroec, Tauler and Suso and the writer of the *Theologica Germanica* in Germany, Bridget of Sweden and Catherine of Siena, and the pervasive influence of Pseudo-Dionysius was still strong. In the fourteenth century the earlier medieval picture of God as a stern and terrible judge to be feared and placated, and of Christ as God's equally fearful vicegerent, had given way, at least in some circles, to a sense of God as love and an understanding of Jesus as suffering love incarnate. There developed what can be called a Jesus cult, centring upon his sufferings on the cross, and including vivid visualizations of the gory details of crucifixion.

THE VISIONS

Lady Julian's visions occurred when she was supposedly on her deathbed. There is reason to think that the illness was an unconsciously self-induced psychosomatic state. She says that she had long had a desire 'to have by God's gift a bodily sickness, and I wished it to be so severe that it might seem mortal, so that I should in that sickness receive all the rites which Holy Church had to give me, whilst I myself should believe that I was dying, and everyone who saw me would think the same, for I wanted no comfort from any human, earthly life'.[12] Further she says that 'When I was young I desired to have that sickness when I was thirty years old',[13] which is when she did have it. In the background

12. Ibid., p. 126, ST1.
13. Ibid., pp. 126–7, ST1.

there is the medieval fascination with death – particularly in Europe north of the Alps[14] – and also the immense importance attributed to a 'good death', with one's sins finally confessed and absolved. And of course people did not then die in a sedated coma in a curtained hospital bed, but at home with their family and neighbours around them. Death was a public event and the deathbed scene a communal affirmation of faith.

The mystical experience which Lady Julian describes was complex, going through a number of stages spread over several days, and a full description of it all is not possible here. The experience took the three forms that are familiar in mystical literature. There were what she calls bodily or corporeal visions, which were apparently visual hallucinations in which she had the experience of, for example, seeing blood flow down a crucifix when the other people present did not. Second, there were what she calls spiritual or inner visions, in which she saw, for example, the Virgin Mary, not however as physically present. And third, words were formed in her mind, she believed by Christ. She is always clear in her account about what is outer and what inner.

At the age of thirty, then, 'God sent me a bodily sickness in which I lay for three days and three nights; and on the fourth night I received all the rites of Holy Church, and did not expect to live until day'.[15] A priest was sent for to be present at her end, and held a crucifix before her. 'Suddenly', she says, 'I saw the red blood trickling down from under the crown, all hot, flowing freely and copiously, a living stream, just as it seems to me it was at the time when the crown of thorns was thrust down upon his blessed head.'[16] Although visualizations of Jesus' crucified body, with the vivid signs of scourging and blood flowing from his wounds, are comparable with scenes in today's horror films, the practice of meditation on the Passion of Christ was then well established and encouraged within the church.

Next an inner vision supervenes upon the outer vision. 'At the same time as I saw this corporeal sight, our Lord showed me a spiritual sight of his familiar love.' This was a vision of 'something small, no bigger than a hazelnut, lying in the palm of my hand'. It seemed so fragile that it was a wonder that it did not 'suddenly fall into nothing'; but 'I was answered in my understanding: It lasts and always will, because God loves it; and thus everything has being through the love of God'.[17] The hazelnut has become the symbol of Julian's revelation of divine love.

The experience then continues in a kaleidoscopic stream of outer and inner visions and auditions. Lady Julian herself distinguishes sixteen. It will be sufficient for our purpose to recall some of the highlights. The

14. Boase, pp. 106–9.
15. Julian of Norwich, p. 127, ST2.
16. Ibid., p. 129, ST2.
17. Ibid., p. 130, ST4.

crucifix is sometimes there in the background but sometimes comes vividly into the foreground in a gruesome picture of the suffering of Christ on the cross. She sees 'spitting to defoul his body, buffeting of his blessed face, and many woes and pains, more than I can tell; and his colour often changed, and all his blessed face was for a time caked with dry blood'.[18] Again, 'as I watched I saw the body bleeding copiously, the blood hot, flowing freely, a living stream, just as I had before seen the head bleed. And I saw this in the furrows made by the scourging, and I saw his blood run so plentifully that it seemed that if it had in fact been happenning there, the bed and everything around it would have been soaked in blood'.[19] Here the hallucination is vivid and powerful, and yet she is aware at the same time that it is not physical reality. This also seems to be the case when, at a later stage, she says, 'The blessed body was left to dry for a long time, with the wrenching of the nails and the sagging of the head and the weight of the body, with the blowing of the wind around him, which dried up his body and pained him with cold, more than my heart can think of, and with all his other pains I saw pain such that all that I can describe or say is inadequate, for it cannot be described.'[20] But the meaning of all this is always clear to her. It is the infinite divine love which bears and transforms these pains for her sake and for the sake of us all. As she says towards the end, concerning her whole experience, 'What, do you wish to know your Lord's meaning in this thing? Know it well, love was his meaning. Who reveals it to you? Love. What did he reveal to you? Love. Why does he reveal it to you? For Love.'[21]

It is Julian's intense awareness of the divine love as tender, gracious (or, as she says, 'courteous') and accepting that led her to conclude that 'as truly as God is our Father, so truly is God our Mother'.[22] God is both 'the power and goodness of fatherhood' and 'the wisdom and lovingness of motherhood'.[23] Again, she speaks of 'our true Mother Jesus'[24] and 'our heavenly Mother Jesus'.[25] To think of the divine in female as much as male terms has long been familiar within Hinduism, where female and male deities equally manifest the infinite reality of

18. Ibid., p. 136, ST7.
19. Ibid., p. 137, ST8. It is interesting to compare this with Catherine of Genoa's account: 'Our Lord, desiring to enkindle still more profoundly His love in this soul, appeared to her in spirit with His Cross upon His shoulder dripping with blood, so that the whole house seemed to be full of rivulets of that Blood, which she saw to have been all shed because of love alone'. (Quoted by von Hugel, I, p. 108.)
20. Julian of Norwich, pp. 141–2, ST13.
21. Ibid., p. 342, LT398–9.
22. Ibid., p. 295, LT59.
23. Ibid., p. 296, LT59.
24. Ibid., p. 298, LT60.
25. Ibid., p. 301, LT61.

Brahman, in itself beyond personality and gender. Thanks to the contemporary feminist and womanist movements Christian thought is beginning to accept that the traditional exclusively male image of God, with all its implicit as well as explicit associations and implications, has been a distortion and that our theology must be rethought on a more inclusive basis. Lady Julian, some six hundred years ahead of her time in this respect, offers suggestions about how to do this. These suggestions are much more radical than the attempts by a number of feminist theologians today to comb through the Bible and the Christian tradition to find occasional exceptions to their overwhelmingly patriarchal character. Better, I would think, frankly to admit this pervasive patriarchalism, consciously to reject it as not binding on Christians today, and then to make a relative new beginning with the aid of such people as Lady Julian.

Interspersed with Julian's bodily and semi-bodily visions of the Passion there are inner visions. For example, 'God brought our Lady to my understanding. I saw her spiritually in her bodily likeness, a simple, humble maiden, young in years, of the stature which she had when she conceived.'[26] And there are moments when words were formed in her mind, 'without voice and without opening of lips'.[27] Perhaps the most famous of these is 'I am the ground of your beseeching',[28] meaning that God is with us in our prayers, both instigating and answering them, a saying which T.S. Eliot builds into 'Little Gidding'. Julian explains this theologically by saying that 'everything which our good Lord makes us to beseech he himself has ordained for us from eternity'.[29] This does not seem to have been something revealed to her but a philosophical speculation on her part, or very likely one that she had received from others. It is not however a good idea because, if followed through, it entails a divine determinism that would undermine human free will.

Returning to revelatory words formed in her mind, Lady Julian was told that in Christ's Passion the devil was being defeated. The devil is in fact a prominent figure in the drama. Writing about a moment towards the end of the experience she says, 'And as soon as I fell asleep, it seemed to me that the devil set himself at my throat and wanted to strangle me, but he could not. And I awoke, more dead then alive . . . And then a little smoke came in at the door, with great heat and a foul stench.'[30] She wondered if there was a real fire, but those around her assured her that there was not. Later 'the devil returned with his heat and his stench, and kept me very busy. The stench was vile and painful, and the physical heat was fearful and oppressive: and I could also hear in my ears chattering and talking, as if between two speakers,

26. Ibid., p. 131, ST4.
27. Ibid., p. 138, ST8.
28. Ibid., p. 248, LT41.
29. Ibid., pp. 248–9, LT41.
30. Ibid., p. 163, ST21.

and they seemed to be both chattering at once, as if they were conducting a confused debate, and it was all low muttering . . . And so they occupied me all that night and into the morning, until it was a little after sunrise; and then all at once they had all gone and disappeared, leaving nothing but their stench, and that persisted for a little while. And I despised them, and so I was delivered from them by the strength of Christ's Passion. For it is so that the fiend is overcome, as Christ said before to me.'[31] For at an earlier point Christ, speaking of his Passion, had formed in her mind the words 'With this the fiend is overcome' and 'You will not be overcome'.[32] Indeed at one point Lady Julian 'saw our Lord scorning [the devil's] malice and despising him as nothing, and he wants us to do the same. Because of this sight I laughed greatly, and that made those around me laugh as well; and their laughter was pleasing to me.'[33]

Looking at the long experience as a whole, phases of the horror of Christ's excruciating pain and of terrifying assaults by the devil alternate with phases of blessed assurance of God's love and providence, putting the devil to scorn. But even though the devil makes a final unsuccessful attack upon her almost at the end, the progression throughout is towards a deeper and more joyful awareness of being in the hands of God's unchanging love. We read at one point that 'suddenly, as I looked at the same cross [i.e. crucifix] he changed to an appearance of joy. The change in his appearance changed mine, and I was as glad and joyful as I could possibly be.'[34] For, says Julian, 'what I am describing now is so great a joy to Jesus that he counts as nothing his labours and his bitter sufferings and his cruel and shameful death'.[35] Again, 'Very merrily and gladly our Lord looked into his side, and he gazed and said this: See how I loved you . . . Our Lord showed this to me to make us glad and merry.'[36] At another point, 'our Lord revealed to me a supreme spiritual delight in my soul. In this delight I was filled full of everlasting surety, and I was powerfully secured without any fear. This sensation was so welcome and so dear to me that I was at peace, at ease and at rest, so that there was nothing upon earth which could have afflicted me.'[37] Peace, rejoicing, happiness, even laughter, have a prominent place within Julian's experience.

In the *Shewings* then, the two sides of human experience in all ages, pain and joy, suffering and happiness, are embraced. Julian did not close her eyes to misery and suffering. She was very conscious that 'in our lifetime we have in us a marvellous mixture of both well-being and woe'.[38] But for her these are united within the present and all-enfolding

31. Ibid., pp. 165–6, ST23.
32. Ibid., p. 164, ST22.
33. Ibid., p. 138, ST8.
34. Ibid., p. 144, ST12.
35. Ibid., p. 145, ST12.
36. Ibid., p. 146, ST13.
37. Ibid., p. 139, ST9.
38. Ibid., p. 279, LT42.

goodness which is God. This phrase 'the goodness which is God' is based on such sayings of Julian as 'the goodness which everything has is God'.[39] But this goodness is somehow the ground of darkness and suffering as well as light and peace. Julian has an utterly realistic awareness of human pain, suffering and misery, vividly focused in Jesus' suffering on the cross, and at the same time an equally realistic awareness of the divine love, again expressed in the cross, which is in the process of turning all evil into good, so that, in her most famous saying, which recurs a number of times, 'All shall be well, and all shall be well, and all manner of thing shall be well'.[40] It is as though suffering and happiness are two sides of the same coin, or two aspects of the same divine work, although we humans can only experience them one at a time. It is this combination of stark physical realism and firm religious realism that is so impressive in Lady Julian. She speaks in the same sentence of 'our mortal flesh, which is sometimes in pain, sometimes in sorrow, and will be so during this life . . . [and] an exalted and blessed life which is all peace and love; and this is more secretly experienced'.[41] One may compare this outlook with that expressed in the Hindu conception of the lord Shiva, who both creates and destroys and whose cosmic dance constitutes the ongoing life of the universe. The conceptualities are very different, and yet both express a similar religious realism in the face of the inextricable intermingling of good and evil in human experience.

39. Ibid., p. 190, LT8.
40. Ibid., p. 225, LT27.
41. Ibid., p. 212, LT19.

14

LADY JULIAN'S FRUITFUL HERESIES

THE FALL–REDEMPTION MODEL

This brings us to Lady Julian's theology, though 'theology' sounds too formal and ecclesiastical a term for the searching reflections that arose out of her vivid and compelling religious experiences. Such reflection was not for her a purely intellectual exercise, playing with a set of inherited symbols and devising new ways of systematizing them, but a persistent attempt to discern the meaning and implications of an experienced reality, which is of course what Schleiermacher, the greatest of the modern theologians, said that theology should be.

Julian affirms several times her adherence to 'all the faith of Holy Church'.[1] She says, 'For the faith of Holy Church, which I had before I had understanding [i.e. before understanding her experiences], and which, as I hope by the grace of God, I intend to preserve whole and to practice, was always in my sight, and I wished and intended never to accept anything which might be contrary to it.'[2] Further, she uses unhesitatingly all the traditional Christian concepts and symbols and would no doubt have been able to pass an examination in basic Christian doctrine, as indeed she may possibly have had to do when nominated to the St Julian anchorage. But that she was conscious of a tension between this and the import of her revelations is already suggested by the fact that she has more than once to deny that there is any such tension! She adopts ideas which, if pursued to their logical conclusions, undermine much of the traditional western orthodoxy of her time. But as a fourteenth-century woman totally integrated into the

1. Julian of Norwich, p. 163, ST21.
2. Ibid., p. 192, LT9.

life of the church, it would have been unthinkable for her to question its official teachings. She certainly did not see herself as a heretic. In order to qualify as this one has not only to accept ideas which do not fit the orthodox pattern, but to follow them through to the point of explicitly breaking that pattern. And when she comes within sight of that point Lady Julian takes refuge in the idea of a mystery that will only be dispelled on the last day.

But consider nevertheless the radical nature of her central insights. R.N. Swanson says that 'her formulations superficially appear to conflict with [the Church's] formal teaching'.[3] But this seems to me to be a considerable understatement. Some of her formulations not only *appear* to conflict with orthodox teaching but clearly *do* conflict with it. The western Christian outlook, formed by Augustine and dominating the medieval church, centres upon the drama of fall and redemption. It emphasizes our sinful and lost state, divine condemnation, the merciful remission of God's just anger through Christ's atoning death, and the eternal condemnation of those outside the true faith. This picture dominated the western Christian imagination for some twelve centuries, although it now lives mainly in the language of the liturgies and, more literally, in the beliefs of the large fundamentalist and evangelical wing of Christianity. Julian, recalling the faith of Holy Church, says that 'by the teaching which I had before, I understood that the mercy of God will be remission of his wrath after we have sinned . . . And therefore I accepted that the remission of his wrath would be one of the chief characteristics of his mercy. But [she says] for anything which I could see or desire, I could not see this characteristic in all the revelation.'[4] Again she speaks of 'that fair, sweet judgment which was shown in all the fair revelation in which I saw [God] assign to us no kind of blame'.[5] She even says that 'our Lord God cannot in his own judgment forgive, because he cannot be angry – that would be impossible'.[6] But she says concerning this insight, 'I could not be fully comforted only by contemplating it, and that was because of the judgment of Holy Church, which I had understood before, and which was continually in my sight . . . [by which] I understood that sinners sometimes deserve blame and wrath, and I could not see these two in God, and therefore my desire was more than I can or may tell, because of the higher judgment which God himself revealed at the same time, and therefore I had of necessity to accept it. And the lower judgment had been previously taught me in holy Church, and therefore I could not in any way ignore the lower judgment.'[7]

Clearly there is a tension here between the teaching of Holy Church, which she cannot reject, and the contrary truth so powerfully revealed

3. Swanson, p. 272.
4. Julian of Norwich, p. 260, LT47.
5. Ibid., p. 257, LT45.
6. Ibid., p. 263, LT49.
7. Ibid., p. 257, LT45.

to her experientially, which she also cannot reject. The resolution, in so far as there is one, seems to be in terms of two points of view, each valid on its own level – the human point of view, embodied in the church's doctrine, and the divine point of view, of which Julian was given a glimpse in her mystical experience. From the human point of view, 'we are sinners and commit many evil deeds . . . so that we deserve pain, blame and wrath', but in her revelations 'I saw truly that our Lord was never angry, and never will be. Because he is God, he is good, he is truth, he is love, he is peace; and his power, his wisdom, his charity and his unity do not allow him to be angry . . . God is that goodness which cannot be angry, for God is nothing but goodness.'[8] Such a distinction between the church's teaching as representing a human viewpoint, and a different divine viewpoint which may be glimpsed in mystical experience, is obviously the thin end of a long heretical wedge. Catholic commentators on Julian often prefer to ignore this, but in my opinion they are failing to do justice to both the complexity and the honesty of Julian's thought.

THE LORD-SERVANT PARABLE

In her understanding of sin then, whilst accepting Augustine's philosophical conception of evil as a privation of good rather than a positive reality, Lady Julian departs from Augustine's teaching that the fall of Adam and Eve was a damnable rebellion against God, deserving infinite punishment. She is closer here to Irenaeus and others of the early Hellenistic Fathers. Irenaeus, for example, in the second century, depicted Adam and Eve as immature childlike creatures whose fall was an understandable error rather than a cosmic crime.[9] Likewise, according to Julian, humanity 'falls into sin through naivete and ignorance. He is weak and foolish in himself.'[10] In the parable of the lord and his servant in chapter 51 of the Long Text, which presumably came to Julian as a further inner vision shortly after her initial experience, the servant, representing Adam and all humanity, falls through sheer bad luck, not through any fault of his own, and is in no way blamed by his lord, who represents God. Further, the fall – which in the parable is a literal fall into a ditch – leaves the servant in a state of confusion and blindness in which he even almost forgets his own love for his lord. This is his fallen and sinful state. 'And the cause [she says] is blindness, because he does not see God; for if he saw God continually, he would have no harmful feelings nor any kind of prompting, no sorrowing which is conducive to sin.'[11] Julian is speaking here, surely, of the

8. Ibid., p. 259, LT46.
9. Irenaeus, 1952, p. 10.
10. Julian of Norwich, p. 260, LT47.
11. Ibid.

'cloud of unknowing' of which her contemporary writes, a cloud between ourselves and God which cannot be pierced by thought but only by love.[12] There is a further analogy to the spiritual blindness of the servant in the ditch, and to the cloud of unknowing between ourselves and God, in the Hindu concept of *maya*, the illusoriness of ordinary self-centred existence, in which we grope in a spiritual blindness from which we can only be liberated by realizing experientially our ultimate unity with the divine.

THE GODLY WILL WITHIN US

So guilt and its atonement, so far from being the central religious fact, are conspicuously absent from Lady Julian's revelations. For her, salvation is not, as in the Augustinian–Calvinist conception, an imputed righteousness bought by a transactional atonement that clears us of guilt, but rather consists in being 'truly in peace and in love, for that is our salvation'.[13] This is akin to the Eastern Orthodox conception of *theosis*, salvation as transformation into the finite 'likeness' of God. For it is one of Julian's distinctive teachings that there is in each of us 'a godly will which never assented to sin nor ever will, which will is so good that it can never will evil'.[14] We have indeed within us, she says, a created analogue of the uncreated divine nature. 'God is endless supreme truth,' she says, 'endless supreme wisdom, endless supreme love uncreated; and a man's soul is a creature of God which has the same properties created.'[15] And so God is not 'wholly other', and we are not totally depraved and alienated and condemned, but on the contrary there is, in George Fox's phrase, 'that of God in everyman'. This basic theme runs through a great deal of mystical religion. The mystics speak, in different conceptualities, of the *imago dei*, or of the divine spark affirmed by Plotinus, Dionysius, Eckhart, Ruusbroec, Suso, Tauler and others, or of the *atman* that in the depths of our being we all are, or of the universal buddha nature, and it is equally strongly affirmed by the Sufi mystics of Islam. In each case the realization of this divine element within us flowers in the salvific transformation which is our highest good.

12. This is the teaching of *The Cloud of Unknowing* by an unknown writer probably roughly contemporary with Julian (*Cloud* 1978). That love reaches straight to God is also the theme of many of the Sufi mystics. Jalaluldin Rumi, for example, writing just a century before Julian and *The Cloud*, says that 'The mystic ascends to the Throne in a moment . . . [for] Love . . . is an attribute of God . . . Love hath five hundred wings, and every wing reaches from above the empyrean to beneath the earth . . . the lovers of God fly more quickly than lightning' (Rumi, 1995, p. 102).
13. Julian of Norwich, p. 264, LT49.
14. Ibid., p. 283, LT53.
15. Ibid., p. 256, LT44.

Returning to Lady Julian, that we have within us this 'godly will' does not mean that we do not, in our present fallen state, sin grievously, and it does not mean that sin is not ugly, evil, and productive of terrible pain. 'For sin is so vile and so much to be hated that it can be compared with no pain which is not itself sin.'[16] Remember also Julian's vivid awareness both of the suffering of Christ and of the frightening assaults of the devil. But nevertheless, everything is taking place within the all-encompassing goodness and love of God. Each moment of the creative process of which we are part, whether happy or painful, can now be seen as a step on a journey that is leading ultimately to a limitlessly good end. And so Julian says that 'if I were to act wisely . . . I should not be glad because of any special thing or be distressed by anything at all, for all will be well'.[17]

UNIVERSAL SALVATION?

This brings us to Lady Julian's cosmic optimism. Her 'all shall be well', which is the other famous saying used in Eliot's 'Little Gidding', occurs first in the Short Text and is elaborated in the Long Text. Baron von Hugel, in *The Mystical Element of Religion*, says that such optimism is present 'in the recollective moments of all the great Mystics'.[18] It arises for Julian as she faces the age-old problem of evil. She follows Augustine in holding that all suffering flows from sin.[19] She holds however that sin and its consequent suffering serve in the end a creative divine purpose. Suffering 'is something for a time, for it purges us and makes us know ourselves and ask for mercy'.[20] It has a soul-making function. This is so because our present life leads on to another in which all shall be well, and all shall be well, and all manner of thing shall be well. Lady Julian's implicit theodicy is thus teleological, embracing a strand of Christian thought which has however never been fully integrated into the tradition as a whole. This is the O *felix culpa*, O fortunate fault which merited such and so great a redeemer. Christ taught Lady Julian that 'I should contemplate his glorious atonement, for this atoning is more pleasing to the blessed divinity and more honourable for man's salvation, without comparison, than ever Adam's sin was harmful'.[21] She reports that 'an inward spiritual revelation of the lord's meaning descended into my soul, in which I saw . . . that his great goodness and his own honour require that his beloved servant, whom he loved so much, should be highly and blessedly rewarded

16. Ibid., p. 247, LT40.
17. Ibid., p. 153, ST16.
18. Von Hugel, II, p. 306.
19. Julian of Norwich, p. 225, LT27.
20. Ibid., p. 149, ST15.
21. Ibid., p. 150.

forever, above what he would have been if he had not fallen, yes, and so much that his falling and all the woes that he received from it will be turned into high, surpassing honour and endless bliss'.[22]

But having said that sin is the condition of a greater good than would have been possible without it, Lady Julian now considers the obvious objection: 'If this be true, then it would be well to sin so as to have the greater reward'.[23] Her reply is simply, but I think quite adequately, that love excludes sin: God 'teaches us that we must hate sin only because of love'.[24] And yet sin is, in Lady Julian's Middle English, 'behovely'. How should we put this into modern English – necessary, unavoidable, profitable? 'Sin is behovely, but all shall be well, and all shall be well, and all manner of thing shall be well'.[25] We are left with the paradox that evil, consisting in sin and the suffering that it causes, is necessary for an ultimately good purpose, and yet that sin as it occurs within the temporal process is nevertheless really sin and evil really evil. She does not try to unravel the relationship between these two facts, but her basic insight is the essence of what in our own day has been called the Irenaean or soul-making type of theodicy.[26] So I anticipate that if there is ever a convention of theodicists through the centuries, Lady Julian will be at the head of those of us who carry a banner proclaiming 'No Theodicy Without Eschatology'! The only amendment that I would suggest to her at this point is that instead of thinking in terms of reward, or of compensation for past sufferings, we should think in terms of fulfilment, a full realization of the highest potentialities of human nature in relation to the divine, brought about through the whole temporal story of creaturely existence, including the unpredictabilities of contingency and free will.

Julian's optimism expresses a western and therefore time-dominated sense of the inescapable reality of both joy and suffering in human life, to which we are reconciled through awareness of the final future when 'all shall be well and all manner of thing shall be well'. We can note at this point that there is a different resolution in the startling Mahayana Buddhist discovery that *samsara* (ordinary life with all its pain and suffering) and nirvana (the state of ultimate blessedness) are identical when life is experienced in a totally unselfcentred way, though, to complete the picture, this existential acceptance of each present moment is itself contained within the larger expectation that all human beings will eventually, through many lives, arrive at that nirvanic state.

22. Ibid., p. 269, LT51.
23. Ibid., p. 247, LT40.
24. Ibid.
25. Ibid., p. 225, LT27.
26. For an account of this see my *Evil and the God of Love*.

Did Lady Julian carry her cosmic optimism to the point of affirming universal salvation? Grace Jantzen says 'no' – 'her affirmation of her belief in the teaching of the Church on this point is clear'.[27] And indeed it is; but the problem is that she then goes on to say other things that are incompatible with that teaching. She begins by saying that 'one article of our faith is that many creatures will be damned, such as the angels who fell out of heaven because of pride, who are now devils, and many men upon earth who die out of the faith of Holy Church, that is to say those who are pagans and many who have received baptism and who live unchristian lives and so die out of God's love. All these will be eternally condemned to hell, as Holy Church teaches me to believe'.[28] Nothing could be clearer than that. But then she goes on, 'all this being so, it seemed to me that it was impossible that every kind of thing should be well, as our Lord revealed at this time. And to this I had no other answer as a revelation from our Lord except this: What is impossible to you is not impossible to me. I shall preserve my word in everything, and I shall make everything well.'[29] She then refers mysteriously to 'a deed which the blessed Trinity will perform on the last day . . . and what the deed will be and how it will be performed is unknown to every creature who is inferior to Christ, and it will be until the deed is done'.[30] All this led Richard Harries to conclude that 'as a loyal daughter of the Church Julian was unwilling to deny the reality of hell; yet every aspect of her thought brings her to the brink of universalism'.[31] This seems to me correct. The whole projectory of her thinking is towards universal salvation, and if the teaching of Holy Church had not restrained her I think that she would certainly have affirmed it.

There are a number of other very interesting elements in Lady Julian's theology. But, in sum, from the point of view of the orthodoxy of her day she was, along with many other Christian mystics, a heretic without knowing it, and indeed without wanting to know it. In her rejection of the fall–redemption model, which made sin and guilt the central human problem and a transactional atonement its solution; in her affirmation of the 'godly will' in virtue of which we are not separated from God by guilt, but rather by the spiritual confusion and blindness of our earthly state; and in her incipient universalism, she was moving in realms of thought that are familiar to the mystics of all traditions but that lie outside the traditional dogmatic system of the church; and of course in her perception that God should be thought of in female as truly as in male terms, she was once again far ahead of her own time.

27. Jantzen, 1987, p. 178.
28. Julian of Norwich, p. 233, LT32.
29. Ibid.
30. Ibid.
31. Harries, p. 58.

15

UNITIVE MYSTICISM: LITERAL UNITY

LITERAL OR METAPHORICAL?

Mysticism has often been defined as the experience of union either with God or with an ultimate non-personal reality. Thus William James says that the 'overcoming of all the usual barriers between the individual and the Absolute is the great mystic achievement. In mystic states we both become one with the Absolute and we are aware of our oneness.'[1] Likewise Evelyn Underhill says that 'mysticism is the art of union with Reality',[2] and R.C. Zaehner says that 'in Christian terminology mysticism means union with God'.[3] Many other similar statements could be cited.

However I shall argue that whilst the final state, far beyond this life, may well be one in which human individuality has finally been transcended, having served its purpose, talk of union with the Ultimate in this life must be understood metaphorically. Most theistic mystics have in fact used 'union' or 'unity' and/or 'deification' or 'divinization' as metaphors for a union of love or an alignment of wills which does not entail literal identity. Others however, usually but not always non-theistic, have intended to speak of a literal numerical identity, a union without distinction. In order to understand where different authors stand on this question we have to be aware of the metaphysical pictures presupposed in their writings. For there are systems which allow for, and even require, a literal union with the Ultimate; others which allow for this but do not require it; and yet others which exclude it.

1. William James, p. 404.
2. Happold, p. 38.
3. Zaehner, p. 32.

As well as reading the mystics against their metaphysical backgrounds we also have to distinguish between texts describing a union which the writer claims to have experienced, and others referring to a unitive state to which the writer's philosophy or theology points, but which the mystic does not profess to have experienced personally.

ADVAITA VEDANTA

At one end of the range of options is the Hindu advaita Vedanta which not only allows for but affirms a union without distinction. At the opposite pole is a strict monotheism which sees God as the sole absolute reality, the creator out of nothing of everything other than God. There is therefore an ineliminable distinction between creator and creature rendering it impossible for the latter ever to become literally identical with the creator. And in between there is the Neoplatonism that lay behind virtually all Christian mysticism up to the time of the Reformation and which was almost equally influential within Jewish and Islamic mysticism. The conception initiated by Plato[4] of the great chain of being descending from God at the summit, through the different levels of creaturely existence, allows for the possibility of the human soul being drawn upwards into the Godhead in a unity without distinction, although it does not necessarily require this. In the early and medieval Christian mystics, as also in the Sufis of Islam, Neoplatonism and monotheism coexisted in a continual tension with one another. It is sometimes difficult for us today, and may sometimes even have been difficult for the mystics themselves, to be entirely clear about where they stood within this spectrum.

In advaitic, or non-dualist, vedantic Hinduism a literal unity of the human soul with the Ultimate is said actually to be experienced by advanced advaitic mystics. This school of philosophy and of spiritual practice holds that there is ultimately only one reality, the eternal changeless Brahman, and that we fleeting conscious selves are 'unreal' in the sense that our separate individuality arises from ignorance (*avidya*) of our true nature. As Radhakrishnan puts it, 'The ego belongs to the relative world, is a stream of experience, a fluent mass of life, a centre round which our experiences of sense and mind gather. At the back of this whole structure is the Universal Consciousness, Atman, which is our true being.'[5] Through prolonged yogic practice we can reach the Atman, which is both individual and universal. Indeed our own nature, in its ultimate depths, is identical with the

4. For the origin and development of the idea, see Lovejoy, 1960.
5. Radhakrishnan, p. 91.

Atman, which is ultimately Brahman. So our present individual conscious existence is a kind of 'dream', the awakening from which is the experience of *moksha*, of identity with the Atman/Brahman. Within the borders of this 'dream' of *maya*, however, everything and everyone is completely real. They occur within a state analogous to a coherent life-long dream in which one does not know that one is dreaming. And if we ask, 'Who is dreaming?', the answer is that it is Brahman that is dreaming, and it is Brahman that each of us will be when eventually we awake!

I shall take as my text for this teaching the *Crest-Jewell of Discrimination* (*Viveka-Chudamani*), traditionally attributed to Shankara, who was alive in about 700 CE. Although Surendranath Dasgupta, in his monumental history of Indian philosophy, thought that the book 'seems to be genuinely attributed to Sankara',[6] more recent scholarship has been inclined to attribute it to an anonymous disciple. But, regardless of authorship, the book enjoys the status of a classic advaitic text, and since it is a succinct expression of Shankara's teaching as known from other writing, I shall use it here.

The *Crest-Jewell of Discrimination* uses the analogy of the air and the jar. If there are a number of clay jars containing only air, and you break the jars, what remains? The answer is, the air, as an unbounded totality: 'The air in the jar is one with the air everywhere. In like manner, your Atman is one with Brahman.'[7] Again Shankara uses the figure, also familiar in Christian and Muslim mystical literature, of a drop of water becoming part of the ocean. Shankara tells of someone who goes into deep meditation:

> His mind was completely absorbed in Brahman. After a while, he returned to normal consciousness. Then, out of the fullness of his joy, he spoke: The ego has disappeared. I have realized my identity with Brahman and so all my desires have melted away. I have risen above my ignorance and my knowledge of this seeming universe. What is this joy that I feel? Who shall measure it? I know nothing but joy, limitless, unbounded! The ocean of Brahman is full of nectar – the joy of the Atman. The treasure I have found there cannot be described in words. The mind cannot conceive of it. My mind fell like a hailstone into the vast expanse of Brahman's ocean. Touching one drop of it, I melted away and became one with Brahman. And now, though I return to human consciousness, I abide in the joy of the Atman.[8]

Again Shankara says, 'I am Reality, without beginning, without equal. I have no part in the illusion of "I" and "You", "this" and "that". I am

6. Dasgupta, p. 79.
7. Shankara, p. 80; cf. pp. 53, 97, 117, 126.
8. Ibid., p. 113.

Brahman, one without a second, bliss without end, the eternal, unchanging Truth.'[9] I shall point out presently the epistemological problem that lurks here, but let me first draw attention to some features of advaitic thought and experience which are illustrated or implied in these passages.

First, in traditional Indian thought philosophy has never been a detached intellectual activity but is the reflective aspect of the religious search for the absolutely real. And its criteria are less verbal consistency and conceptual clarity than experiential knowledge and the fruits of that knowledge. Shankara says, 'the only absolute proof is direct and immediate experience, within your own soul',[10] or again, 'Liberation does not come by merely saying the word "Brahman". Brahman must be actually experienced.'[11]

Second, the way to the awareness of union with Brahman is by transcending our natural self-centredness. This is a common theme of the mystics of all traditions. 'There must be' says Shankara, an entire giving-up of all actions which are done from personal, selfish desire.'[12] For 'the spiritual seeker cannot attain liberation as long as any trace of the ego remains in him.'[13] Accordingly, 'With a controlled mind and an intellect which is made pure and tranquil, you must realize the Atman directly, within yourself. Know the Atman as the real I. Thus you cross the shoreless ocean of worldliness, whose waves are birth and death. Live always in the knowledge of identity with Brahman, and be blessed.'[14] The phrase 'the ocean of worldliness whose waves are birth and death' reminds us that in the Hindu picture of the universe, the process of repeated reincarnations continues until final liberation is reached, bringing a final freedom both from the domination of the empirical ego and from its karmic impetus to further ego existence.

Third, the theme of joy runs through Shankara's text. This is a feature of most of the mystics in most traditions. Shankara speaks of 'the Atman, which is endless joy (*ananda*)'.[15] He refers to the goal as 'the highest bliss',[16] and says that the awakened person is 'illumined when he enjoys eternal bliss',[17] and that the Atman, which is our true nature, 'never ceases to experience infinite joy',[18] and so on.

And fourth, whilst ego-transcendence, culminating in self-awareness as the universal Atman, can only be achieved by individual effort – though effort supported by a long tradition embodied in a community of faith – it has significant social consequences, which are of course expressed in the texts in terms of the existing structures of Indian

9. Ibid., p. 115.
10. Ibid., p. 112.
11. Ibid., p. 41.
12. Ibid., p. 42.
13. Ibid., p. 83.
14. Ibid., pp. 53–4.
15. Ibid., p. 103.
16. Ibid., p. 39.
17. Ibid., p. 104.
18. Ibid., p. 53.

society. 'Give up pride of caste, family and rank and abstain from deeds of self-interest',[19] says Shankara; for 'caste, creed, family and lineage do not exist in Brahman'.[20] Indeed the aim of the liberated person is 'to realize that which is his ultimate good and to be constantly engaged in doing good to others'.[21] Such liberated souls, he says, 'bring good to mankind, like the coming of spring . . . It is the very nature of these great souls to work, of their own accord, to cure the troubles of others; just as the moon, of its own accord, cools the earth when it is scorched by the fierce rays of the sun'[22]. This refers of course to *jivanmuktas* (liberated souls), who are living in society, rather than to the celibate ascetic or renouncer who, traditionally in the last phase of life, has left the world to live in solitude.

Shankara himself seems to have led a very active life. He not only wrote vast commentaries on the Upanishads and the *Bhagavad Gita*, but travelled for many years throughout India as a teacher, and – according to tradition – founded monasteries at the four 'corners' of the sub-continent and also at Kanchipuram, south of Madras, where he died. This kind of energetic creativity and leadership is characteristic of many of the great mystics. The line of Shankaracharyas presiding over these foundations has continued through the centuries, and I once had an audience with the then Shankaracharya of Kanchipuram. He was an old man with a beautiful face radiating delight, and although with a status roughly equivalent at least to that of a cardinal or an archbishop, apparently lived in the utmost simplicity both in his surroundings and in his clothing and manner. He spoke enough English to be friendly and welcoming, but not enough for philosophical discussion. The meeting was in effect a *darshan* – that is, benefiting spiritually from being in a saint's presence – but hospitably adapted to receiving a non-Hindu.

As a further social implication of the advaitic philosophy, the underlying unity of humanity as different individuations of the one universal Atman entails that the other can never be finally alien or unchangeably an enemy. Shankara says, 'The one Atman appears as many, because of the variety of its outer coverings.'[23] This is the religious basis for *ahimsa*, developed by Gandhi as a non-violent resistance which appeals to the good in the heart of the enemy. But more about this in chapters 20–22.

Let us now return to Shankara's explicit statements quoted above about unity with the Ultimate: 'The ego has disappeared. I have realized my identity with Brahman', and 'I am Brahman'. Or again, 'the wise man reaches that highest state, in which consciousness of subject and object is dissolved away and the infinite unitary consciousness alone

19. Ibid., p. 96.
20. Ibid., p. 75.
21. Ibid., p. 131.
22. Ibid., pp. 37–8.
23. Ibid., p. 92.

remains – and he knows the bliss of Nirvana while still living on earth'.[24] Innumerable similar advaitic texts could be cited. Understood literally, they express a claim to have achieved a numerical oneness with Brahman and to be now living in that state of union.

AN EPISTEMOLOGICAL PROBLEM

There is a problem inherent in this claim. One can never feel confident when suggesting that people in a much higher spiritual state than oneself are mistaken in their understanding of their own experience. But it is nevertheless quite possible, indeed inevitable, when trying to describe the indescribable, to use language metaphorically rather than literally. I think that this must be the case when a mystic declares that he or she has experienced union without distinction with Brahman or with God. The reason is this. An experience that is reported, and that has therefore been remembered, even if it cannot be adequately captured in words, is by definition an episode in the history of the reporter. The mystic undergoes the experience and is subsequently able to remember having done so. But in that case the mystic cannot have ceased to exist as a distinct stream of memory-bearing consciousness. There can have been no literal losing of individual identity. If the finite consciousness of the mystic had been dissolved in the Infinite, like a drop of water becoming part of the ocean, there would be no unbroken thread of finite consciousness continuing through the experience and subsequently able to recall it. Thus it seems to me that if individual identity is indeed lost in the ocean of Brahman this must be a state from which there is no return, and hence no possibility of its being reported by a still living mystic.

If this is so, the fully enlightened person's experience is not the final state to which the advaitic philosophy points, but is perhaps the nearest approach to it possible in this life. As Louis Dupré puts it, 'such a total elimination of personal consciousness remains an asymptotic ideal never to be reached but to be approached ever more closely.'[25] I would add that whilst there can only be movement towards this in our earthly life, there is, according to advaitic teaching, a final state in which total union will at last be achieved. The approach to it that we see in living *jivanmuktas* is apparently a state in which the world is decreasingly experienced and evaluated as centring upon oneself. Instead he or she is conscious of the ever-changing world from a particular point within it, but without privileging that point in such a way as to be led to put one's own interests above those of others.

24. Ibid., p. 43.
25. Dupré, p. 248.

My conclusion thus far then, is that the advaitic philosophy does postulate a final loss of individual identity in total unity with the infinite reality of Brahman, and that this can be approached but not fully attained in our present life, or indeed during the long series of lives leading to eventual enlightenment. But in their exuberant use of metaphorical language about this most desirable of states, this 'pearl of great price', advaitic mystics have spoken of their present existence as though it were already the ultimate unity. The Buddhist tradition, on the other hand, distinguishes between nirvana and *parinirvana*. The former, which can be attained in varying degrees in this life, is a state beyond ego-centredness expressed in a serene joy, in loving-kindness (*metta*), and in compassion (*karuna*) for all life; whilst the latter is the state of a fully awakened one, a Buddha, beyond earthly existence and with no karmic residue leading to further rebirths.

NEOPLATONISM

There are unmistakable parallels between the eastern Vedantic and the western Neoplatonic pictures of reality. Dom Bede Griffiths says that 'Neoplatonism, as found in Plotinus and later developed by St Gregory of Nyssa and Pseudo-Dionysius the Areopagite, is the nearest equivalent in the West of the Vedantic tradition of Hinduism in the East'.[26] The Neoplatonic One, like the Vedantic Brahman, is ineffable (or as I would rather say, is transcategorial reality), beyond the range of our human conceptual systems. And the mystic path is one of purification of the ego and its self-centred desires and concerns in order to find our true nature in unity with the Ultimate. The classic Vedantic saying, *tat tvam asi*, 'that art thou', means that each of us ultimately *is* Brahman.[27] Catherine of Genoa provides a direct Christian parallel: 'Once stripped of all its imperfections, the soul rests in God, with no characteristic of its own, since its purification is the stripping away of the lower self in us. Our being is then God.'[28] Or again, 'My *me* is God.'[29] The sixteenth century *Theologica Germanica* says that when one empties oneself of everything – of will, wisdom, love, desire, knowledge – then one knows that 'I, poor fool that I was, imagined it was I, but behold! it is and was, of a truth, God!'[30] There are innumerable other examples expressing a range of nuances. Denys Turner says that 'some version of the soul's ultimate identity with God is the common stock in trade of the whole Western mystical tradition, at least until as late as the sixteenth century'.[31]

26. Pseudo-Dionysius, p. 32.
27. *Chandogya Upanishad* VI, 9.4; Radhakrishnan, p. 460.
28. Catherine of Genoa, p. 80.
29. Underhill, p. 222.
30. Chapter 5.
31. Turner, p. 143.

It is unlikely that the analogies between Neoplatonist metaphysics on the one hand, and Vedantic and Buddhist metaphysics on the other, are merely coincidences, although the extent of trans-cultural sharing remains guesswork. There were historical channels along which influences could have flowed in both directions. Contact between the Mediterranean world and India goes back a very long way: the Indian gods Indra, Mitra and Varuna are mentioned in cuneiform Hittite inscriptions dated around 1350 BCE. About 515 BCE the Persian emperor Darius conquered the Indus Valley, and when some two hundred years later Alexander the Great also invaded the sub-continent, he left behind a number of Greek settlements. There is evidence of trade between the Mediterranean world and India in the first and second centuries CE, with remains of a Roman trading station found as far east as Pondicherry, and coins of Augustus, Tiberius and Nero have been found up and down the east coast of India. So it is evident that in the period in which Neoplatonism developed there had already been centuries of east–west contact. Dean Inge, referring to the western end of the relationship, says, 'There is no doubt that the philosophers of Asia were held in reverence at this period . . . [C]ertainly there are parts of Plotinus, and still more of his successors, which strongly suggest Asiatic influences.'[32] Michael von Bruck also speaks of Neoplatonism as 'an important bridge to Indian culture'.[33] However despite this no specific borrowing in either direction has been identified, and it remains possible that we should see the idea of an ultimate divine–human unity as a universal, or at least a very widespread, insight occurring independently within different traditions. Thus von Bruck speaks of 'underlying structures which express common human, spiritual relationships',[34] and Rudolph Otto in his classic study of mysticism says that 'in mysticism there are indeed strong primal impulses working in the human soul which as such are completely unaffected by differences of climate, of geographical position or of race. These show in their similarity an inner relationship of types of human experience and spiritual life which is truly astonishing.'[35] So when eastern and western mystics encountered each others' ideas, they naturally welcomed and found support in them.

32. Inge, p. 101.
33. Bruck, p. 103.
34. Ibid., p. 117.
35. Otto, 1957, p. xvi.

16

UNITIVE MYSTICISM: METAPHORICAL UNITY

CHRISTIAN NEOPLATONISM

Neoplatonists generally shared the Indian assumption that philosophy is a spiritual search rather than an intellectual exercise, and accepted religious experience as a major source. Indeed Mary Clark says that 'Neoplatonism was the first theology constructed on the basis of religious experience'.[1] That basis continued to support Christian faith, particularly among the mystics. In the great mystical flowering of the fourteenth century 'we find in them an unfaltering conviction that our communion with God must be a fact of experience, and not only a philosophical theory'.[2] This is what sets mystical theology apart from the purely intellectual creation of theological systems. The same is true of the Jewish mystics, of whom David Blumenthal says that 'whilst some forms of mystical literature are really types of Talmud [or, we could say, of biblical exegesis] and philosophy . . . most, if not all, of mystical literature reflects an actual or anticipated experience on the part of the writer'.[3] But whilst Christian Neoplatonism is indissolubly connected with mystical experience, it also provided the intellectual framework of western mystical thought for many centuries. A.N. Whitehead once said in a memorable exaggeration that western philosophy consists in 'a series of footnotes to Plato'.[4] But it is not an exaggeration to say that during the early and medieval periods, the picture of the universe accepted by Christian mystics, and the forms of religious experience that they reciprocally reflected and shaped, were a series of echoes of Neoplatonism.

1. Clark, p. 366.
2. Inge, p. 167.
3. Blumenthal, 1978, p. 186.
4. Whitehead, p. 53.

The Greek philosopher Plotinus (205–70 CE) was a major conduit through which Neoplatonism entered the life stream of Christianity. Plotinus' disciple, Porphyry, wrote of his master that 'his end and goal was to be united (*henothenai*) [with the One] . . . Four times while I was with him he attained that goal.'[5] Plotinus himself speaks in an autobiographical passage in the *Enneads* of his 'acquiring identity with the divine'.[6] Was this the experience of a literal or a metaphorical unity? Bernard McGinn, in his authoritative and still growing history of western mysticism, says that 'most recent interpreters claim that a careful study of Plotinus actually indicates that he does not teach any form of annihilation of the soul or absolute identity with the Supreme'.[7] This is certainly true of most of the great Christian, Muslim and Jewish mystics who have spoken of union with God. In the intensity of their devotion and their overwhelmingly vivid awareness of God's presence, they have often expressed themselves in the extravagant language of love, freely exercising poetic licence and employing vivid metaphors and similes which are not however, if questioned, intended to be understood literally. This applies to much the greater part of their language of union. But on the other hand some of them do at least seem to speak entirely soberly and with philosophical precision of an ultimate union with God. We must therefore leave open the possibility that, in some cases, the tension between biblical monotheism and Neoplatonism was resolved in favour of the latter, and that these writers mean exactly what they say; and the fact that they were so often suspected of heresy is consonant with this possibility.

Following the historical path laid out by McGinn, we can say that the first major Christian figure to speak of union with God was one of the desert fathers, the late fourth-century Evagrius. He presents a version of the Neoplatonist picture of souls falling out of a primal unity with God and then, aided by divine grace, gradually returning to that unity through ascetic and contemplative practices. In expressing this he uses the familiar simile of the drop and the ocean, with its implication of an eventual union without distinction: 'When minds flow back to [God] like torrents into the sea, he changes them all completely into his own nature, color and taste. They will no longer be many but one in his unending and inseparable unity, because they are united and joined with him. And as in the fusion of rivers with the sea no addition in its nature or variation in its color or taste is to be found, so also in the fusion of minds with the Father no duality of natures . . . comes about.'[8] It is difficult to be certain whether a literal unity with God is intended here. Either way, there is no suggestion that Evagrius claimed to have

5. McGinn, 1991, p. 44.
6. IV, 8.1; MacKenna, p. 357.
7. McGinn, 1991, p. 54.
8. Ibid., p. 154.

experienced such union. But although he was in some important respects entirely orthodox – in his understanding of Christ, for example, he opposed various current heresies – Evagrius' writings did arouse suspicion, and the second Council of Constantinople in 553 CE condemned fifteen propositions, some of which were derived from his writings. One modern commentator, Urs von Balthasar, says that 'the mystical teaching of Evagrius in its fully developed consistency stands closer to Buddhism than to Christianity'.[9] Others disagree; but that Buddhism was known in the early church is evident from Clement of Alexandria's remark about 200 CE that 'some, too, of the Indians obey the precepts of Buddha; whom, on account of his extraordinary sanctity, they have raised to divine honours'.[10]

PSEUDO-DIONYSIUS

Pseudo-Dionysius, thought to have been a Syrian monk writing about 500 CE, and whom we met in chapter 9, speaks of the divinization of the soul and of the mystic's goal as 'to be at one with God'.[11] In *The Divine Names* he says that 'somehow, in a way we cannot know, we shall be united with him',[12] and that 'the most divine knowledge of God, that which comes through unknowing, is achieved in a union far beyond mind'.[13] Such phrases, which seem to suggest a union to be attained in mystical experience, are not however as prominent in his writings as we would expect if they are intended to be taken literally, and they are probably best understood metaphorically in the light of his statement that 'the soul is brought into union with God himself to the extent that every one of us is capable of it'.[14] For a state that is capable of degrees is more analogous to a union of love or of wills than to union without distinction. However, metaphorical language could well be based on religious experience; and Dionysius does at one point speak not only of 'perspicuous and laborious research of the scriptures' but also of 'that more mysterious inspiration, not only of learning but also experiencing the divine things',[15] and of the moment when the mind 'is made one with the dazzling rays, being then and there enlightened by the inscrutable depth of Wisdom'.[16] What is not entirely clear, however, is whether he had himself received this experience.

9. Von Balthasar, p. 193.
10. *Stromateis* I. 15; Roberts and Donaldson, p. 316.
11. *Celestial Hierarchy*, chapter 3.2; Psuedo-Dionysius, p. 154.
12. Chapter 1; ibid., p. 52.
13. Chapter 7.3; ibid., p. 109.
14. *Divine Names*, chapter 13.3; ibid., p. 130.
15. Ibid., chapter 2.9; ibid., p. 65.
16. Ibid., chapter 7.3; ibid., p. 109.

John Scotus Eriugena in the ninth century uses the phrase 'ineffable unity'.[17] Later, the fourteenth-century Meister Eckhart says that 'if I am to know God directly, I must become completely He and He I: so that this He and this I become and are one I'.[18] Using the drop of water analogy he says that the soul 'is more intimate with [God] than a drop of water put into a vat of wine, for that would still be water and wine; but here, one is changed into the other so that no creature could ever again detect a difference between them'.[19] In another familiar analogy he says that God 'is light and when the divine light pours into the soul, the soul is united with God, as light blends with light'.[20] Ruusbroec and Suso in the fourteenth century also spoke of union with God. Ruusbroec, for example, writes of 'unity without difference . . . There . . . all exhalted spirits melt away and come to naught by reason of the blissful enjoyment they experience in God's essential being, which is the superessential being of all beings.'[21] He certainly seems to be speaking here of a unity without distinction. But that only shows how easy it is to make the mistake of taking the mystics' language at face value.[22] For Ruusbroec says a little later that 'no created being can be one with God's being and have its own being perish. If that happened, the creature would become God, and this is impossible, for God's essential being can neither decrease nor increase and can have nothing taken away from it or added to it.'[23] Again, 'Yet the creature does not become God, for the union takes place in God through grace and our homeward-turning love: and therefore the creature in its inward contemplation feels a distinction and an otherness between itself and God.'[24] Suso, a disciple of Eckhart, likewise declares that the good and faithful servant 'disappears and loses himself in God, and becomes one spirit with Him, as a drop of water which is drowned in a great quantity of wine. For even as such a drop disappears, taking the colour and taste of wine, so it is with those who are in full possession of blessedness.' However he then adds that 'His [the human person's] being remains, but in another form, in another glory, and in another power'.[25] Clearly he is not speaking here of a numerical identity in which the mystic's personality is obliterated, but rather of a spiritual identity in which it is transformed. St John of the Cross says that in attaining to unity with God 'the soul is indeed

17. McGinn, 1994, p. 116.
18. Sermon 99; Underhill, p. 420.
19. *Talks of Instruction*, 20; Eckhart, 1941, p. 29.
20. Sermon 52; Eckhart, 1941, p. 163.
21. *Clarification*, Part III; Ruusbroec, p. 265.
22. This is a mistake that Nelson Pike makes in his otherwise brilliant book on unitive mysticism; Pike, 1992.
23. *Clarification*, Part III; Ruusbroec, pp. 265–6.
24. *Book of Truth*, 11; Underhill, p. 423.
25. *Eternal Wisdom*, 4; Underhill, p. 424.

God by participation'; but he makes it clear in the same paragraph that this union is capable of degrees and that the soul remains 'as distinct from the Being of God as it was before'.[26] And, to give just one more example, Bernard of Clairvaux wrote that 'The union between God and man is not unity . . . For how can there be unity where there is a plurality of natures and difference of substance?The union of God and man is brought about not by confusion of natures, but by agreement of wills . . . this unity is effected not by coherence of essence but by concurrence of wills.'[27]

Another simile used by several of the mystics, making the same point, is the way in which fire can penetrate and transform a lump of iron. Thus the seventeenth-century Jabob Boehme says, 'Behold a bright flaming piece of iron, which of itself is dark and black, and the fire so penetrateth and shineth through the iron, that it giveth light. Now, the iron doth not cease to be; it is iron still: and the property of the fire retaineth its own propriety: it doth not take the iron into it, but it penetrateth and shineth through the iron . . . In such a manner is the soul set in the Deity.'[28]

I take it that this metaphorically unitive state is one in which self-concern has been transcended and in which the consciousness is filled instead with the divine reality. The human self still exists, but instead of being aware of itself it is aware only of the all-encompassing divine presence. The theistic mystics are, as W.H. Auden said, 'trying to describe . . . a state in consciousness so filled with the presence of God that there is no vacant corner of it detachedly observing the experience'.[29] It is this that has also been called deification or divinization.

DEIFICATION

Deification (*theiosis*) is one of the main metaphors used by Christian mystics, particularly in the eastern church. It too derives from Neoplatonism. Plato himself seems to have thought of the soul as naturally divine, so that the process of 'divinization' is a return to what one really is. But when the second-century Clement of Alexandria wrote that 'the Word of God became man, that thou mayest learn from man how man may become God',[30] and when the fourth-century Athanasius wrote that ' "the Word became flesh" that He might make man capable of Godhead',[31] and again when Augustine a generation later said that 'the Son of God was made a partaker of mortality so that mortal man

26. *Mount Carmel*, II, 5.7; Peers, p. 182.
27. Butler, p. 114.
28. Underhill, p. 421.
29. Woods, p. 385.
30. *Protrepticus*, 1; Roberts and Donaldson, p. 174.
31. *Against the Arians*, II. 21.59; Schaff and Wace, p. 380.

might partake of divinity',[32] they did not mean that humans are literally to acquire the defining attributes of deity – eternity, omnipotence, omniscience, etc. They were thinking in terms of the distinction drawn by the Hellenistic Fathers, particularly Irenaeus[33] and Clement of Alexandria,[34] and later Origen, between the image (*eikon, imago*) and the likeness (*homoiosis, similitudo*) of God. In modern terms, the image of God is our existence as intelligent ethical animals with a spiritual nature capable of responding to our creator. As such we are however only at the beginning of a long process of development towards the 'likeness' of God, which is our perfecting by the Holy Spirit. It is this perfecting that is called in the eastern Christian tradition deification or divinization. This has never meant literally becoming God, but a growing into the full human nature divinely intended for us.

THE LOVE POETRY OF THE MYSTICS

Yet another stream of metaphorical language derives from human sexuality. The one moment of love poetry in the scriptures was seized upon by a succession of mystics to express the soul's love for God. Indeed what is canonically called the Song of Solomon is probably the main key to the metaphor of union in Christian mystical literature; and it is a union of love, even erotic love, but not of literal identity. Much of the literature within both the western and the eastern churches was commentary on this ancient text, applying its often beautiful imagery to the relation between the soul and either God or Christ. Those who commented on the Song of Songs, or who took up the theme of the soul's marriage to Christ, include not only Origen but also Chrysostom, Gregory of Nyssa, Ambrose, Jerome and Cassian in the fourth century, Augustine in the fourth and fifth, Gregory the Great in the sixth and seventh, Peter Damien in the eleventh, Bernard of Clairvaux, Hugh of St Victor and a host of others, including for the first time a number of women writers (such as the author of *A Teaching of the Loving Knowledge of God*) in the twelfth century, and many other major figures since then, including Ruusbroec and Suso in the fourteenth and Teresa of Avila in the sixteenth century. As typical examples, Bernard of Clairvaux quotes the opening verse of the Song, 'Let him kiss me with the kisses of his mouth,' and asks, 'Who is it speaks these words? It is the Bride. Who is the Bride? It is the Soul thirsting for God.'[35] And Teresa of Avila even speaks of 'the Spiritual Marriage of the Bridegroom [i.e. Christ] with your soul'.[36]

32. *Homily on Psalms*, 52.6; McGinn, 1991, p. 251.
33. *Against Heresies*, 5.6.1; Roberts and Donaldson, p. 523.
34. *Stromata* 2.22; Roberts and Donaldson, p. 376.
35. Sermon 7; Underhill, p. 137.
36. *Interior Castle, Seventh Mansion*, 1.1.

As a different kind of example of human love language applied to the divine, the sixteenth-century mystic Francis de Sales uses the analogy of a mother feeding her baby:

> See how its mother . . . takes it, clasps it, fastens it, so to speak, to her bosom, joins her mouth to its mouth, and kisses it . . . at such a moment there is perfect union. Thus too . . . our Lord shows the most loving breast of his divine love to his devout soul, draws it wholly to himself, gathers it in, and, as it were, enfolds all its powers within the bosom of his more than motherly comfort. Then, burning with love, he clasps the soul, joins, presses, and fastens it to his sweet lips and to his delightsome breasts, kisses it with the sacred 'kiss of the mouth', and makes it relish his breasts, 'more sweet than wine'.[37]

Teresa of Avila also speaks of her experience of the 'wound of love', a theme that recurs frequently in Christian mystical literature:

> Beside me, on the left hand, appeared an angel in bodily form . . . In his hands I saw a great golden spear, and at the iron tip there appeared to be a point of fire. This he plunged into my heart several times so that it penetrated my entrails. When he pulled it out, I felt that he took them with it, and left me utterly consumed by the great love of God. The pain was so severe that it made me utter several moans.[38]

She uses the marriage imagery to the full: 'When our Lord is pleased to take pity on the sufferings . . . endured through her longing for Him by this soul which He has spiritually taken for His bride, He, before consummating the celestial marriage, brings her into this His mansion or presence chamber'.[39]

Although Teresa herself would not make the connection, the sexual character of the experience is self-evident in a culture which has absorbed the insights of Sigmund Freud. And why not?As I have argued in chapter 12, religious experience always receives its specific form from the conceptual and imaginative resources of the experiencer. Sexual imagery is surely as good as any other. But if we ask why this particular imagery is so prominent within Christian mysticism, Dean Inge's answer must be right: 'There is no doubt', he says, 'that the enforced celibacy and virginity of the monks and nuns led them, consciously or unconsciously, to transfer to the human person of Christ (and to a much slighter extent, to the Virgin Mary) a measure of those feelings which could find no vent in their external lives.'[40] From a naive realist perspective this would be damning, but from a critical realist point of

37. Cohn-Sherbok, 1994, p. 132.
38. Ibid., p. 166.
39. *Interior Castle, Seventh Mansion*, 1.3; p. 170.
40. Inge, p. 270.

view it creates no problem. For this is what we could expect if such experiences, whilst obviously imaginative projections, are at the same time responses to the universal presence of the Real.

THE JEWISH KABBALAH

Jewish mysticism flourished mainly in the medieval period, and its history is as complex as it is fascinating. A number of schools began at different times, each initiated by a major spiritual figure, and most of these movements later died out, although they had always contributed something to the continuing tradition. The subject thus has to be treated either at great length or rather briefly; and I must regretfully follow the latter course. I shall restrict consideration to the Kabbalah (or Qabbalah). It is generally held that this avoided any idea of literal divine–human unity. Thus a major authority on the subject, Gershom Scholem, wrote that 'it is only in extremely rare cases that ecstasy signifies actual union with God in which the human individuality abandons itself to the rapture of complete submersion in the divine stream. Even in this ecstatic frame of mind, the Jewish mystic almost invariably retains a sense of the distance between the Creator and his creature.'[41] On the other hand Moshe Idel has more recently claimed that 'unitive descriptions recur in Kabbalistic literature no less frequently than in non-Jewish mystical writings, and the images used by the Kabbalists do not fall short of the most extreme forms of other types of mysticism'.[42] A key term is *devekut*, 'cleaving' or 'adhesion' to God. In ecstatic Kabbalism, Idel says, 'mystical union is presented as a process of assimilation to the Divine'.[43] He cites a leading representative, the thirteenth-century Abraham Abulafia, who used the formula 'he and He become one entity'. Again Rabbi Isaac of Acre used the metaphor, familiar from both Christian and Hindu sources, of water falling into water: 'She [the soul] will cleave to the divine intellect [i.e. God], and it will cleave to her . . . and she and the intellect become one entity, as if somebody poured out a jug of water into a running well, that all becomes one.'[44]

As with the Christian and Muslim mystics, the question is whether this unitive language is being used literally or metaphorically. I have argued earlier that if such language is intended literally, as indicating a total union without distinction, it cannot properly refer to a state of the still living and embodied mystic, but rather to an ultimate state beyond this life. And Rabbi Isaac seems to have thought that the point at which 'all becomes one' is to be reached only through the doorway of death.

41. Scholem, 1955, pp. 122–3.
42. Idel, p. 60.
43. Ibid., p. 64.
44. Ibid., p. 67.

Idel says that 'the great endeavor of the mystic is to attain the state of union without, nevertheless, being absorbed and lost in the divine abyss. Sinking is envisioned here as a perilous possibility inherent in the unitive process. However, at least in the case of Moses, death – which I suppose is parallel to sinking – is portrayed as a higher mystical step that Moses attempted to achieve; it was denied him only because he was needed to lead the people of Israel, an activity consisting of corporeal acts.'[45]

On balance then, it seems that whilst the language of union has been used as freely by Jewish as by other mystics, it is used metaphorically of religious experience in this present life.

THE SUFIS OF ISLAM

Unitive language has, once again, been used as much by the Sufis as by Christian and Jewish mystics. Al-Hallaj, for example, uses the drop of water image in his poem:

> Thy Spirit is mingled in my spirit even as wine is
> mingled with pure water.

Again:

> I am He whom I love, and He whom I love is I:
> We are two spirits dwelling in one body.
> If thou seest me, thou seest Him,
> And if thou seest Him, thou seest us both.[46]

Rumi likewise speaks in his mystical poetry of union with God:

> With Thy Sweet Soul, this soul of mine,
> Hath mixed as Water doth with Wine,
> Who can the Wine and Water part,
> Or me and thee when we combine?[47]

This union is a completed return to the divine–human unity that existed before creation when creatures existed only in the mind of God – an idea which the Sufis justified by their interpretation of the qur'anic verse in which God speaks to the children of Adam before he created them (7. 171). The restored union is the final point of a process of turning from self to God which begins with prayer (*dhikr*), eventually achieves full self-naughting (*fana*), and so becomes life which is part of the life of God (*baqa*). Speaking of this process, the ninth- and tenth-century Sufi

45. Ibid., p. 67–80.
46. Nicholson, p. 151.
47. *Festival of Spring*; Underhill, p. 426.

master Junayd of Baghdad says that 'the creature's individuality is completely obliterated' and that he is 'naughted to self'.[48] Again Rumi writes, 'No one will find his way to the Court of Magnificence until he is annihilated,' and again, 'With God, two I's cannot find room. You say "I" and He says "I". Either you die before Him, or let Him die before you.'[49] Such language is common among the Sufis. However, this 'death' of the self is not a ceasing to exist, but its transformation into spiritual union with the divine life. Rumi says, 'The spirit becomes joyful through the I-less I.'[50] The self-naughted person lives, and lives in fullness of energy and joy; but it is now the divine life that is being lived in and through the fully surrendered servant of Allah. And as in the case of the Christian mystics, union is often seen as the most appropriate available metaphor. As the tenth-century Sufi Al-Ghazali says, the mystics 'after their ascent to the heavens of Reality, agree that they saw nothing in existence except God the One . . . Nothing was left to them but God . . . But the words of lovers when in a state of drunkenness must be hidden away and not broadcast. However, when their drunkenness abates and the sovereignity of their reason is restored – and reason is God's scale on earth – they know that this was not actual identity.'[51]

The one problematic moment was of course the famous, or infamous, utterance of the tenth-century Al-Hallaj, '*Ana 'l-Haqq*,' 'I am the Real,' i.e. 'I am God,' for which Al-Hallaj was executed as a blasphemer or, as some Muslims prefer to say, as 'the martyr of mystical love'. The irenical Al-Ghazali later suggested that what Al-Hallaj meant was that 'he is so completely absorbed in al-Haqq [the Real] that there is no space in him for one other than [God]'.[52] And he pointed out that 'one's speaking of a union (between two objects) and saying, "the one is the other", is not possible except by expanding (the meaning of the words) and using them metaphorically, which is in accordance with the practice of the Sufis and poets'.[53]

There has however been an enormous discussion of Al-Hallaj's words, and of the extent to which he thought in terms of some kind of divine incarnation in human life, both in himself and in others who had attained to *baga*. For there is a sense in which, for a number of the Sufis, God is incarnate in varying degrees throughout human life, and indeed throughout the whole visible universe. Rumi's remarkable poem about this is too long to quote here, but R.A. Nicholson summarizes it when

48. *Kitab al Fana*; Zaehner, p. 166.
49. Chittick, pp. 179, 191.
50. Ibid., p. 193.
51. *Mishkat al-Anwar* 121.3; Zaehner, pp. 157–8.
52. Al-Ghazali, 1987, p. 99.
53. Ibid., p. 133.

he says that Rumi 'describes how the One Light shines in myriad forms through the universe, and how the One Essence, remaining ever the same, clothes itself from age to age in the prophets and saints who are its witnesses to mankind'.[54] Divine incarnation in this sense is not however intended (as within Christianity by the Council of Chalcedon) in the literal terms of an individual having two natures, one human and the other divine. We have to think rather of the metaphorical sense of identity that was used in, for example, Jesus' saying to those who, in the parable of the sheep and the goats, had fed the hungry and visited the prisoners and sick, 'as you did it to one of the least of these my brethren, you did it to me'.[55] We find the same metaphorical sense of identity in Rumi's poem in which God rebukes Moses, saying, 'I am God, I fell sick, thou camest not.' Moses expostulates, 'O Lord, Thou never ailest. My understanding is lost: unfold the meaning of these words.' And God replies, 'Yea; a favourite and chosen slave of Mine fell sick. I am he. Consider well: his sickness is My sickness.'[56] In such parables God is self-identified with human beings in that the way to serve God is to serve one's neighbours in their need.

The upshot of this discussion of the mystics' language of union is that it should generally be construed metaphorically. The mystics do not intend a literal numerical unity without distinction, but a self-naughting, a transcending of the ego point of view, so that, in the words of chapter 10 of the *Theologia Germanica,* one is to the Eternal Goodness what one's own hand is to oneself. This is a transformation from natural self-centredness to a new orientation centred in the divine reality. And when mystics in any tradition claim to have attained a literal oneness with the Ultimate, I have pointed out (pp. 141–2) that, if they had, they could not have existed within it as distinct memory-bearing consciousnesses capable of subsequently reporting the experience. Such a unity, beyond separate individuality, may well, I shall suggest in chapter 26, be the ultimate state after individuality has finally achieved its perfection in a total self-transcendence. But that state does not occur in the present life.

54. Nicholson, p. 152.
55. Matthew 25:40.
56. Rumi, 1995, p. 65.

17

THE DARK SIDE

THE DARK SIDE OF THE CULTS

We have seen that religious and mystical experience is not necessarily a response to the Transcendent. It can also be human delusion, and sometimes very dangerous human delusion.

Some recent and contemporary small religious movements, or cults, for example, have been based on delusions that have been extremely harmful, often to their own adherents, sometimes to others, sometimes to both. In 1978 some nine hundred men, women and children died in a combination of mass suicide and murder under the charismatic leadership of the Rev. Jim Jones in Jonestown, Guyana. In 1987 the bodies of thirty-three people involved in a religious cult in South Korea were found in a factory attic after an apparent suicide–murder pact in Yongin, near Seoul. In 1993 David Koresh and about eighty members of his Branch Davidian cult died by fire during a bungled police attack on their ranch at Waco, Texas. In 1994 fifty-three members of the Order of the Solar Temple died in simultaneous murder–suicide rituals in France and Canada. In 1995 the Aum Shinrikyo sect put sarin gas in the Tokyo underground system, resulting in twelve deaths and thousands of cases of sickness. The same year sixteen charred bodies of members of the Order of the Solar Temple were found in a forest in south-western France, and five more died in 1997 in an apparent suicide pact in a small town near Quebec, Canada. Also in 1997 there was the horrific mass suicide of Heaven's Gate members in a luxury mansion near San Diego, California. (This was the end of March. I happened to be in nearby Palm Springs at the time and well remember the continuing shock as more and more details came out from the police. The suicides, who had given up their homes and work in other parts of the country, believed that they would be beamed up to a great spaceship in the sky, leaving the rest of humanity to perish on earth.) In early 1998 a group of the same or a similar cult were prevented by the police from committing mass suicide on the Canary Island of Tenerife. In such cases common sense, both practical and ethical, enables religious and non-religious people alike to be confident that the leaders and the led were dangerously deluded. But their faith – which was in the broadest sense a religious faith – must have been reflected in the ways in which they experienced their lives and the events around them, and this was clearly a delusory experience.

It is however worth adding at this point that religious sects and cults are not, as such, necessarily harmful. On the contrary, they can often be beneficial to their members, precipitating a move from a purely secular to a religious outlook, for 'converts to new religious movements are overwhelmingly from relatively irreligious backgrounds'.[1] But even when beneficial, the new movements usually provide only a temporary halting place on the individual's spiritual journey. For such groups as the Hari Krishnas (International Society for Krishna Consciousness), the Moonies (Unification Church), the Children of God (now the Family of Love), modern paganism, and many more, generally have a relatively narrow belief basis and practice. This can be helpful to some people at some point in their lives, but lacks the comprehensiveness of the great traditions, which are sufficiently inclusive and internally varied to provide a spiritual home throughout a lifetime of growth. So it is not surprising that cults typically have a revolving-door membership, with new members joining and others leaving all the time, so that 'many people have "gone through" the movements, but only a few have stayed'.[2] However, the 'going through' may well have met the individual's spiritual needs at that time. Further, 'a growing body of research has indicated that those who join the movements are no more likely to be psychologically disturbed than are the majority of their peers'.[3] Indeed it is easy to forget that, depending on upbringing, what is to one person solid truth can seem to another pure fantasy. For example, just as those of us who are not Mormons tend to regard as fantasy the 1827 story of Joseph Smith being directed by the angel Moroni to some golden plates, which subsequently disappeared, filled with writing which he translated with the aid of special stones into the text of the *Book of Mormon*, so non-Christians (and indeed some Christians) regard as fantasy the story that Jesus, having died on the

1. Stark, p. 178.
2. Barker, p. 34.
3. Ibid.

cross, came back physically to life, spent forty days on earth with his disciples, and then ascended bodily into the sky from a hillside outside Jerusalem. We should therefore be tolerant of our neighbours' 'fantasies' so long as these do not lead them to harm anyone, and the smaller and newer movements should not be persecuted or treated with contempt. To do so is often a case of people living in a large, ancient, and therefore respectable glass house throwing stones at people in smaller, new, temporary glass houses!

THE DARK SIDE OF THE GREAT RELIGIONS

Whilst the damage done by some cults has usually (though not always) been restricted to their own followers, the great world religions, with their much greater power over much greater numbers of people, have been responsible for evil on a much vaster scale. Even Buddhism – the religion which on the whole has the cleanest record in this respect – was used in the first century BCE to support the invasion of Sri Lanka by Buddhist kings on the Indian mainland.[4] Indeed, in virtually every war that has ever been fought, God has been believed by each set of combatants to be on their side. It seems that the only cause that God really supports is the arms industry! The twentieth century has seen huge numbers of young men of many nations of both east and west in the grip of religiously intensified loyalties that enabled them to commit cruel, merciless violence, even against helpless civilians. In a number of the most brutal conflicts of the last half of the twentieth century, religious allegiances have injected a justifying religious dimension, so that religion has provided the mast to which the two sides have nailed their colours. For, as Pascal said, 'Men never do evil so completely and cheerfully as when they do it from religious conviction.'[5] A major example is the mutual Hindu, Muslim and Sikh massacres in the Punjab after the partition of India in 1947, and in sporadic communal conflict and violence in India ever since. Again, when in May 1998 India and then Pakistan conducted underground nuclear tests, India's bomb was referred to as a Hindu and Pakistan's as an Islamic bomb. Similarly, India's long-range missiles are named Prithvi and Agni after ancient Hindu kings, whilst Pakistan's is named after Ghauri, one of the early Muslim invaders of India. Other examples abound: the Jewish–Arab wars in Israel, Palestine and Lebanon; the long and costly war between (Sunni) Iran and (Shi'ite) Iraq; the Serbian (Christian Orthodox) and Bosnian and Kosovo-Albanian (Muslim) conflicts in former Yugoslavia; the generations of Catholic–Protestant violence in northern Ireland; the

4. Bowker, pp. 15–17.
5. Tracy, p. 86.

continuing conflict in the Sudan . . . And going back in history, the rapid expansion and consolidation of Islam in the seventh to ninth centuries into a vast empire, stretching from the western Mediterranean and North Africa into central Asia, was initially accomplished by force of arms. In the Crusades of the eleventh to thirteenth centuries, Christian knights blessed by the Pope and by local bishops, seeking fame and fortune from the imagined riches of Jerusalem and eager for the indulgences to be earned in this holy enterprise, led armies marching under the banner of Christ. They first slaughtered the Jews in the cities that they entered, then further east slaughtered Greek Christians, and eventually slaughtered Muslims with a savagery that has haunted relations between Christianity and Islam ever since. And of course the invaded Muslim countries responded in kind, so that in two centuries of intermittent war, both sides committed equally horrible atrocities. This entire multi-generational episode launched by Christian Europe was completely unjustified and, in the end, politically completely pointless. As Steven Runciman says in concluding his monumental three-volume history of the Crusades, 'Seen in the perspective of history the whole Crusading movement was a vast fiasco.'[6] After a huge expenditure of lives it left the situation on the ground unchanged. But it was not a harmless fiasco, for it involved the slaughter of great numbers of innocent people, and left a still continuing legacy of mutual distrust. And in the seventeenth century, during the Thirty Years War between Catholic and Protestant powers, the competing armies ravaged much of central Europe, plundering as they marched and leaving farms, villages, towns and cities in ruins. The western colonizing aggression of the sixteenth to nineteenth centuries into South America, Africa, India and the Middle and Far East justified itself as the extension of Christian civilization into heathen darkness.[7] In all these cases there were powerful motives of economic exploitation, commercial expansion, political aggrandizement, individual greed and ambition, all covered over in the public consciousness by a religious–racist rationale.

As well as being used to justify the mass killing of innumerable people, religion has also been directly responsible for the torture and death of individuals who did not fit into the pattern of Christendom – pagans, Jews, theological dissidents and social deviants branded as witches. To begin with the pagans (i.e. followers of a wide variety of local Roman and nature religions), after the church progressively achieved power through the conversion of the emperor Constantine in the fourth century, its victory over paganism reminds one of nothing so much as the Nazi persecution of the Jews in Germany in the 1930s. This

6. Runciman, p. 392.
7. For more about this see James Morris 1973, particularly chapter 3, and for a summary of other information, Hick 1987.

has been brought prominently to light by research of the last twenty years. It was increasingly advantageous career-wise to be a member of the church, and increasingly dangerous to remain outside – in 415 and 425 CE laws were passed reserving all places in the imperial service to Christians. Pagan books were publicly burned; militant monks 'afire with holy zeal' led mobs to destroy pagan shrines and temples; and under Justinian a number of non-Christians were beheaded or crucified. In 579, for example, a prominent pagan figure, Anatolius, was 'tortured, torn up by wild beasts, and crucified, while his aide died of his tortures'.[8] The whole story is very different from the older picture of a Europe converted by the superior merits of the all-conquering new faith: the church was indeed all-conquering, but more by political and economic pressure and monkish violence than by the preaching of the gospel. And then there were the Jews. To mention only some of the dark moments, in 1144 the Jews of Norwich, England, were accused of using the blood of murdered Christian children in their Passover bread, and this blood libel spread throughout Europe, unleashing a wave of hatred; in 1182 the King of France cancelled all Christian debts to Jewish creditors; in 1190 the Jewish community in York, England, were burned to death in the city's castle; the Fourth Lateran Council in 1215 decreed that Jews should wear distinguishable clothing; in 1290 the entire Jewish community of England was expelled; the Spanish Inquisition forcibly converted Jews to Christianity with threats of torture and death, the Grand Inquisitor, Torquemada, playing his notorious part in the late fifteenth century. And of course the old accusation of deicide lingered on in the background, adding weight to the secular anti-Semitism of the nineteenth and twentieth centuries, leading to the Holocaust of the 1940s. During the medieval period the Catholic Inquisition busily rooted out heretics, such as the Cathars, more than two hundred of whose leaders were burned after the siege of their castle at Montsegur in 1242. But Protestants were no less ready to persecute and burn. In England, Latimer and Ridley were burned at the stake in Oxford in 1555 and Cranmer the following year. Many Catholic priests in England were hounded down and killed during the sixteenth century. In Calvin's Geneva, Servetus was burned as a unitarian heretic in 1553. And during the 'great witch craze' between 1450 and 1700, 'millions were persecuted and tens of millions terrified during one of the longest and strangest delusions in history',[9] with perhaps a hundred thousand women burned or drowned – all of this instigated and supported by the churches.

8. MacMullen, p. 28.
9. J.B. Russell, p. 419.

HARMLESS ECCENTRICITIES

As almost comic relief from the terrible violence and hatred of these unholy wars and persecutions, there are forms of religious experience which are bizarre by the standards of ordinary sane behaviour, but are nevertheless probably in themselves quite harmless. Thus in the New Testament church 'speaking with tongues', consisting in an ecstatic uttering of unintelligible noises mimicking a language, occurred in many congregations, and the phenomenon continues today within the large and growing pentecostal wing of Christianity. The practice was criticized by St Paul as much less valuable than was assumed by those who found themselves speaking in tongues (I Corinthians 14). There have been many subsequent charismatic episodes throughout Christian history. Leaping across the centuries, early Methodism, sweeping through England in the mid-eighteenth century, the age of Enthusiasm, was often accompanied by similarly harmless hysterical manifestations. In his journal for 7 July 1735, John Wesley describes a congregation listening to the eloquent evangelist George Whitefield: 'No sooner had he begun . . . to incite all sinners to believe in Christ, than four persons sank down close to him, almost at the same moment. One of them lay without either sense or motion. A second trembled exceedingly. The third had strong convulsions all over his body, but made no noise unless by groans. The fourth equally convulsed, called upon God with strong cries and tears.'[10] In our own time the church has seen a series of charismatic revivals which include not only speaking in tongues but other much more bizarre phenomena. In the now widespread Vineyard movement, 'one of the distinctive features . . . is a "time of ministry" where one can observe trembling, crying, laughing, screaming, shaking, falling to the ground, people with sensations of electricity, heat and cold, and so on'; and its offshoot, the Toronto Blessing, has 'spread in a contagious way to different parts of the world. It is accompanied by profound effects on individuals and unusually dramatic phenomena such as barking like a dog, clucking like a chicken, roaring like a lion.'[11]

Once, as a child of about twelve, I experienced a physical manifestation of the power of the Spirit as conveyed by a charismatic preacher. This was the then famous Welsh evangelist George Jeffreys, founder in 1926 of the Four Square Gospel Alliance, later the Elim Pentecostal Churches. Jeffreys was also a healer, though whether his healings went beyond a powerful but temporary placebo effect, I do not know. When conducting a revival mission in Scarborough, where we lived, Jeffreys and several of his colleagues stayed in my grandmother's

10. Middlemiss, p. 28.
11. Ibid., p. xii.

house. When they left there was a farewell prayer meeting in her dining room, and we children were included. I was kneeling at a chair when Jeffreys, coming round the circle, laid his hands on my head. I immediately felt a strong physical effect, like an electric shock except that it was not a sharp jolt but a pervasive sensation spreading down through my body. I was in floods of tears, not through sadness or fright, but just through a tremendous emotional release. This would have been some time in the early 1930s, but it was an experience that I have never forgotten. It leaves me with the knowledge that such physical manifestations do undoubtedly occur, and that they can be entirely harmless and even sometimes beneficial to those who experience them.

There are however important negative aspects of this charismatic type of Christianity. Whilst these movements may well be helpful to some, they tend to be individualistic and introverted, with a concentration on personal holiness that can turn attention away from the issues of social justice and injustice, both national and international. In this respect they fit all too well Karl Marx's description of religion as the opium of the people. They are also generally anti-rational, despising careful thought, intellectual consistency and critical reflection. Adherents accordingly tend to be credulous, vulnerable to the authority of charismatic leaders, and given to absolute but unjustifiable certainties.

Such unjustifiable certainties often include belief in special psychic powers or revelations. As one of innumerable examples, early in 1994 Sofia Richmond (Sister Marie), a 'mystic astronomer' who believed that God had placed a Prophetic Telescope in her mind, published an alarming prediction in quarter-page newspaper advertisements in Britain. 'These predicted global destruction during the run up to Comet Shumaker hitting Jupiter in July 1994. According to her predictions a huge fragment would head towards earth, planes would stop flying, many people would die, governments would fall, there would be starvation and world-wide destruction . . . None of these events occurred on the appointed day . . . The way she coped with the situation was by using *ad hoc* theories: "Sister Marie is very glad that all the prayers of people who asked God to stop any dangerous effects from the Comet/Jupiter collision, were answered in July 94." '[12] And there have been many other comparable religious delusions involving weeping madonnas, bleeding crucifixes, visions in the sky, milk-drinking Hindu images, and so on.

More trivial cases of religious self-deception occur every day as people experience their own practical judgements and moral insights as

12. Ibid., p. 205.

divine guidance. For example – to take a case from the Religious Experience Research Unit files – an aircraft mechanic in the RAF, posted to the Far East, was faced with a long line of aircraft to service, and had to decide which to deal with first as most urgently in need of attention. He says, 'We were short staffed in my trade. I trusted God to guide me to the right plane and in my mind came a quiet voice. I obeyed the code letters and raced to that aircraft. As I did, my heart was filled with joy to the brim. After the trouble was over I worked it out to 360 aircraft checked without the mistake of servicing the wrong one. I can write a small book on how God has guided me and also fill it with everyday happenings which I know come from our Maker.'[13] Evidently the aircraft mechanic had not considered the implications of his conviction that God was guiding him to the right planes. He was involving God in a military operation – in this case probably against people trying to throw off colonial rule – and thus assuming both that God is a God of war and that God was on his side. Further, he did not consider why, if God helped him in this way, God did not do many other things to bring about a speedier and less costly victory. In short, he failed to use the common sense that no doubt operated in the rest of his life. I can illustrate this thoughtlessness again from an experience of my own. I was once flying from Washington to London, hoping very much to arrive fairly closely on time. However, we were delayed on the ground for over two hours before taking off, and it looked as though we would inevitably arrive late in London. But during the flight the pilot announced over the loudspeakers that there was the strongest west-to-east wind that he had ever experienced, and that we would be able to land on time after all, which we did. If I had believed that God miraculously intervenes on request, and had prayed for divine assistance, I would no doubt have reported a divine intervention on my behalf and would have sincerely thanked God for the miracle. It would not have occurred to me that the wind which speeded eastward flights across the Atlantic was to the same extent delaying all the westward flights! Ordinary common sense should be enough to rule out the idea of one's being specially divinely favoured.

All such cases, but particularly those involving great historical evils, make it extremely clear that some criterion is needed by which to distinguish authentic from delusory forms of religious experience.

13. Maxwell, p. 116.

18

THE CRITERION

THE FRUITS IN HUMAN LIFE

How in terms of our big picture can we distinguish between veridical and delusory religious experiences – between those that are and those that are not cognitive responses to the Transcendent? And indeed, is this a clear-cut distinction – may not religious experience often be a mixture of both?

The central criterion can only be the long-term transformative effect on the experiencer. A momentary experience, or an experience lasting minutes or even hours, is only important if its significance is integrated into one's ongoing life. If, as in the case of the great mystics, their altered states of consciousness have a transforming and energizing effect in their lives, leading to a stronger centring in God, the Holy, the Real, and a greater love and compassion for their fellows, this is the evidence, accepted within each of the great traditions, of their openness to the Transcendent. It is of course the latter element, the love and compassion expressed in their actions, that we are able to observe and for which we therefore rightly look. This has always been evident to the mystics themselves. Tauler said that 'works of love are more acceptable to God than lofty contemplation'.[1] If those who report mystical experiences are selfish, greedy, dishonest, we cannot believe that their experiences were due to the impact upon them of the ultimately Real. But if they are increasingly filled with unselfish love and practical compassion, we *can* believe that they are responding to the presence of the Ultimate. Eckhart said that 'if a man were in such a rapturous state as St Paul once

1. Inge, p. 188.

entered, and knew of a sick man who wanted a cup of soup, it would be far better to withdraw from the rapture for love's sake and serve him who is in need'.[2] Eckhart himself lived a busy and productive life, becoming, because of his outstanding energies and abilities, Prior of Erfurt, Vicar of Thuringen, Provincial of the Domincan Order in Saxony, Vicar of Bohemia, and Professor at Cologne. W.R. Inge says that 'all the great mystics have been energetic and influential, and their business capacity is specially noted in a curiously large number of cases. For instance Plotinus was often in request as a guardian and trustee; St Bernard showed great gifts as an organizer; St Teresa, as a founder of convents and adminstrator, gave evidence of extraordinary practical ability; even St Juan of the Cross displayed the same qualities; Fenelon ruled his diocese extremely well; and Madam Guyon surprised those who had dealings with her by her great aptitude for affairs.'[3] Among these, St Teresa of Avila's new centring in God was expressed in her successful reformation of the Discalced Carmelite convents. She created a new Carmelite house in Avila and then went on to found others, seventeen in all, surmounting a wall of male ecclesiastical and political opposition by her energy, skill and determination. Again, Ignatius Loyola was a man of incredible energy and achievement: William James describes him as 'assuredly one of the most powerful practical human engines that ever lived'.[4] Catherine of Genoa was a nurse, then matron of a hospital, doing much administrative work and dealing with large sums of money. And so on.

Evelyn Underhill thought that the actively practical lives of mystics was a distinctively Christian phenomenon,[5] but this is not in fact so. Presumably the greatest of the eastern mystics has been Gautama the Buddha who, out of compassion for multitudes lost in ignorance of their true nature, spent a long life travelling around India teaching great numbers of people, always adapting his method to those to whom he was speaking. According to the story of his enlightenment, he initially decided against going out into the world to teach the demanding but liberating truth because the people were too blinded by self-concern to receive it. But then one of the gods came to him to plead for the world. There are, he said, some who are not blind, and the world will perish if the Buddha does not go forth to save it. So eventually he went, moved by compassion for a perishing world.[6] He was thus a *bodhisattva*, one who has attained but who postpones his own 'entry' into nirvana in order to remain in the world for the sake of others. Many of the

2. Eckhart, 1941, p. 14.
3. Inge, pp. xi–xiii.
4. William James, p. 399.
5. Underhill, p. 172.
6. *Digha Nikaya* II, 36; Davids, 1959, pp. 30–1.

Buddha's followers over the centuries have been active missionaries, taking the *dharma* from India into China and throughout south-east Asia, founding monasteries and universities – there are the ruins of what is probably the oldest university in the world, a Buddhist foundation, at Nalanda in Bihar. Another great Indian mystic, Shankara, founder of the school of advaita Vedanta, also spent a long life travelling round India, teaching and founding monasteries. The Ramakrishna mission, inspired by Swami Vivekenanda, is today well known for its educational and social work. Practical concern for the needy has never been a western monopoly.

Half-way between what we call the east and what we call the west, Jesus, a truly God-filled mystic, gave himself to others in teaching and healing and finally in his death; his follower St Paul, who also saw visions and heard voices, lived a heroic missionary life. The prophet Muhammad, who received the Qur'an in mystical auditions, likewise lived an active life of both teaching and political leadership. In fact virtually all the historically famous mystic-saints have been active in the world and have contributed to the shaping of human history.

OPERATING THE CRITERION

In making judgements about the authenticity of religious experience then, we look for the marks of spiritual transformation. For although we cannot describe absolute Reality as it is in itself, we *can* describe its effects on the lives of men and women. According to our big picture, the world religions are human responses to that absolute Reality, embodying its 'impact' upon us. And they all report this impact – whether they speak of revelations, theophanies, enlightenment, illumination, awakening – as benign, loving, compassionate, merciful, as well as totally demanding. They also all affirm the original goodness of our human nature when not distorted by a primeval fall or by spiritual blindness.

The mahatmas of the different traditions have been men and women in whom that original goodness has been recovered to a notable degree. They have undergone, to a much greater extent than the rest of us, the salvific transformation from self-centredness to a new centring in the ultimately Real as known to them in their own tradition. They thus reflect in themselves something of the higher reality to which our minds are normally largely closed. In the metaphor of Jalaluldin Rumi they are the shadow of God on earth.[7] And so we use them as the markers by which to judge the validity of religious experience. We shall be looking

7. Chittick, p. 136.

at some of them more closely in Part V, The Saints Come Marching In.

This human fruit of awareness of the Transcendent has always been the decisive criterion used within the world religions. It has however often been supplemented, or rather restricted, by a doctrinal test. For example, Teresa of Avila, speaking of the faithful Christian soul, said that 'all the revelations it could imagine, even were it to see the heavens opened, would not cause it to budge an inch from the Church's teaching . . . for . . . the soul must be convinced that a thing comes from God only if it is in conformity with Holy Scripture'.[8] The church's control over her own mind was so complete that she was in no danger of departing from its teaching. On the contrary, it determined the form taken by her mystical experiences, even to the extent that the necessity for God to be a Trinity was revealed to her.[9] But her doctrinal test presupposes an unacceptable Christian exclusivism that rules out the entirety of Buddhist, Hindu, Jewish, Muslim and other forms of mystical experience. Indeed it would even rule out a good deal of Christian mysticism, for a number of major Christian mystics have been suspected of heresy, including Evagrius, Eckhart, St John of the Cross, Molinos, Madam Guyon, Marguerite Porete, George Fox.

But within the borders of Christian orthodoxy, as this was understood in late medieval Christendom, Teresa of Avila used the much more universal moral-and-spiritual-fruits criterion. It was accepted within the monasteries and nunneries that false as well as genuine religious experiences occurred, that these were sometimes hard to distinguish, and that one should therefore be constantly on guard against the deceits of the devil. That a revelation has come from God, and not from the devil, is assured for Teresa by its observable continuing effects in the soul. As Rowan Williams says, she 'makes it very clear that, as far as she is concerned, the criteria of authenticity do not lie in the character of the experience itself but in how it is related to a pattern of concrete behaviour, the development of dispositions and decisions'.[10] At one point she uses the analogy of someone who encounters a stranger who leaves her a gift of jewels. If someone else later suggested that the stranger had been an apparition, the jewels left in her hand would prove otherwise. Likewise, in the case of her visions, 'I could show [any doubters] these jewels – for all who knew me were well aware how my soul had changed: my confessor himself testified to this, for the difference was very great in every respect, and no fancy, but such as all could clearly see. As I had previously been so wicked, I concluded, I could not believe that, if the devil were doing this to delude

8. Teresa of Avila, 1960, pp. 238–9.
9. William James, p. 397.
10. Williams, p. 147.

me and drag me down to hell, he would make use of means which so completely defeated their own ends by taking away my vices and making me virtuous and strong; for it was quite clear to me that these experiences had immediately made me a different person.'[11]

In treating the mahatmas as our living criteria of Real-centredness we are of course moving in a dialectical circle. We are identifying them as visible human responses to the Real, as manifested within this or that tradition, and we are identifying the Real as that to which they are visible responses. This is not a vicious circle. Every large-scale hypothesis shares this logical character. Consider for example the foundational hypothesis that in sense perception we are conscious of a real material environment. Our 'evidence' for this is that we experience this environment; and we mean by this environment that which we thus experience. We cannot, in our basic beliefs, escape from an ultimately circular doxastic position.

TRUSTING RELIGIOUS EXPERIENCE

But why should we step into the circle of religious faith in the first place? There is no logical necessity for this, but there is a good experiential ground and a rational permissibility. For the fifth dimension of our own nature inclines us to respond to the fifth dimension of the universe, and the fruits of this response are self-evidently such that we value and desire them. Philosophically however, we have to distinguish between the first- and third-person points of view. I shall argue that those who do – sometimes and to some degree – participate in the wide and varied stream of human religious experience are rationally justified in living on the basis of a religious understanding of the universe. But I do not argue that those who, as of now, do not know what it is to experience life religiously ought to trust the reports of others. They *may* be so impressed by some of the saints or mahatmas that they are drawn to explore the religious possibility. But the ambiguity of the universe means that they are not rationally obliged to do so. So in what follows I am only asserting the epistemic right of the religious person to live in terms of a religious rather than a naturalistic faith.[12]

It is a basic principle of life that we trust and act upon our experience except when we have reason to distrust it. We know that seeing can be deceptive – there are misperceptions, hallucinations, mirages, conjuring tricks. But nevertheless our experience of our environment is normally

11. Teresa of Avila, 1960, pp. 238–9.
12. This line of argument is today a major topic within the philosophy of religion, two of its leading proponents being, in different ways, William Alston (1991 and earlier articles) and Alvin Plantinga (1983 and 1997); and it is one for which I have myself argued ever since my first book, *Faith and Knowledge*, in 1957.

reliable, otherwise we could not have formed the distinction between veridical and delusory perceptions. We are evolutionarily programmed to act on the assumption that what appears to be so is indeed so, unless there are indications to the contrary. When we see food we proceed on the basis that it is food, and not a mirage. When we see a charging lion, or an onrushing car, we assume that it is real and we get out of the way. To be rational is to think and act in terms of reality, and the vast mass of human experience has taught us to trust appearances except when we have some positive reason not to. This has been dubbed the principle of credulity,[13] or as I prefer to say, the principle of rational credulity.

Our cognitive experience (i.e. experience that is apparently *of* something) forms a seamless unity. We all experience the trees and hills and lakes around us. 'Primal' peoples experienced some of those trees and hills and lakes as indwelt by living spirits. Later, people have experienced their dependence upon a divine creative and sustaining power, or have, like Wordsworth, experienced the natural world as mediating 'something far more deeply interfused whose dwelling is the light of setting suns, and the round ocean and the living air, and the blue sky, and in the mind of man'.[14] Others have experienced a divine presence focused in the image of a Hindu god, or of Christ on the cross, or of the Virgin Mary, or in the bread and wine of the Mass; or in living in accordance with the Torah or the Qur'an; or as superimposed upon their natural and social environment and suffusing their experience as a whole. Yet others have experienced visions of deity in its many forms – Isaiah's vision in the temple of 'the Lord sitting upon a throne, high and lifted up; and his train filled the temple . . .',[15] or Arjuna's vision of Vishnu: 'If the light of a thousand suns should effulge all at once, it would resemble the radiance of that god of overpowering reality. Then and there, Arjuna saw the entire world unified, yet divided manifold, embodied in the God of gods,'[16] or in visions of deity as incarnated in Christ or in Krishna; and in many other forms. Others experience unity with God or with Brahman or with the universal buddha nature. The principle of rational credulity applies impartially to these as to all other forms of apparently cognitive experience, but always subject to the all-important proviso that counter indications can overrule the prima-facie rationality of believing on this basis.

The application of the principle of rational credulity in our everyday acceptance of sense experience is uncontroversial. In contrast, whereas we all trust sense experience, many see good reasons to suspect, or

13. The term was introduced by Richard Swinburne in *The Existence of God*, 1979.
14. From 'Lines composed a few miles above Tintern Abbey'.
15. Isaiah 6:1.
16. *Bhagavad Gita*, XI:12–13; Bolle, p. 127.

dismiss, religious experience. What, then, are the contrasting features that evoke this distrust?

1. Experience of the natural environment is forced upon us, as we noted earlier, whereas experience of any supra-natural environment seems to be optional.
2. Sense experience occurs universally, religious experience not. We all continuously experience the three dimensions of space and the fourth dimension of time, but a fifth spiritual dimension is only experienced by some, and (in most cases) only intermittently.
3. Sense experience has a public character, so that we can confirm or disconfirm the validity of one another's perceptions. If we all have the experience of seeing a woman wearing a red dress sitting in the armchair, she exists. But if only one of the twelve people in the room has that experience, it is a hallucination. Religious experience does not share this public character. (From a critical realist point of view, the mystics' reports, and the less intense experiences of ordinary believers, can in fact be mutually confirming. But this is a much more restricted area of confirmation than in the case of sense perception.)

These differences are all variations on the same theme. Because sense experience is compulsory it is universal and therefore public. But religious experience is uncompelled and hence not universal and public. Does not this glaring contrast render it rational to trust our sense experience but not our religious experience?

The answer, I suggest, is 'no'. For, as I suggested earlier (pp. 37–8), these differences all follow from a difference between the supposed objects of sense and religious experience respectively. Our awareness of the physical world has to be compulsory if we are successfully to survive within it as vulnerable fleshly organisms. But, according to our big picture, the religious ambiguity of the universe makes possible a free response to the Transcendent by finite spiritual creatures. In theistic terms, the divine presence must not be forced upon our consciousness. For, as Pascal wrote, 'willing to appear openly to those who seek Him with all their heart, and to be hidden from those who flee from Him with all their heart, [God] so regulates the knowledge of Himself that He has given signs to Himself, visible to those who seek Him, and not to those who seek Him not. There is enough light for those who only desire to see, and enough obscurity for those who have a contrary disposition.'[17] Putting it in more universal terms, intellectual freedom is

17. Pascal, p. 118.

an aspect of our spiritual nature, the fifth dimension of our being. Our capacity to respond or fail to respond to the impact of the Real, both as moral claim and as spiritual presence, is essential to what we are. And the differences between sensory and religious experience follow from this. If our big picture is basically correct, this is what we should expect. It cannot therefore constitute a reason to reject that big picture and the role of religious experience within it.

Finally, an important clarification. Is a living response to the Real confined to religious persons? No. Are saints/mahatmas necessarily religious persons? No. As John Wesley said, 'the merciful God regards the lives and tempers of men more than their ideas'.[18] I have defined religious experience as experience that is structured by religious concepts. But the 'impact' upon us of the universal presence of the Real does not *have* to be structured by religious concepts. This was normal in the period when the religions included virtually everyone. But today there are also 'secular' saints, particularly in the political field; Nelson Mandela, for example, although a devout Methodist in his youth, should probably today be counted as one. What is all-important is not the set of ideas in people's minds, but their openness and response to the claim upon them of the ultimately Real as encountered in the inextricably interrelated moral and political needs of humanity.

18. Thompson, p. 99.

PART V

THE SAINTS COME MARCHING IN

19

ONE LIVING SAINT IS WORTH TEN DEAD ONES

SAINTS, MAHATMAS AND OTHERS

'Saint' is a distinctively Christian term, but the other great traditions also recognize special individuals who are looked up to as exemplars of an authentic response to the Transcendent – the *rishi* (Vedic sage), *jivanmukta* (liberated soul), *mahatma* (great soul), and *guru* (teacher) of Hinduism; the *arahant* (one who has attained nirvana) of Theravada Buddhism and the *bodhisattva* (who has attained but remains in the world to help others) and the *roshi* (Zen master) of Mahayana Buddhism; the sage (*shen*) of Confucianism; the *tsaddiq* (just man) and other exemplary figures of Judaism; the *wali* (friend of God) of Islam, particularly within the Sufi strand. For convenience, I shall bring all these together under the label of saint.[1] I do not however want to invoke such associations of the word as haloes, shrines, relics, pilgrimages and saint's days. For whilst some of the official Christian saints have clearly been saints in the sense that I intend, many others were canonized on the slenderest evidence for political or ecclesiastical–political reasons. I am referring instead to men and women of all traditions who are much more advanced than the rest of us in the transformation from natural self-centredness to a re-centring in God, the Real, the Ultimate.

THE FOUNDERS

One naturally thinks first of the supremely great figures at the origins of the world traditions – Moses, Zoroaster, Gautama, Mahavira,

1. For a comparative study of 'sainthood' in the world's religions see Kieckheffer, 1988.

Confucius, 'Lao-Tzu', Jesus, Muhammad, Nanak – those whom John Macquarrie has called the Mediators.[2] However we have to recognize that they are now remote in time and only known to us through a cumulative haze of legend formed by the adoration of centuries. We have – though with varying degrees of assurance – some of their selected and remembered words and deeds, which deeply move and inspire us. And because we need heroes, exemplars, gurus, figures whom we can look up to, trust and follow, generations of devotees have magnified them beyond historical warrant and have often ended by absolutizing them.

The individual on whom the strongest such adoration has been focused is undoubtedly Jesus of Nazareth. For traditional Christian faith he was sinless, perfect, divine. But in actual fact we know far too little about him for this to be a historical judgement; it can only be an affirmation of faith. '[The New Testament scholar] G.H. Streeter once calculated that, apart from the forty days and nights in the wilderness (of which we are told virtually nothing) everything reported to have been said or done by Jesus in all four gospels would have occupied only some three weeks, which leaves the overwhelmingly greater part of his life and deeds unrecorded'[3] – and many more recent scholars would put the known time-span at considerably less than three weeks. This leaves ample scope for the creative imagination. The psychiatrist Anthony Storr, discussing this phenomenon, says that 'if the world had possessed a detailed biographical account of Jesus, an authentic picture of what he was like as a man, it is quite possible that Christianity would not have been established as a world religion. I am not suggesting', he adds, 'that Jesus would have been shown up as dishonest or inauthentic; but simply indicating that a person is more easily made into a mythical figure if the outlines of his personality are blurred.'[4] The same is true of the other founders. Because of the historical uncertainties of our pictures of these supreme religious figures, and because of the idealizing tendency of our minds, I want to focus instead upon less epoch-making but more recent and contemporary individuals.

LIVING SAINTS

To us (although not of course intrinsically) one living saint is worth ten dead ones. And the Christian saints are all, by definition, dead – no one is canonized until long after his or her death. But I am more interested at this point in saints who are alive now, or at least within living memory. The drawback – if it is a drawback – in these cases is that they are not as flawless as the dead saints! We know too much about them.

2. Macquarrie, 1995.
3. Nineham, 1977, pp. 188–9.
4. Storr, p. 147.

But in reality saintliness is a matter of degree, and not even the greatest saints are perfect. They all have their unsaintly aspects and moments.

A number of writers today turn to literature when exploring the possibilities of human nature, quoting Dostoyevsky, Albert Camus, Flannery O'Connor and many others. These did indeed have very valuable insights. But to be sure of the heights to which humanity can rise, one real person counts for more than many fictional ones. As Gandhi once said, speaking of the rare kind of businessman who always deals honestly and who will not cheat or exploit or injure others, 'the type ceases to be imaginary as soon as even one living specimen can be found to answer to it'.[5] Living and directly remembered saints are part of the known human reality; they are living sacraments, 'outward and visible signs' of the Transcendent. We have probably all been aware of elements or moments of saintliness in people whom we know well or whom we have more briefly encountered. It is this degree of saintliness, observed at first hand, that enables us to accept the authenticity of the much more significant figures of the past who founded the great world traditions, or reformed them, or who still function as their great exemplars. So I can believe in certain aspects of Jesus' message partly because the same intrinsic authority of moral insight was incarnated in our own century in Mohandas Gandhi. And I can believe in what Gandhi called Truth partly because I have seen that Truth incarnated, though to a lesser extent, in others, including one about whom I shall write later.

THE PROFILE OF THE SAINT

William James' 'composite photograph of universal saintliness, the same in all religions', is excellent, except that whilst he does not exclude the political form of saintliness he does not sufficiently stress it. This is understandable, for the phenomenon of the political saint has become much more prominent since his time. James lists the four cardinal features of, first, 'a feeling of being in a wider life than that of this world's selfish little interests; and a conviction, not merely intellectual, but as it were sensible, of the existence of an Ideal Power'; second, 'a sense of the friendly continuity of the ideal power with our own life, and a willing self-surrender to its control'; third, 'an immense elation and freedom, as the outlines of the confining selfhood melt down'; and fourth, 'a shifting of the emotional center towards loving and harmonious affections, towards "yes, yes," and away from "no," where the claims of the non-ego are concerned'.[6]

5. Gandhi, 1968, IV, p. 254.
6. William James, pp. 268–70.

To these we must add more explicitly, I think, the rare attribute, evident in the greatest saints, of spiritual joy. This is not to be confused with the natural temperamental gaiety and happiness with which some people have the very good fortune to be endowed. As William James said, 'There are [people] who seem to have started in life with a bottle or two of champaigne inscribed to their credit.'[7] They are not necessarily, however, less self-centred or more Real-centred than others with a naturally dourer temperament. But Teresa of Avila is representative of the great mystics of all traditions in having experienced the overwhelming joy of release from the ego as it becomes open to the Transcendent. This, she says, 'gave me a joy so great that it has never failed me even to this day, and God converted the aridity of my soul into the deepest tenderness. Everything connected with the religious life caused me delight; and it is a fact that sometimes, when I was spending time in sweeping floors which I had previously spent on my own indulgence and adornment, and realized that I was now free from all those things, there came to me a new joy, which amazed me, for I could not understand whence it arose.'[8] This experience – either a quietly glowing inner peace and serenity or an outwardly manifest radiance of joy – is characteristic of the true mahatmas and saints. It is this that William James refers to as an 'immense elation and freedom'. Julian of Norwich, whose awareness of the divine reality took the form of visions and auditions of Christ on the cross, tells how 'suddenly, as I looked at the same cross he changed to an appearance of joy. The change in his appearance changed mine, and I was as glad and joyful as I could possibly be . . . Our Lord showed this to me to make us glad and merry.'[9] Evelyn Underhill, describing Francis of Assisi, Ruusbroec, Catherine of Siena, Richard Rolle, Catherine of Genoa, and John of the Cross, speaks of the 'inextinguishable gladness of heart', the 'gaiety, freedom, assurance, and joy',[10] that seems to be a characteristic of the 'unitive' state which they reached after a long, arduous, and sometimes painful pilgrimage.

When we turn to the Hindu world we find that the ultimate, Brahman, is spoken of as *sat–chit–ananda*, being–consciousness–bliss, and that the experience of union with Brahman is an experience of this bliss. 'I know nothing but joy, limitless, unbounded. The ocean of Brahman is full of nectar – the joy of the Atman.'[11] Again Shankara speaks of the goal of mystical practice as 'the highest bliss' and declares that in our deepest nature one 'never ceases to experience infinite joy'.[12] Again, the Buddha taught: 'He that crushes the great "I am" conceit – this, even this, is happiness supreme.'[13] One of the perfections of the

7. Ibid., p. 144.
8. Teresa of Avila, 1960, p. 77.
9. Julian of Norwich, pp. 144–5.
10. Underhill, pp. 437, 440.
11. Shankara, p. 113.
12. Ibid., pp. 39, 53.
13. *Udana* II, 1; Woodward, 1948, p. 13.

bodhisattva is joy (*mudita*). And so the contemporary Buddhist monk Nyanaponika says, 'Let us teach real joy (*mudita*) to others. Many have unlearned it. Life, though full of woe, holds also sources of happiness and joy, unknown to most. Let us teach people to seek and to find real joy within themselves and to rejoice with the joy of others! Let us teach them to unfold their joy to ever sublimer heights.'[14] The Sufis of Islam are full of the joy of living in the divine love, which they describe poetically in 'a great variety of images, most of them connected with love and wine'. 'Oh, my spirit is joyful over Thee – may my spirit never be without Thee!', sings Rumi.[15]

At the same time, we must not imagine that the mahatmas/saints are perpetually cheerful, never weighed down by the pain and injustice around them. On the contrary, the more involved they are in the life and suffering of the world, the more they share its sorrows. For instance Gandhi, whilst he bubbled over with fun and delight much of the time, was emotionally devastated by the slaughter in the Punjab in the wake of the partition of India. And the more introverted mystics have generally been through their dark night of the soul, enduring a period of mental suffering and doubt from which they only emerged after a long ordeal.

Nevertheless, despite its 'dark nights', and its agonies of suffering with those who suffer, the saintly or enlightened or awakened life is one that we can see to be intrinsically good and desirable, a state in which we would dearly love to be. We spontaneously feel that such individuals are incarnating some of the higher possibilities of our common human nature. We sense that they are not only more unselfcentred but also, paradoxically, more truly fulfilled than ourselves. But in order to empathize with them we need to have participated, at least to some small degree, in their experience of the Transcendent, and to have experienced, again in however slight a degree, something like their inner illumination and joy. It is when we have known in some tiny momentary way that of which they speak, that we are entitled to trust their much greater and stronger and more continuous experience of the Divine, the Holy, the Real. This is why I have presumed to mention from time to time some of my own very, very slight 'mystical' experiences. There have so far for me been only two all-too-brief moments of participation in the inner joy of openness to the Transcendent. The first came in the aftermath of an evangelical conversion when a young law student. I was sitting on the top deck of a bus somewhere in the middle of the city of Hull, England. To quote what I later wrote, 'As everyone will be very conscious who can themselves remember such a moment, all

14. Nyanaponika, 1996, p. 225.
15. Chittick, pp. 246, 244.

descriptions are inadequate. But it was as though the skies opened up and light poured down and filled me with a sense of overflowing joy in response to an immense transcendent goodness and love. I remember that I couldn't help smiling broadly – smiling back, as it were, at God – though if any of the other passengers were looking they must have thought that I was a lunatic, grinning at nothing.'[16] The other time when I have been glancingly touched by this extraordinary joy that turns earth into heaven or, as the Buddhists say, *samsara* into nirvana, was in my room in Oriel College, Oxford, when a graduate student. I woke up one day in this state of utter overflowing happiness, gratitude and inner freedom, which however faded during the morning. Such fleeting experiences as these are nothing in comparison with that of the mahatmas. What is for us ordinary people a momentary flash is for them the light in which they live for large parts of their lives. But these brief and tantalizing moments are nevertheless important because they make us take seriously the accounts that we have of the mahatmas.

MODERN POLITICAL SAINTS

In the ancient world and down to and well beyond the end of the medieval period, power was concentrated in the hands of national and local rulers, so that saintly individuals, of whatever tradition, generally had no political power or the political responsibility that goes with it. There was no possibility of their changing the existing political and economic structures to create a more just and equal society in which human potential could be liberated. And so their saintliness typically took either an inner contemplative form, or was expressed in ascetic lives and/or acts of charity to needy individuals – the poor, the sick, the outcasts (such as lepers), the handicapped, and widows and orphans. But with the rise of democracy, and the struggles for freedom from colonial powers and from evil dictators, political power and responsibility have become much more widely distributed, and mahatmahood has increasingly taken political forms. As Harvey Cox has said, 'the world has taken the place of the wilderness as the classical testing ground for sanctity and purification'.[17] One immediately thinks not only of Gandhi but also of Vinoba Bhave in India, Martin Luther King in the United States, Archbishop Oscar Romero in San Salvador, the international statesman Dag Hammarskjöld, Nelson Mandela and Desmond Tutu in South Africa; and there are many, many others who are less well known because they operate within more local situations.

16. Goulder, pp. 40–1.
17. Sharma, 1993, p. 392.

But at the same time, contemplative saintliness continues, and has equal value and validity. Both are necessary to express the fullness of the human response to the Real, and I shall describe later a contemplative saint whom I have known. But in the nature of the case, such solitary or enclosed contemplatives are (with a few exceptions, such as Thomas Merton and Thich Nhat Hanh) barely known to the public.

There are then these spiritually impressive twentieth-century figures – far more, needless to say, than those I have mentioned. They never think of themselves as saints, but when we encounter such people, most of us cannot help feeling that they are living in response to a higher level of reality than the purely natural.

20

GANDHI: A CASE STUDY

MY LIFE IS MY MESSAGE

We should begin with Gandhi himself because, in contrast to many significant thinkers, it is impossible to separate his thought from his life. Indeed once, when asked what his message was, he replied that his life was his message.[1] This was not a boast, but something that those who had to do with him already knew. He tried to persuade others to accept his basic insights only after he had first lived them out in a career which was, throughout his adulthood, a continuous series of what he called 'experiments with Truth'.

The tremendous impact which Gandhi made upon so many people, challenging them to change their outlook and in quite a number of cases to change the course of their lives, came from the fact that what he taught was morally compelling and that he was visibly living it out, often at great cost to himself and finally at the cost of his life. He once said, 'The act will speak unerringly,'[2] and it was undoubtedly his acts that made his words believable, drawing others into practical commitment. They had either to respond to the challenge of non-violent persuasion in action or dismiss him as an impractical dreamer, a deluded fanatic, or a political schemer. Thus Winston Churchill, protesting in 1931 against Gandhi's presence in the independence negotiations, famously said, 'It is alarming and also nauseating to see Mr Gandhi, a seditious Middle Temple lawyer, now posing as a fakir of a type well known in the East, striding half-naked up the steps of the viceregal palace, while he is still organizing and conducting a defiant campaign of

1. Brown, p. 80.
2. Chatterjee, p. 73.

civil disobedience, to parley on equal terms with the representative of the King-Emperor.'[3] However, Churchill had at times an almost pathological attitude to Gandhi and to India: he once even announced, 'I hate Indians. They are a beastly people with a beastly religion.'[4] At one time General Smuts of South Africa thought of Gandhi somewhat as Churchill did. But much later, in conversation with Churchill, he said of Gandhi, 'He is a man of God. You and I are mundane people. Gandhi has appealed to religious motives. You never have. That is where you have failed.'[5]

More charitably, but no less emphatically, Lord Willingdon, when Governor of Bombay, described Gandhi as 'honest, but a Bolshevik & for that reason very dangerous'.[6] Presumably anyone seeking Indian independence was for him a Bolshevik. And again, despite Gandhi's efforts throughout his public life to promote mutual Hindu–Muslim acceptance and tolerance, he has been blamed by some Muslims for the violent upheavals of the partition that he had so strenuously opposed. The long-term blame must lie mainly with the British practice of 'divide and rule' – playing off the Hindu and Muslim communities, and also the different elements within the Hindu community, against one another, and the princely states against the centre, in order to retain control over them all. Gandhi pointed to 'the shameless manner in which, for sustaining the spoliation of India, British statesmen are setting one party against another'.[7] And Churchill, for example, did not conceal the fact that he 'regarded the Hindu–Muslim feud as the bulwark of British rule in India'.[8]

But during the end-game the situation was more complex. On the ground Hindus, Muslims and Sikhs had generally lived together peacefully as neighbours in the same villages. But with the prospect of early independence the political leaders drew apart into increasingly hostile camps. Although Gandhi had always preached the equality of religions, and although Nehru and the Congress leadership as a whole were committed to a future secular state, these ideals never penetrated the mass consciousness deeply enough to determine the course of events. In the months leading up to Independence the Muslim population was gripped by an understandable fear that the supposedly secular India would in reality be Hindu dominated. Suspicion fanned real or imagined incidents into deliberate insults and threats, and local happenings were magnified by rapidly spreading rumour, with enmities flaring into violence. The demand for a separate Muslim state, Pakistan, became irresistible and partition inevitable.

The myth-making tendency of the human mind has long affected the public image of Gandhi. Some western enthusiasts have uncritically

3. Payne, p. 404.
4. French, p. 170.
5. Chadha, p. 382.
6. Brown, p. 118.
7. *Young India*, 1 March, 1928.
8. Lawrence James, p. 540.

glorified his memory, filtering out his human weaknesses, and the popular picture of him among devotees in India has attained mythic proportions so that he is counted by many among the divine *avatars* or incarnations. But on the other hand he is sufficiently recent for the man himself still to be visible behind these clouds of adoration. There are people now living who knew him and, further, his is probably the most minutely documented life that has ever been lived. There are about five thousand books of 'Gandhiana'.[9] There is a gigantic mass of detailed information in such publications as the eight-volume biography by D.G. Tendulkar (1951–4) and the four volumes by Gandhi's secretary Pyaralel (1956–80), and there are more recent and more balanced biographies, such as the superb one by Judith Brown (1989). But new full-scale biographies continue to appear, the latest being that of Yogesh Chadha in 1997. Gandhi's own writings, including letters and notes, speeches, interviews, newspaper articles, pamphlets and books, fill ninety-three volumes of *The Collected Works of Mahatma Gandhi* published by the Government of India. Hundreds of people who knew him have published books and articles about him. So the available historical materials enable us to form a reasonably accurate and rounded picture of a life that was lived so recently and so publicly and that has been recorded so fully and from so many different angles.

Gandhi himself would have nothing to do with his own idealization. He rejected the title of Mahatma which, he said, had often deeply pained him and had never pleased him.[10] He said, 'I myself do not feel like a saint in any shape or form.'[11] In the earlier days his followers called him *Bhai* (brother), and as he grew older *Bapu* (father), and referred to him as Gandhiji – the *ji* being a common mark of respect. He was acutely, sometimes painfully, conscious of his own faults. He blamed himself for many misjudgements and mistakes, including the major one that he called his 'Himalayan blunder' – his call to the people in 1919 to practise mass non-violent resistance before they were ready for it.[12]

A VERY HUMAN SAINT

There were then problematic sides to Gandhiji's character. On the one hand he was a magnetic personality, with no inner barriers between himself and others, radiating love and full of humour, a person whom it must have been immensely exciting and inspiring to be with. As Margaret Chatterjee says, 'All who were close to Gandhi have testified to his irresistible sense of fun, his bubbling spirits which seemed to well

9. French, p. 18.
10. Gandhi, 1968, I, pp. xvii–xix.
11. *Young India*, 20 January 1927.
12. Gandhi, 1968, II, p. 702.

up from an inner spring in the face of all adversity,'[13] though it is also true that at the end of his life he was filled with deep sorrow and despair at the disastrous partition of India, and at the failure of both politicians and populace to act out his teaching of non-violence and mutual love.

Gandhi was also blessed with an enviable capacity for concentration. One observer wrote:

> So many people could be constantly crowding around him that if perchance he could snatch a few moments of spare time, he would spend them wholly in his work of reading and writing. One was simply amazed to find how in the midst of all this confusion he could keep his head cool and get through the scheduled course of his work . . . And yet everyday, whether in his room or in the train, he would go on calmly and patiently writing articles for the *Navajivan* and *Young India*, while all round him people were making a noise and the crowds were howling outside.[14]

Louis Fischer, who spent some time with him in one of the ashrams, says, 'Gandhi accepted people as they were. Aware of his own defects, how could he expect perfection in others?'[15] 'Life at Sabarmati Ashram [Fischer says] and, after 1932, at Sevagram in central India, was serene, simple, joyous, and unconstrained. Nobody stood in awe of him. Until he was too old, he sat in the scullery every morning with the ashramites peeling potatoes; he did his share of other chores as well.'[16] At the same time he insisted on certain standards of behaviour – cleanliness, punctuality, participation in the work of the ashram, including at least half an hour of spinning every day. However, 'with all his strictness about the personal conduct of his co-workers . . . he was completely tolerant toward their thinking'.[17]

Gandhi was indeed a living paradox, both attractive and yet domineering, and in admiring him we ought to be aware of both sides of his character. His moral insights were so strong and uncompromising that he imposed them upon his followers by the sheer force of conviction. Such was his overwhelming charisma that he could be a dictator within his immediate circle. Even Jawaharlal Nehru, who was a major international statesman in his own right, said that on occasions Gandhi's inherent authority 'reduces many of his intimate followers and colleagues to a state of mental pulp'![18] And beyond his inner circle he was capable of manoeuvring to get his way within the Congress movement. For example, in 1938–9 Subhas Chandra Bose was elected, against Gandhi's wishes, as Congress President. Bose believed in gaining freedom by violence, and later led the Indian National Army, composed

13. Chatterjee, p. 108.
14. Brown, p. 160.
15. Fischer, pp. 213–14.
16. Ibid., p. 213.
17. Ibid.
18. French, p. 264.

of prisoners of war held by the Japanese, in their advance through South-East Asia, aiming at the conquest of the British in India. Gandhi rejected Bose's outlook and in 1939 deliberately engineered his downfall as Congress President. It was this kind of clever political manoeuvring, as well as his undoubted skill in negotiations, that led to Gandhi being regarded by some as sly and devious or, in the words of a recent English critic, 'a ruthlessly sharp political negotiator'.[19] Lord Willingdon, when Viceroy, said, 'He may be a saint, he may be a holy man; he is I believe quite sincere in his principles; but of this I am perfectly certain, that he is one of the most astute politically-minded and bargaining little gentlemen I ever came across.'[20] French, who quotes this, speaks of 'the plaster Mahatma encapsulated in Richard Attenborough's 1982 film'.[21] Another recent historian of the period says, 'Behind the facade of the prophet-cum-saviour was an astute political brain.'[22] But these recent secular historians seem not to have studied Gandhi's day-to-day utterances and activities. He certainly had a sharp political brain, but no one who has examined the records could think that the religious aspect of Gandhi's life was a mere facade. Some, probably thinking of saintliness as inherently detached from politics, see Gandhi's considerable political skill as incompatible with his reputation for saintliness. But why should not a saint be highly competent in practical affairs? It is clear that Gandhi was politically formidable, combining appeal to reason and evidence with an instinct for the symbolic actions that would rally the Indian masses behind him. What to some was low cunning was to others Gandhi's ability so often to outwit those – whether the British rulers or rival Indian leaders – who were trying to outwit him.

But he was undoubtedly sometimes a very difficult person to deal with. His devoted secretary, Mahadev Desai, in a moment of exasperation once composed the verse:

> To live with the saints in heaven
> Is a bliss and a glory,
> But to live with a saint on earth
> Is a different story.[23]

Perhaps most importantly Gandhi's family found him hard to live with. He had absorbed the traditional Indian understanding of the wifely role: 'A Hindu husband regards himself as lord and master of his wife who must ever dance attendance on him.'[24] Accordingly Fischer says, 'A tension marred his early relations . . . [But] Gradually, as lust, in

19. Ibid., p. 17.
20. Ibid., p. 86.
21. Ibid., p. 17.
22. Lawrence James, p. 524.
23. Brown, p. 286.
24. Gandhi, 1968, I, p. 275.

Gandhi's words, yielded to love, they became a model couple, she the acme of service, he a paragon of consideration . . . Being herself and being at the same time a shadow of the Mahatma made her a remarkable woman, and some who observed them for long years wondered whether she had not come nearer to the *Gita* ideal of non-attachment than he. He was too passionate to be the perfect yogi.'[25] Gandhi himself came to recognize this when he said, 'Her determined submission to my will on the one hand and her quiet submission to the suffering my stupidity involved on the other, ultimately made me ashamed of myself and cured me of my stupidity in thinking that I was born to rule over her; and in the end she became my teacher in non-violence.'[26] Again, his relations with his sons were sometimes tragic. 'As he was more severe with himself than with anybody else, so he was severest with his own boys,' says Fischer.[27] His oldest son, Harilal, overwhelmed by the demands falling upon a son of the Mahatma, rebelled against him and eventually went badly to pieces. Fischer summarizes the sad story: 'While [Harilal's] wife lived, he was outwardly normal. But when she died in the 1918 influenza epidemic, and when Gandhi frowned on his remarriage, Harilal disintegrated completely. He took to alcohol and women; he was often seen drunk in public. Under the influence of drink, penury, and the desire for vengeance, he would succumb to the offers of unscrupulous publishers and attack his father in print, signing "Abdullah", a Moslem name. He had become Moslem. Conversion to Islam, drunkenness, and profligacy were probably Halilal's effort to hurt his father.'[28] For Gandhi himself, Islam was as authentic a way to God as Hinduism, but in this case the motive for conversion was insincere. The sad figure of Harilal in middle age, looking prematurely old, publicly discredited, consumed by resentment and alcohol, was a tragedy for which Gandhi himself must bear his degree of responsibility; and indeed Fischer says that 'Gandhi blamed Harilal's misdeeds on himself'.[29] Manilal, the second of the four sons, was also estranged for a while from his father, but later reconciled, and at the famous march on the salt factory in 1930, whilst Gandhi himself was in prison, Manilal was in the front row of the *satyagrahis* when, in the words an American reporter, 'Suddenly at a word of command, scores of native policemen rushed upon the advancing marchers and rained blows on their heads with their steel-shod lathis. Not one of the marchers even raised an arm to fend off the blows. They went down like ten-pins. From where I stood I heard the sickening whack of the clubs on unprotected skulls. The waiting crowd of marchers groaned and sucked in their breath in sympathetic pain at

25. Fischer, p. 206.
26. Roy, p. 224.
27. Fischer, p. 206.
28. Ibid., p. 209.
29. Ibid., p. 211.

every blow. Those struck down fell sprawling, unconscious or writhing with fractured skulls or broken shoulders . . . The survivors, without breaking ranks, silently and doggedly marched on until struck down.'[30] This terrible event, in which scores of people inspired by Gandhi's gospel of non-violence voluntarily put their lives at risk for India's freedom, was a turning point in the wider world's view of the British raj. It proved to be the beginning of the end of foreign rule.

Gandhi's vow of *bramacharya* at the age of thirty-seven has been criticized by many western writers, although in the Indian religious context it was recognized as a dedication of all his energies to the service of others. He defined *bramacharya* as 'control of the senses in thought, word and deed',[31] but it was generally understood to mean specifically sexual continence. Although acceptable in the culture in which Gandhi and Kasturbai were brought up, we today can only see it as a grave defect that he made his *bramacharya* decision unilaterally, even though, he says, Kasturbai had no objection.[32] Concerning his sexuality, the one thing that many westerners know about Gandhi, even if they know very little else, is his deliberate testing of his *bramacharya* vow for a while in old age by sleeping under the same blanket with young women disciples. He believed that his power as a spiritual and political leader depended on his inner soul-power, which in turn depended on absolute faithfulness to his vows, so that in the 1947 crisis of Hindu–Muslim strife in Bengal he had to be victorious in testing this most demanding of vows.[33] This is largely incomprehensible to the western mind, and yet it made sense at the time to Gandhi. However, given the inevitability of hostile publicity, we must count it as one of his blunders, and he was persuaded to end the experiment. But the inner spiritual force that he had thus maintained in his own way was entirely real and extremely powerful. In riot-torn Calcutta 'Gandhi and H.S. Suhrawardy, the former prime minister of Bengal, walked arm in arm through streets tense with religious frenzy. Suhrawardy drove an automobile with Gandhi as his passenger through riotous areas. Violence seemed to melt away wherever they passed. Thousands of Moslems and Hindus embraced one another shouting, "Long Live Mahatma Gandhi".'[34] Again, 'That more lives were not lost in Bengal owed much to the pervasive influence of Mahatma Gandhi, who had moved to Calcutta before Independence Day. There he had taken up residence in one of the city's many poor districts, living among the Untouchables and the dispossessed and threatening to fast to death should violence break out. Miraculously, there was no repetition of the mass murders that had disfigured Calcutta a year earlier and the whole province of Bengal

30. Ibid., p. 273.
31. Gandhi, 1968, I, p. 314.
32. Ibid., I, p. 310.
33. See Sharma, 1989.
34. Fischer, p. 477.

remained reasonably calm.'[35] One of the Viceroy's staff wrote that 'hardened press correspondents report that they have seen nothing comparable with this demonstration of mass influence. Mountbatten's estimate is that he achieved by moral persuasion what four Divisions would have been hard pressed to have accomplished by force.'[36]

But to return to Gandhiji's failings, in his earlier years in particular he experimented with many fads concerning health, diet, natural cures and sanitation. Some of his eccentricities, such as his strict vegetarianism, are now regarded by many as good practice. But others were failed experiments which he himself later repudiated. For example, speaking of his 'earth and water and fasting treatment in cases of wounds, fevers, dyspepsia, jaundice and other complaints,' he says, 'But nowadays I have not the confidence I had in South Africa, and experience has even shown that these experiments involve obvious risks.'[37]

A ROCK-LIKE INTEGRITY

In the case of the great figures of the distant past, any flaws are now hidden by the devotion of centuries. But it is precisely because Gandhi is close enough for us to be aware of his real human weaknesses, blunders and eccentricities that his spiritual greatness stands out so convincingly. Both his human limitations and his remarkable capacity for spiritual growth are evident in the way he developed over the years. He was not born a mahatma but became one through his response to circumstances. The shy youth in Porbandar grew through his encounter with the west as a law student in London, and then developed rapidly in response to racial discrimination in South Africa into an assured and formidable non-violent activist. His ideas gradually became clearer and more compelling, and as the acknowledged leader of the movement for Indian independence he became a charismatic personality who impressed everyone who met him and who directly and indirectly influenced millions. With all his failings he still emerges as one of the truly great human beings of the modern world.

When one trawls through the vast collection of Gandhi's utterances – very few can have read the whole of the ninety-three substantial volumes – one meets a great deal of repetition, not in words but in substance, because the same issues were raised again and again by different people. In addition to constantly pressing home the central themes of *ahimsa*, non-violence, and the need to purify India to be worthy of its freedom, Gandhi was also continually fielding both small

35. Royle, pp. 195–6.
36. Brown, p. 379.
37. Gandhi, 1968, II, p. 458.

and large questions, such as 'Isn't even swatting a fly violence?'; 'Is the mercy killing of a wounded cow permissible?'; 'Can marauding tigers be shot?'; 'What about euthanasia?'; 'What should the Abyssinians have done when Mussolini's troops invaded their country?'; 'What ought to happen to war criminals?'; 'What to do when the masses can rise to the tactic of non-cooperation with the British raj but not to a commitment to total non-violence in every aspect of life?' and so on and so on. He was constantly in direct interaction with others, and what stands out so impressively is the massive consistency of his basic convictions. He was by no means always consistent on detailed issues, but totally consistent on his central message, the call to live in selfless response to Truth, *sat*, true reality. To attain ultimate union with that reality was the central Hindu quest. But one of Gandhi's special insights was that this quest can take the form of the service of truth in its more immediate and relative forms – truthfulness in thought and speech, truthfulness in dealing with one's opponents, truthfulness in presenting a case, truthfulness in every aspect of life. Another form of this insight is that the deluded state in which humanity normally lives, in Hindu terms *maya*, takes social, political and economic forms. This was brought home to Gandhi in South Africa when he was thrown off the train at Pietermaritzburg as a non-white barrister presuming to travel in a first-class compartment. It dawned on him that racism was a spiritual delusion embodied in an entrenched social system. As Rex Ambler says, 'The great illusion, the social maya, as we may call it, is that human beings are fundamentally different from one another, and that some are inherently superior to others and are, thereby, entitled to dominate them . . . His life's work was largely devoted to the exposure of that illusion and the realization of the hidden Truth of human oneness.'[38]

Within the rock-like consistency of conviction, Gandhi's approach to life was always one of openness to new experiences and new encounters, always ready to grow into a different and fuller understanding. To quote Judith Brown, 'He saw himself as always waiting for inner guidance, to which he tried to open himself by prayer, a disciplined life, and increasing detachment not only from possessions but also from excessive care about the results of his earthly actions. He claimed to be perpetually experimenting with satyagraha, examining the possibilities of "truth force" as new situations arose. He was, right to the end, supremely a pilgrim spirit.'[39] And speaking of the last phase she adds 'The later 1930's saw the ageing Gandhi still an optimist – about human nature, himself and Indian public life. But he was coming to terms with the passing years painfully and not without struggle, his hope often

38. Ambler, p. 93.
39. Brown, p. 80.

temporarily darkened by events as clouds blot out the sun but cannot finally remove it . . . His profound spiritual vision of life as a pilgrimage generated in him a mental and emotional agility which responded to change as an opportunity to be welcomed rather than resisted with fear.'[40] We can say that he embodied his own ideal of the optimist: 'The optimist lives delighting in thoughts of love and charity and, since there is none whom he looks upon as his enemy, he moves without fear.'[41] In this optimistic openness Gandhi was continually outgrowing his own former self and always looking with hope to the future. At one point in 1937, when his movement seemed to be failing, he wrote in a letter, 'In the dictionary of a seeker of truth there is no such thing as being "not successful". He is or should be an irrepressible optimist because of his immovable faith in the ultimate victory of Truth which is God.'[42]

Gandhi was not a theoretical thinker and his pronouncements were nearly always made *ad hoc* in particular situations and were open to revision in the future. And so he freely discarded statements of his own when they no longer applied or when he had come to see things differently. He said frankly, 'My aim is not to be consistent with my previous statements on a given question, but to be consistent with truth as it may present itself to me at a given moment.'[43] Further, he was a strongly intuitive thinker whose basic insights welled up with imperative force from the 'inner voice' of his unconscious mind. These intuitions came shining in their own light as the impact of Truth, utterly devoid of doubt or ambiguity, hence their power not only in his own life but also in the lives of so many whom he influenced. But Gandhi was well aware that there can be evil as well as good intuitions, and this is why he insisted so strongly on the purification of the self by discipline, vows, and a renunciation of wealth and possessions. 'A pure heart', he said, 'can find and see the truth.'[44] It was because he knew that he was sincerely striving for *moksha*, for unity with the Divine, that he believed that the 'inner voice' of Truth sometimes illuminated his mind.

Lest Gandhi's reliance on intuition should suggest that he was vague or muddle-headed, I should add that he clearly had a high order of intelligence, as well as an unwavering respect for facts and considerable forensic skill. He had been called to the Bar in London and had practised for many years as a successful barrister in South Africa. Whenever he approached the authorities, whether on behalf of some local group or of India as a whole, with a case for redress or reform or for independence, he always did so on the basis of careful research. For example, in 1916 Gandhi was asked to help the indigo plantation workers of Champaran in Bihar, who were being grossly exploited,

40. Ibid., pp. 312–13.
41. *Navajivan*, 23 October 1921.
42. Brown, p. 283.
43. Ibid.
44. Iyer, II, p. 195.

often by absentee landlords. He took up their cause and was soon arrested and imprisoned for refusing to obey a judicial order excluding him from the district. The news spread rapidly and a large crowd gathered in his support. But instead of inciting a riot Gandhi had his followers help to calm and control the crowds. 'In this way [the authorities] were put at ease, and instead of harassing me they gladly availed themselves of my and my co-workers' co-operation in regulating the crowds. But it was an ocular demonstration of the fact that their authority was shaken. The people had for the moment lost all fear of punishment and yielded obedience to the power of love which their new friend exercised.'[45] When the magistrate wisely released him Gandhi set up a centre to which thousands of peasants came to record their evidence, which was then carefully checked and collated. Using this he wrote an exact and damning report as a result of which an official enquiry was held and reparation was at last made to the peasants. 'The *tinkathia* system [under which the peasants were forced to devote three-twentieths of their land to indigo] which had been in existence for about a century was thus abolished, and with it the planters' *raj* came to an end.'[46] This was the first major victory of Gandhi's method of rational and non-violent persuasion, and it made his new type of leadership known throughout India.

45. Gandhi, 1968, II, p. 614.
46. Ibid., II, p. 634.

21

THE POLITICS OF TRUTH

GOD IS TRUTH, TRUTH IS GOD

It is time now to look at Gandhi's famous statement that Truth is God. He did not mean primarily truth in the sense that comes most naturally to the western mind, namely truths, true propositions. He says explicitly that he meant it in the Indian religious sense of *satya*, which means, in a variety of English phrases, being, reality, that which alone truly is, the ultimate. At the beginning of *From Yeravada Mandir* Gandhi wrote, 'The word *Satya* (Truth) is derived from *Sat*, which means "being". Nothing is or exists in reality except Truth. That is why the term *Sat* or Truth is perhaps the most important name of God.'[1] God is not then a Person, but is beyond the personal/impersonal distinction as the ultimate reality underlying all things. That Gandhi often spoke of this reality in personal terms as guiding, protecting, commanding etc. is also characteristic of much Indian thought, in which Vishnu, Shiva, Rama, Sita and the innumerable other gods and goddesses are thought of as manifestations of the formless (or ineffable) ultimate reality, Brahman. But because we are persons we generally need to personify that reality. As Gandhi said, 'as we cannot do without a ruler or a general, such names as "King of Kings" or "The Almighty" are and will remain generally current'.[2] But Truth 'is That which alone is, which constitutes the stuff of which all things are made, which subsists by virtue of its own power, which is not supported by anything else but supports everything that exists. Truth alone is eternal, everything else is momentary. It need not assume shape or form.'[3]

1. Gandhi, 1968, IV, p. 213.
2. Ibid.
3. Iyer, II, p. 576.

Everything that Gandhi said shows that he was primarily a seeker after God, Truth, the Ultimate, and a politician because this led him into the service of his fellows and so into conflict with any form of injustice. For him there was in practice no division between religion and politics, for true religion expresses itself politically, and the only way to achieve lasting political change is through the inner transformation of masses of individuals, beginning with oneself. The great aim of his life was, in his own words, to 'see God face to face',[4] though seeing God face to face 'is not to be taken literally . . . God is formless'.[5] And the place where he 'saw' God was in responding to the needs of the poor, the downtrodden, the marginalized, the outcastes. He says of his time at Champaran, 'It is no exaggeration, but the literal truth, to say that in this meeting with the peasants I was face to face with God, Ahimsa and Truth.'[6] And so he could say that his great aim, which he believed should be everyone's aim, was to attain the inner liberation that expresses itself in love for all. When a foreign visitor once asked him why he was spending his life on behalf of India's poverty-stricken villagers he said, 'I am here to serve no one else but myself, to find my own self-realization through the service of these village folk. Man's ultimate aim is the realization of God, and all his activities, social, political, religious, have to be guided by the ultimate aim of the vision of God. The immediate service of all human beings becomes a necessary part of the endeavour simply because the only way to find God is to see Him in His creation and to be one with it. This can only be done by service to all.'[7] In the Truth that he encountered there was ultimately no distinction between one's own salvation and that of others.

The Hindu tradition recognizes three paths to unity with Brahman. *Jnana* yoga is the way of knowledge and insight; *bhakti* yoga is the way of devotion; and *karma* yoga is the way of action, originally ritual action but developing through the centuries into action in general. Following the *Bhagavad Gita,* this last was Gandhi's way. As Judith Brown says, 'He was never at rest in the purely contemplative tradition, but believed passionately that as sparks of truth, of ultimate reality, lay in each person, so the truth-seeker must find truth, must find his God, in encounter with and compassion for his fellow-men.'[8] In his ashrams the day began and ended with prayer, readings (mainly from the *Gita*), hymns (including some Christian hymns) and often a short talk by Gandhi. But worship for him also took the form of spinning, sweeping the floor, cleaning the latrines, nursing the sick, attacking some specific injustice or planning some aspect of the campaign for independence. It is important to understand that for Gandiji *swaraj*, freedom, was not

4. Gandhi, 1968, I, p. xix.
5. Iyer, I, p. 587.
6. Gandhi, 1968, II, pp. 615–16.
7. *Harijan*, 29 August 1936.
8. Brown, p. 83.

simply or even primarily a matter of political independence, but the transformation of both individuals and society from selfishness to true community. In his manifesto *Hind Swaraj* he lays down as the first principle, 'Real home-rule is self-rule or self-control',[9] which can alone bring about permanent change. But self-rule required that people could first see and feel the value of mutual help. And so during the Champaran campaign Gandhi's co-workers were also busy setting up schools in six villages in the district and at the same time teaching the people methods of cleanliness and good sanitation.

A HINDU CRITIC OF HINDUISM

As we have seen, Gandhi was not a systematic thinker, but one for whom action came first with theory following behind. When in his letters and dialogues some general principle or philosophical concept was under discussion, he quickly brought the conversation round to its practical implications. But at the same time his life and thought unfolded within the context of an inherited Hindu worldview.

Although a devoted Hindu, Gandhi was strongly opposed to many aspects of traditional Hindu culture, such as animal sacrifices in the temples,[10] child marriages,[11] and untouchability. 'Untouchability', he said, 'is a soul-destroying sin. Caste is a social evil.'[12] For whilst he generally acknowledged the traditional caste division of labour, he did not see it as religiously based, and he increasingly criticized its harmful aspects. Indeed in his practice he overturned them. In his ashrams people of all castes, colours, nationalities and religions ate and worked together, everyone, including Gandhi and his family, joining equally in the manual labour traditionally allocated to the *sudras* (the lowest caste), and such dirty jobs as latrine cleaning traditionally done only by the outcastes. He regarded untouchability as a 'useless and wicked superstition',[13] and was revolted by its defence in terms of the doctrine of karma.[14] In his eyes there was no difference between a Brahmin and an outcaste;[15] and he defended marriages between people of different castes.[16] He refused to wear the sacred thread of a caste Hindu because 'If the *Shudras* may not wear it, I argued, what right have the other *varnas* [castes] to do so?'[17] And whilst he supported the traditional Hindu reverence for the cow, 'Cow protection, in my opinion, included cattle-breeding, improvement of the stock, humane treatment of bullocks, formation of model dairies, etc.'[18] In short, Gandhi's moral insights had far greater authority for him than established traditions,

9. Gandhi, 1968, III, p. 201.
10. Ibid., IV, p. 251.
11. Ibid., V, p. 445.
12. Ibid., V, p. 444.
13. Brown, p. 58.
14. Gandhi, 1968, V, pp. 404–5.
15. *Indian Opinion*, 20 May 1905.
16. Brown, p. 290.
17. Gandhi, 1968, II, pp. 585–6.
18. Ibid., II, p. 636.

and in his maturity he had no hesitation in sweeping away long-accepted ideas and practices that he regarded as harmful excrescences on the body of Hinduism.

Gandhi did however cleave to certain basic Hindu beliefs which were the source of his practical intuitions. In setting these out in order I am taking separately ideas that belong together as aspects of a single integrated body of belief, but it may be helpful to focus on them one by one.

The first is that each of us in our deepest nature is identical with the universal *atman*, which, in the depth of our being, is common to us all, although divided in this life into innumerable different bodies and consciousnesses. Gandhi said that 'the chief value of Hinduism lies in holding the actual belief that *all* life (not only human beings, but all sentient beings) are one, i.e. all life coming from the One universal source, call it God, or Allah, or Parameshwara'.[19] Accordingly he wrote, 'I subscribe to the belief or the philosophy that all life in its essence is one, and that the humans are working consciously or unconsciously towards the realization of that identity.'[20] Again he said, 'I believe in *advaita*, I believe in the essential unity of man and for that matter of all that lives.'[21] His focus was not upon the advaita Vedanta philosophy as such – he never allowed himself to become enmeshed in technical philosophical debates – but on its concrete significance. 'What though we have many bodies?' he asked, 'We have but one soul.'[22] Again, 'Souls seem to be many; but underneath the seeming variety, there is an essential oneness.'[23] Accordingly, 'To be true to such religion one has to lose oneself in continuous and continuing service of all life.'[24] The political implication for Gandhi of the unity of life was that no one can be totally alien and irredeemably an enemy, and that 'one's true self-interest consists in the good of all'.[25] 'I, for one, bear no ill-will against the British or against any people or individual. All living creatures are of the same substance as all drops of water in the ocean are the same in substance. I believe that all of us, individual souls, living in this ocean of spirit, are the same with one another with the closest bond among ourselves. A drop that separates soon dries up and any soul that believes itself separate from others is likewise destroyed.'[26]

The second closely related belief underlying Gandhi's work is that there is a divine element in each of us. As he learned from the *Bhagavad Gita*, 'I [Vishnu] am the *atman* dwelling in the heart of all beings.'[27] In more universal terms, 'the Power that pervades the universe is also

19. Iyer, I, p. 451.
20. Chatterjee, p. 106.
21. *Navajivan*, 15 February 1925.
22. *Young India*, 4 December 1924.
23. Iyer, I, p. 451.
24. Ibid., I, p. 461.
25. Ibid., II, p. 122.
26. *Indian Opinion*, 29 April 1914.
27. Gandhi, 1968, IV, p. 305.

present in the human heart'.[28] This means in practice that in all situations of conflict there is something in the opponent that can be appealed to, not only a common humanity but, in the famous Quaker phrase (and Gandhi felt great affinity with the Quakers), 'that of God in every man'. 'I have a glimpse of God', he said, 'even in my opponents.'[29] So, once again, no one can be utterly and finally an enemy because none are without that divine spark within them. 'People may consider themselves to be our enemies,' Gandhi said, 'but we should reject any such claim.'[30] He was however well aware that appearances are often against such an outlook. Referring to Nazism and 'the bloody butchery that European aggressors have unloosed' he wrote:

> In the face of this, how can one speak seriously of the divine spirit incarnate in man? Because these acts of terror and murder offend the conscience of man; because man knows that they represent evil; because in the inner depths of his heart and of his mind, he deplores them. And because, moreover, when he does not go astray, misled by false teachings or corrupted by false leaders, man has within his breast an impulse for good and a compassion that is the spark of divinity.[31]

A third, again integrally related, aspect of Gandhi's faith is *ahimsa*, non-killing, and more generally, non-violence. This is an ancient Hindu, but more particularly Jain, principle. It obviously coheres with the belief that all life is ultimately one and that there is a divine element in every person. It follows that in injuring others we are injuring the whole of which we are ourselves a part, and injuring the ultimate Truth or Reality which we call God.

NON-VIOLENCE

Ahimsa is the point at which Gandhi's philosophy becomes political and has a continuing significance for the whole world. It means in practice that, in the midst of injustice, the right way to deal with oppressors – whether the South African government in its treatment of the 'coolies' or the British raj dominating and exploiting the people of India – is not violent revolt but an appeal to the best within them by rational argument together with disobedience to unjust laws, even when this involves suffering, violence and imprisonment. Willingness to suffer for the sake of justice, appealing as it does to the common humanity of both oppressor and oppressed, is the moral power for which Gandhi coined the word *satyagraha*, the power of Truth. He believed that a policy of non-aggression in the face of aggression, of calm reason in response to

28. Ibid., V, p. 380.
29. Iyer, I, p. 438.
30. Ibid., I, p. 530.
31. *Modern Review*, October 1941.

blind emotion, of appeal to basic fairness and justice, together with a readiness to suffer for this, are more productive in the long run than meeting violence with violence. He was convinced that there is always something in the other, however deeply buried, that will eventually, given enough time, respond. For 'non-violence is the law of our species as violence is the law of the brute. The spirit lies dormant in the brute and he knows no law but that of physical might. The dignity of man requires obedience to a higher law – to the strength of the spirit.'[32] But in order for this to happen the *satyagrahi* must have the courage to face the oppressor without fear. Without such courage, which Gandhi was able to evoke in many of his followers, genuine non-violent action is impossible. 'Non-violence', he said, 'is a weapon of the strong. With the weak it might easily be hypocrisy.'[33] But a *satyagrahi* can be non-violent precisely because he does not fear the oppressor. 'Fear and love', Gandhi said, 'are contradictory terms . . . My daily experience, as of those who are working with me, is that every problem would lend itself to solution if we are determined to make the law of truth and non-violence the law of life.'[34]

However, he was not opposed to the use of force in all circumstances. For example he was seriously physically assaulted in South Africa in 1908, and when one of his sons later asked what he ought to have done if he had been there, Gandhi replied that in that situation he should have used force to rescue his father.[35] He accepted that violence was necessary in restraining violent criminals, and he said, 'I would support the formation of a militia under *swaraj* [self-rule].'[36] 'In life', he said, 'it is impossible to eschew violence completely. The question is, where is one to draw the line?'[37] But in general, 'non-violence is infinitely superior to violence'.[38]

In the colonial India in which Gandhi most notably applied his principles, he had to carry the masses with him. And so a great deal of his time was spent in 'consciousness raising' by public speaking, often to great crowds throughout the country, by a constant stream of newspaper and journal articles, and by interviews with individuals and groups from both India and abroad. He knew that the ideal of total non-violence, which involves loving one's enemy, was not going to be attained by the masses in any foreseeable future. He said that 'for me the law of complete Love is the law of my being. Each time I fail, my effort shall be all the more determined for my failure. But I am *not* preaching this final law through the Congress or the Khalifat organization. I know my own limitations only too well. I know that any

32. Iyer, II, p. 299.
33. Ibid., I, p. 294.
34. Ibid.
35. Ibid., II, p. 298.
36. Ibid., II, p. 391.
37. Ibid., II, p. 257.
38. Ibid.

such attempt is foredoomed to failure.'[39] But although perfect *ahimsa* was an ideal rather than a present reality, something approaching it, namely non-violent non-cooperation with the foreign ruler, was possible, and would eventually bring about the nation's freedom. He said, 'I know that to 90 per cent of Indians, non-violence means [civil disobedience] and nothing else.'[40] Again, 'What the Congress and the Khalifat organizations have accepted is but a fragment of the implications of that law [*ahimsa*]. [But] Given true workers, the limited measure of its application can be realized in respect of vast masses of people within a short time.'[41] He was able to convince a critical mass of his fellow countrymen that a hundred thousand Englishmen could only rule three hundred million Indians as long as the Indians weakly submitted to their rule. If they had the courage to withdraw their co-operation, and deliberately disobey unjust laws – such as the salt tax – the British raj would be helpless and the imperial rulers would see that their position was both morally and politically untenable. Although in 1930 there were 29,000 Congress activists in jail, the government could not imprison millions; and although there might be further outbursts of violence, like the terrible Amritsar massacre in 1919, or the more recent Peshawar incident in 1930 when armoured cars were used against a crowd of demonstrators, or again in the same year, the air force's bombing of villages supporting Abdul Gaffar Khan, known as the Gandhi of the North-West Frontier,[42] the world would react against this and in the end the imperial power would be defeated and would have to depart. Gandhi said, 'Once the British Government are sure that they can no longer hold India, all the difficulties that are now being put forth on their behalf will vanish like darkness before dawn.'[43] And in the end this is what happened. After the 1939–45 war the Labour government of Clement Attlee came to power in Britain and made the momentous decision to grant Indian independence. It was evident that the demand and expectation for this were growing to the point at which only brute force could check it, and this in an India in which the whole administrative machinery had been gravely weakened during the war. The conscript British soldiers wanted to go home and had no enthusiasm whatever to stay on in India to sustain an imperial rule. In 1946 the Viceroy, General Archibald Wavell, reported to London that 'our time in India is limited and our power to control events almost gone'.[44] Further, members of the new British government, including the prime minister, Clement Attlee, had over the years been convinced of the justice of the demand for Indian independence. The new Secretary of State for India, Lord Pethic-Lawrence, was a friend of Gandhi and

39. *Young India*, 9 March 1922.
40. Iyer, II, p. 363.
41. *Young India*, 9 March 1922.
42. Lawrence James, pp. 527–8.
43. *Harijan*, 16 March 1940.
44. French, p. 245.

Nehru, as was the dominant intellect of the Labour party, Stafford Cripps. The last Viceroy, Lord Mountbatten, who was sent out to bring independence about, admired Gandhi and regarded Nehru as a worthy prime minister of a free India.

And so at this late stage circumstances conspired to bring about early independence. In that immediate situation independence was the work, not of Gandhi and the Congress, but of the collapse of British power. But on a longer view this final situation was made possible by the progressive achievement of the independence movement during the previous thirty years. It was Gandhi and his colleagues who had made Indians proud of their culture and confident of their capacity for self-rule, and who had built up the finally irresistible expectation and demand for independence.

Throughout the long struggle Gandhi provided the inspiration, the moral authority, and the immense unifying symbolic power. But in the detailed negotiations during the final phase it was mainly Pandit Jawaharlal Nehru and Sardar Vallabhbhai Patel who moulded the settlement on the Congress side – Nehru the brilliant, sophisticated, charismatic disciple of Gandhi, chosen by him as Congress President at this critical juncture, and Patel the shrewd, tough, forceful, uncompromising political operator. And so the raj ended as Gandhi had always said it would, with the British voluntarily handing over power and leaving in friendship, despite the strong opposition at home by old-style imperialists led by Winston Churchill. Instead of going in bitterness and enmity, the British went with great pomp and ceremony, leaving an India which has proudly continued to this day to be a member of the British Commonwealth. It seems very unlikely that history would have taken this course but for Gandhi's influence during the previous thirty years, somewhat as, more recently, it seems very unlikely that apartheid in South Africa would have ended so peacefully but for the personal influence of Nelson Mandela.

22

GANDHI'S TRUTH FOR US TODAY

We can now try to formulate the main lessons of Gandhi's life and thought for ourselves today. Gandhi himself believed that his basic message would only have its main impact many years after his own death. It is certainly a mistake to think of him only in the context of the movement for Indian independence, inseparable though his memory is from that. But he did not see political independence as such as his great aim, but rather a profound transformation of Indian society. True *swaraj* meant freedom from greed, ignorance, prejudice; and most of Gandhi's time was spent in trying to educate and elevate the masses, dealing with basic questions of cleanliness, sanitation and diet, combating disease, and fostering mutual help and true community. As Judith Brown writes, 'He visualized a total renewal of society from its roots upwards, so that it would grow into a true nation, characterized by harmony and sympathy instead of strife and suspicion, in which castes, communities, and both sexes would be equal, complementary and interdependent.'[1] Thus Gandhi's vision went much further than the immediate political aims that he shared with his colleagues in the Indian National Congress. What elements of his long-term project are relevant today?

NON-VIOLENT CONFLICT RESOLUTION

First is the Gandhian approach to conflict resolution, based on a belief in the fundamental nature of the human person. Not however of human nature as it has generally manifested itself throughout history, but of its further potentialities, which can be evoked by goodwill, self-giving love,

1. Brown, p. 213.

and a sacrificial willingness to suffer for the good of all. As Lamont Hempel puts it, 'Gandhi's crowning achievement may have been his ability to inspire *homo humanus* out of *homo sapiens*'.[2] But this was only in a number of individuals, not in society as a whole. Individuals continue to be inspired by Gandhi's teaching and example. But neither India nor any other state has based its policies on Gandhian principles. It is particularly tragic that his own country has failed to live up to his ideals. The rise of the Hindu supremacist movement – which was responsible for Gandhi's assassination – has intensified communal tensions, culminating in the destruction of the Ayodhya mosque in 1992. And the Hindu nationalist government which represents that movement has now destabilized the whole region by five nuclear explosions in underground tests. All this would make Gandhi weep. Unregenerate human nature has triumphed once again over what Gandhi called Truth, as it has against the teachings of enlightened religious leaders in every century.

Nevertheless the attempt to inspire humans to rise to true humanity must never cease. It involves an unwavering commitment to fairness, truthfulness, open and honest dealing, willingness to see the other's point of view, readiness to compromise, readiness even to suffer. In the familiar but in practice disregarded words of Jesus, it requires us to love our enemies and to turn the other cheek rather than retaliate. Such a response refuses to enter the downward spiral of mutual recrimination, hatred and violence. The lesson of history is not that this has been tried and failed, but that the failure has been in not trying it.

We have had sufficient glimpses of dedicated non-violence in action to realize its power. We have seen it in the work of Martin Luther King, in the spirit of reconciliation inspired by Nelson Mandela in the new South Africa, and in many small local actions in many places amidst situations of conflict. But *ahimsa* as practical politics is a long-term strategy. It took time, patience, ceaseless effort and example to evoke the limited realization that non-violent action in India, even simply as a tactic, is more effective than violent revolt. It is thus pointless to ask how Gandhi would have fared in, for example, Nazi Germany. He would no doubt have been quickly eliminated. The more useful question is what would have happened if someone like him had been at work in Germany during the previous twenty years. For in hindsight we can see that both of the world wars were unnecessary. The 1914–18 war was blundered into by short-sighted politicians and generals, and developed under its own impetus into the mindless slaughter of millions. The settlement after it, again reached by short-sighted and sometimes

2. Hempel, p. 5.

vindictive politicians, created the conditions within which Hitler would come to power, leading to another world war which might otherwise never have happened, again involving the slaughter of millions. The Gandhian approach to peace could obviously not be implemented in the midst of such a war, but if implemented during the previous decades it might have changed the course of events so that there would have been no war. This was not impossible. For immensely intelligent pragmatists, such as John Maynard Keynes, were advocating on purely practical economic grounds some of the policies that Gandhi would have wanted to promote.

Going further back in the same stream of moral insight, we can say that if Christian Europe and North America had lived by the teachings of Jesus, the history of the west would not have been soaked in the blood and violence which have so often characterized it. And the same is true of the east if it had lived by the teachings of the Buddha and Confucius and the Hindu sages of India. But the ideal must continue to be witnessed to, and practised whenever there are people able to do so.

GREEN THINKING

Another implication of Gandhi's thought concerns ecology, the preservation of the earth and the life on it. Here Gandhi was far ahead of his time, anticipating the Green movement of today. To quote James Gould, 'Gandhi has emphasised opposite values to those of the consumer society: the reduction of individual wants, the return to direct production of foodstuffs and clothing, and self-sufficiency rather than growing dependency. As the limits of growth and the inherent scarcity of resources broke upon the world in the 1960s, the Gandhian idea of restraint suddenly made sense.'[3] E.F. Schumacher, author of the influential *Small Is Beautiful*, regarded Gandhi as the great pioneer in insisting that the rampant growth of capitalist industrialism is incompatible with a sustainable world ecosystem. He said, 'Gandhi had always known, and rich countries are now reluctantly beginning to realise, that their affluence was based on stripping the world. The USA with 5. 6% of the world population was consuming up to 40% of the world's resources, most of them non-renewable. Such a life-style could not spread to the whole of mankind. In fact, the truth is now dawning that the world could not really afford the USA, let alone the USA plus Europe plus Japan plus other highly industrialised countries. Enough is now known about the basic facts of spaceship Earth to realise that its first class passengers were making demands which could not be

3. Hick and Hempel, p. 12.

sustained very much longer without destroying the spaceship.'[4] Gandhi saw this in terms of his native India, then still a developing country in which many of the people in the hundreds of thousands of villages lived in extreme poverty. In 1928, referring to these villages, Gandhi wrote that 'under British rule, millions of children are starving for want of nourishing food and they are shivering in winter for want of sufficient clothing'.[5] And so instead of building up modern industries with labour-saving machinery in the cities, drawing the villagers into the urban slums, he urged basic employment for all. He wanted 'production by the masses rather than mass production'. Every policy should be judged by its effects on the multitude of ordinary citizens. For example cottage industries such as spinning required very little capital equipment and should be encouraged and supported throughout the vast rural areas. But the opposite has happened. When asked whether Gandhi has turned out to be right, Schumacher 'pointed out that the number of rich, even very rich, people in India had increased as had the number of desperately poor people. He added that the situation in India reflected the situation of the world as a whole and Gandhi would undoubtedly consider this a sign of grievous failure.'[6] We should not of course assume that if Gandhi had lived a generation later he would have been advocating the same return to the spinning wheel – as we have already noted, his mind was always on the move, taking account of changing circumstances. He would presumably have accepted the industrialization of India, but would have sought to humanize it.

In the matter of aid to impoverished countries, Gandhi was at least a generation ahead of his time. In 1929 he wrote, 'The grinding poverty and starvation with which our country is afflicted is such that it drives more and more men every year into the ranks of the beggars, whose desperate struggle for bread renders them insensible to all feelings of decency and self-respect. And our philanthropists, instead of providing work for them and insisting on their working for bread, give them alms.'[7] But that aid should be given in such a way as to free the recipients to help themselves is now an accepted principle in international aid circles.

THE POSITION OF WOMEN

Gandhi's 'feminism' – though that is not a term he used – is also of interest today in shifting the focus from the transformation of women to the transformation of men. On the negative side, Gandhi never wholly broke free from the assumptions of the ancient patriarchal

4. Hoda, p. 141.
5. Iyer, I, p. 506.
6. Hoda, p. 140.
7. Gandhi, 1968, II, p. 647.

culture of India, but in this context his concern for the position of women in society was well ahead of his time. He had been impressed when in England by the courage and dedication of the suffragettes, although he did not approve of their resorts to violence. And when women responded to his call in South Africa and India, showing themselves as willing as the men to face violent police action and jail, Gandhi saw that they had a unique contribution to make. To quote Ranjit Kumar Roy, early on 'Gandhi realised that the success of this *Satyagraha* had been due to the new moral force that women's entry brought into the movement. Indeed the presence of women had generated public support and mobilised the "apathetic and the marginally interested" to join the movement. Gandhi was quick to understand that women could become the "leader in the *Satyagraha* which does not require the learning that books give but does require the stout heart that comes from suffering and faith" .'[8] Further, because for Gandhi true liberation always went much further than political independence, to the humane transformation of society, he 'believed that by taking part in the nationalist struggle, women of India could break out of their long imposed seclusion'.[9] His conception of the kind of gender revolution that is needed strikes a chord today. The wholehearted adoption of *ahimsa* can be seen as making for a gentler and less aggressive masculinity. Sushila Gidwani puts the point challengingly in this way: 'Gandhian feminism aims at changing men to become qualitatively [more] feminine while the modern feminism aims at changing women to become qualitatively [more] masculine.'[10] Gandhi not only wanted to change the traditional Indian – and not only Indian – male attitude to women, but also to change the prevailing conception of ideal masculinity.

RELIGIOUS PLURALISM

Finally, another aspect of Gandhi's thought which has implications for today is not novel in the east – it was familiar from the Vedas and from the work of such great ecumenical spirits as Kabir, Nanak, the Sufis of Islam, the Buddhist emperor Asoka and many more – but is highly controversial within Christianity, though much less so today in many circles than in Gandhi's time. This is his understanding of the relation between the great world faiths. 'The time has now passed', he said, 'when the followers of one religion can stand and say, ours is the only true religion and all others are false.'[11] In his youth Gandhi lived within a very ecumenical community. His family were Vaishnavites, but would

8. Roy, p. 224.
9. Ibid., p. 226.
10. Gidwani, p. 233.
11. *Indian Opinion*, 26 August 1905.

freely visit Shaivite temples, and they had Jain, Muslim and Parsi friends and neighbours. Gandhi was particularly influenced by a Jain, Raychandbhai, who introduced him to the idea of the many-sidedness of reality (*anekantavada*), so that many different views may all be valid, including religious views. Gandhi shared the ancient Hindu assumption that 'religions are different roads converging at the same point. What does it matter that we take different roads so long as we reach the same goal? I believe in the fundamental truth of all great religions of the world. I believe they are all God given and I believe they were necessary to the people to whom they were revealed.'[12] He regarded it as pointless, because it is impossible, to grade the great world faiths in relation to each other. 'No one faith is perfect. All faiths are equally dear to their respective votaries. What is wanted, therefore, is a living friendly contact among the followers of the great religions of the world and not a clash among them in the fruitless attempt on the part of each community to show the superiority of its own faith over the rest.'[13] Again, 'Hindus, Mussalmans, Christians, Parsis, Jews are convenient labels. But when I tear them down, I do not know which is which. We are all children of the same God.'[14] However, his 'doctrine of the Equality of Religions', as it has been called, did not move towards a single global religion, but enjoins us all to become better expressions of our own faith, being enriched in the process by influences from other faiths.

These then are ways in which Gandhi's thinking was ahead of his own time and alive in our time: non-violence in dealing with opponents; non-confrontational politics; ecology and what has been called 'Buddhist economics'; feminism; and the relation between religions. Underlying all this, as an available source of inspiration for each new generation, is Gandhi's indomitable faith in the possibility of a radically better human future if only we will learn to trust the power of non-violent openness to others and to the deeper humanity, and indeed deity, within all. To most people this seems impossible. But Gandhiji's great legacy is that his life has definitively shown that, given true dedication, it *is* possible in the world as it is.

12. Scotney, p. 239.
13. *Young India*, 23 April 1931.
14. *Harijan*, 18 April 1936.

23

AN ACTIVIST AND A CONTEMPLATIVE

KUSHDEVA SINGH

Kushdeva Singh was born in the Punjab in 1902. He grew up during the Indian struggle for independence which, like so many others of his generation, he ardently supported. When its leader, Mahatma Gandhi, visited Lahore whilst Kushdeva was a medical student there, 'I along with two other students went to meet him to pay our respects. He pointedly asked me a question, What would you like to be? My reply was that I would like to be a doctor. To this he replied that to become a doctor would be your profession. I am asking you what you would like to *be*, and I replied that I would like to be a good citizen. He was so happy with my reply that he said that if every Indian were to become a good citizen, the British could not rule over the country for a day.'[1] Kushdeva was later one of the vast multitude who travelled to Delhi from all over India to attend Gandhi's funeral in 1948. He said, 'The supreme lesson of Gandhi's life is that a mere man with high aspirations and ceaseless effort can grow into a formidable personality, and with his utter fearlessness and devotion to the cause of humanity can achieve the summit of human endeavour.'[2]

The previous year he had put his own Gandhian outlook into practice during the terrible violence in the Punjab immediately after independence, when probably about a million people – Muslims, Hindus and Sikhs – perished in the mutual slaughter.[3] When I was with Kushdeva Singh more than twenty years later I knew nothing of what he had done at the time of independence, for he did not speak about

1. Kushdeva Singh, 1983, p. 2.
2. Ibid., p. 5.
3. No one knows the precise number and estimates vary from 700,000 to two million, but one million seems to be a reasonable estimate; French, p. 329.

himself. But I find that in Patrick French's recent history of that period he mentions 'Kushdeva Singh, a Sikh doctor who became famous for evacuating Muslims to safety from a small town near Simla'.[4] I also did not know that the Indian government had awarded him the Order of Merit (Civil) in recognition of this. Later, in 1973, Kushdeva Singh wrote an account of events the memory of which, he said, 'is still as fresh in my mind as if they occurred only yesterday'.[5]

In 1947 he was Medical Superintendent of the Hardinge TB Sanitorium at Dharampore in the Simla hills. The people of Dharampore were mainly Hindus and Muslims, with a few Sikhs, and 'there was always quietness and peace in the atmosphere. Complete communal harmony prevailed among the people.'[6] But shortly after partition, Hindus and Sikhs from what was now Pakistan began to pour into the Indian Punjab and refugee camps were set up. Kushdeva Singh was a leader in organizing food, clothing and shelter for camps at nearby Ambala and then in Dharampore itself. Soon stories began to circulate of the horrendous murder of Hindus fleeing from Pakistan, and the growing hatred that this evoked was turned against the local Muslims. A shopkeeper began to manufacture and sell daggers, which were eagerly bought for three or four rupees by young men of both the Hindu and Muslim communities, and guns were sold to the wealthy for seven hundred to a thousand rupees by British officers leaving India. Soon a Muslim was murdered by a Sikh and a Hindu, and the communal tension became acute, with muttered threats to murder all the Dharampore Muslims. They now knew that they must leave their homes, jobs and possessions and try to make their way to Pakistan, even though Muslims travelling west were being slaughtered on the same scale and with the same ferocity as Hindus travelling east.

Kushdeva Singh was probably the only Sikh in that region to be trusted by the Muslims and they sought his help. He was a tall, commanding figure, holding the rank of major from his wartime service in the Indian army medical corps, and able by his personal authority to get things done. He arranged trucks to take the Muslim families to a transit camp at Subathu. 'Next day two trucks arrived at about ten o'clock in the morning. The Muslims were getting ready to leave. It appeared as if all would go well. But it was not to be. I got disturbing information that some of the [Hindu] refugees and miscreants had blocked the road from Dharampore to Subathu at four different places with tree trunks and coaltar drums. Some refugees were also seen moving about near those blockades. I was further informed that the

4. French, p. 352.
5. Kushdeva Singh, 1973, p. 11.
6. Ibid., p. 13.

truck drivers had been bribed.'[7] So he changed the evacuation plan without telling anyone, even the Muslims themselves. When they were almost ready to leave he sent the two truck drivers to his hospital on some pretext, produced two new drivers, and told them to drive immediately to Dagshai, which was in a different direction and where there was a cantonment in which the Muslims would be protected until they could move on further. The ruse succeeded, although the infuriated mob promptly looted all the now empty Muslim houses.

Kushdeva next went to nearby Kasauli where the Muslim community had decided to leave as soon as possible. They wanted to take their possessions with them but he advised them not to since this would almost certainly attract an attack on the journey. He also advised them not to use the road but to go on foot by a bridle-path through the hills. They agreed to do so, sending their possessions separately by truck. The trucks were ambushed and everything stolen, but the refugees themselves reached their destination safely. Kushdeva also personally escorted some Muslim women to Delhi and worked successfully in many ways to enable the local Muslim community to escape safely to Pakistan, in spite of constant danger to himself from people blinded by hatred.

Two years later he was returning by air from Oslo, where he had been doing postgraduate work on tuberculosis, and decided to stop at Karachi on the way. Memories of the carnage were vivid and emotions were still running high. It was therefore astonishing that a turbaned and bearded Sikh should turn up at Karachi. He was asked on arrival if he had come on some mission. Yes, he had come on a goodwill mission. Did he then represent some society? Yes, he was a member of the largest society in the world – the society of mankind. He had come to Pakistan on his way back to India because he did not accept that the relationship between the two countries should continue to be one of enmity. At the airport he was recognized by some Muslim policemen who had known him back in Dharampore and whose families he had rescued. Word of his presence spread rapidly among those he had helped to escape, their friends and relations, and he was greeted with delight and feasted by a growing number of his former neighbours. The Superintendent of Police, Abdul Waheed Khan, was among them, and when Kushdeva's plane was ready next morning 'I embraced Waheed and took leave of him and proceeded towards the plane. The constables accompanied me right up to the plane, and, when I was about to enter the aircraft, all of them stood in a line and presented a salute. I acknowledged with folded hands and tears dripping from my eyes.'[8] In a letter to a Muslim in

7. Ibid., p. 26.
8. Ibid., pp. 40–1.

Pakistan, he said, 'In my opinion we all, whether Hindus, Muslims or Sikhs, are the sons of the same One God, whom you call *Allah*, Hindus call *Ram* and Sikhs call *Wahiguru*. I respect Islam as much as my own religion because I know both are the same. I also know that a true Muslim or a true Sikh or a true Hindu would never have done what was quite common in the last communal riots.'[9] Gandhi had said the same, and Kushdeva Singh was on the same spiritual 'wavelength' as the Mahatma.

Kushdeva was by profession a medical doctor. Because of the widespread tuberculosis in the Punjab he became a TB specialist, but he did far more than carry on an individual practice. He was responsible for creating several TB clinics in the moderate climate of the Simla hills and pioneering the use in India of the latest treatments. He was an immensely energetic, effective and dedicated public servant and was given the Nishan-I-Iftikhar Medal of the Punjab and the national award of Padam Shri, as well as the Indian Red Cross Gold Medal and the Tuberculosis Association of India Gold Medal, none of which, however, I learned from him whilst I was with him in Patiala as a visiting professor at Punjabi University. I discovered all this later whilst writing this chapter.

What I did know was that he was responsible for creating and energizing a range of caring institutions in Patiala, not only a TB sanitorium but also a home for the destitute dying, a home for women excluded from their families, and an orphanage. He took me round these one day, driving at breakneck speed in his ancient car. At the home for the dying he introduced me to the woman in charge, 'This is my sister Anita.' Then at the orphanage to the woman in charge there, 'This is my sister Sushila,' and at the sanitorium, 'This is my brother Darshan,'[10] and so on. At first I wondered if his whole family was involved. But since I was myself introduced as his brother John, and at the orphanage as uncle, I soon realized that for Kushdeva we were all one family.

He was also involved in the big political issue in the Punjab, the demand of the Akali Dal, the Sikh nationalist party, for an independent Punjab – Khalistan, the Sikh state. He was opposed to this and was deeply concerned by the exploitation of religion for political purposes. He wrote that 'since your last visit in 1971 the corruption has slowly and slowly entered the temples of the religions, because of the politicians' hunger for power through all means, including religion'. He published a pamphlet on the Khalistan question, arguing that a Sikh homeland 'would have been a landlocked state of five or six districts,

9. Ibid., p. 61.
10. These are fictitious names because I regret that I do not now remember their real names.

sandwiched between India and Pakistan, and our status in India would have been that of foreigners. The only persons who would have benefited from it would have been a few power-hungry politicians for whom the glow of freedom means ministerial chairs only.'[11] In a letter in 1984, after the bloody siege of the Golden Temple at Amritsar, he said, 'Akali Dal tried to cheat the Government by putting their deeply political demands under the garb of religious demands. Their acceptance would have led to the disintegration of the country. The Akali Dal then prepared for confrontation by massing arms collected from a neighbouring country [Pakistan]. Again they used the holiest shrine of the Sikhs to fight out their political battle. Akali leadership is bitter with me, but I can't help in speaking and writing at all cost. I have no malice with anyone.' Because of his public opposition to the Khalistan movement a young man once came to visit Kushdeva Singh, intending to assassinate him. But after talking with him for some time he was so impressed that he confessed his purpose, which he now saw to be wrong, and departed leaving his knife behind.

Kushdeva was a Sikh in the original mould of Guru Nanak (1469–1539 CE), the founder of the Sikh tradition, who was a profoundly ecumenical spirit, living at a time when this spirit flourished in northern India. Nanak composed what became part of the Sikh morning prayer:

> There is but one God. He is all that is.
> He is the Creator of all things and He is all-pervasive.
> He is without fear and without enmity.
> He is timeless, unborn and self-existent.
> He is the Enlightener
> And can be realized by grace of Himself alone.
> He was in the beginning; He was in all ages.
> The True One is, was, O Nanak, and shall for ever be.[12]

This gives something of the flavour of the Sikhism that is expressed in Kushdeva Singh's own mystical poetry, much of it in English. Guru Nanak, he said, 'proclaimed the Oneness of God, and brotherhood of man irrespective of any distinction whatsoever, and equal status to women in all spheres of human activities'.[13] Kushdeva's own distinctive theme is that of finding God in everyday life:

> People go to their temples
> To greet Me;
> How simple and ignorant are My children
> Who think that I live in isolation.

11. Kushdeva Singh, 1982, p. 18.
12. Harbans Singh, pp. 96–7.
13. Kushdeva Singh, 1982, p. 1.

Why don't they come and greet Me
In the procession of life, where I always live,
In the farms, the factories, and the market,
Where I encourage those
Who earn their living by the sweat of their brow?

Why don't they come and greet Me
In the cottages of the poor
And find Me blessing the poor and the needy
And wiping the tears of widows and orphans?

Why don't they come and greet Me
Among those who are trampled upon
By those proud of pelf and power,
And see Me beholding their suffering and pouring out compassion?
And why don't they come and greet Me
Among women sunk in sin and shame
Where I sit by them to bless and uplift?

I am sure
They can never miss Me
If they try to meet Me
In the sweat and struggle of life
And in the tears and tragedies of the poor.[14]

The poem is a reflection of Kushdeva's own experience of finding God in the service of those in special need in his own place, Patiala. 'Religion', he said, 'is based on eternal faith in and unshakeable love of God, and an over flowing urge from within to serve the living beings – men, animals, birds, insects and all that is life, because of there being oneness of life pervading the whole universe.'[15] This was for him not just a beautiful idea, but the stuff of his daily activity.

What indelibly impressed me about Kushdeva Singh was the degree to which he had moved beyond self-concern, so that the transcendent Reality that he experienced as the divine Thou of the Sikh tradition became manifest in his life and personality. In a letter written near the end of his life, he says 'I am still living, a physical wreck, but I am more than happy and contented.' One of his poems is on immortality:

Some people pray to become immortal.
If they think of becoming immortal
Along with this mortal frame,

14. Kushdeva Singh, 1974, pp. 31–2.
15. Ibid., p. 55.

> They are aspiring for something which is impossible,
> Because this mortal frame must perish.
>
> But if however they want to become immortal
> Through their mortal frame,
> That is possible,
> Because a life led in complete dedication
> Becomes life-eternal, deathless.
> It lives on in the Infinite.
>
> A life lived for one's self is like a pond
> That stagnates, stinks and dries up,
> But a life lived for Him
> Is an ocean, ever fresh and perennial,
> That never exhausts.[16]

As to what happens after death, Kushdeva Singh believed, like other religious Sikhs, in reincarnation. He said in a letter, 'Dr Kushdeva Singh once dead will never be born as such, but the soul shall have some other covering.' He died in 1988. This is the last that I heard from him before his final illness:

> 'The ball no questions of Ayes or Noes makes,
> But right or left as strikes the player goes,
> And He that tossed it down into the field
> He knows about it all – He knows.' (Omar Khayyám)
> This fully applies to the story of my life. In His graciousness He not only blessed me with a human figure, but chose me for a ball to play with. The player enjoyed the play, and the ball in turn enjoyed the surprisingly beautiful, ever changing phenomenon, the world. After playing for over eighty-two years the player has closed the game, and the ball is slowing its speed to come to a halt. At least for the time being. The ball in all sincerity offers you its parting affection and regards for the close ties of friendship over the decades. Yours affectionately, Kushdeva Singh.

NYANAPONIKA MAHATHERA

We now move into a very different religious world, from theistic Sikhism to non-theistic Buddhism.

A Mahathera is a 'great monk' in the Theravada Buddhist tradition, the title coming after having been ordained for twenty years. This particular monk was born in Germany in 1901, and (in the words of the head of his order) 'his body succumbed to the universal law of

16. Ibid., p. 40.

impermanence which holds sway over all conditioned things'[17] in 1994, just after his ninety-third birthday and having just completed his fifty-third rains retreat. Many monks did 'a loving-kindness meditation' for him, wishing him a smooth transition to his new existence.

Nyanaponika lived in a forest hermitage in the Udawattakle Forest Reserve just outside Kandy in Sri Lanka, and it was as a visiting scholar at Peradeniya University, Kandy, in 1974 that I came to know him, to my great spiritual profit.

His original name was Siegmund Feniger, born of Jewish parents living near Frankfurt. He was always religiously inclined and learned Hebrew to study the sacred texts at first hand. As he grew however, and read voraciously in many fields, he began to have disturbing doubts about some of the traditional Jewish teachings. Doubt led him to search for new insights and he found these when he began to read about Buddhism. Although he had never met a Buddhist and was entirely self-taught, by the age of twenty he identified himself as a Buddhist. When the family moved to Berlin in 1922 he was able to join a Buddhist group and gain access to a much wider range of Buddhist literature. He came to know of some German Buddhists who had settled in the east – in Burma and Sri Lanka – and decided that one day he would himself become a monk in that part of the world. This did not happen, however, until later. In 1933 Hitler came to power in Germany and the persecution of the Jews began. Now in his early thirties, and working in a bookshop in Berlin, Siegmund joined the Central Committee of German Jews for Help and Self-Protection. He wanted to get his widowed mother out of Germany, and in 1935 they moved to Vienna, where they had relatives. He was already in correspondence with a German Jew who a generation earlier had become a Buddhist monk in Sri Lanka, Nyanatiloka, and in 1936 Siegmund set sail for the east. The Venerable Nyanatiloka Mahathera, as he then was, met him when he landed at Colombo, and took him to his Island Hermitage in a lagoon near the small town of Dodanduwa on the south-west coast. He lived there as an *upasaka* or lay disciple preparing for ordination, and a year later became a *bikkhu* or monk, being given the name of Nyanaponika, which means inclined to knowledge. It was then that he studied Pali, the ancient language of the Buddhist scriptures, and also learned English. He was later to translate parts of the Pali canon into German and English and to write on Buddhism in both languages.

When the Nazis invaded Austria in 1938, Nyanaponika arranged for his mother to come to Sri Lanka, where she lived with Sir Ernest and

17. Bodhi, 1995, pp. ix–x.

Lady De Silva, patrons of the Island Hermitage. Nyanaponika regularly came to visit her in Colombo and she eventually became a Buddhist herself, taking the Three Refuges – the Buddha, the Dharma and the Sangha. When the second world war broke out in 1939, Nyanaponika was interned as a German, in spite of being a German Jew. He was held in a camp in Ceylon, as it then was, and later at Dehra Dun in the Himalayan foothills in India, from 1941 to 1946. During his internment he translated the *Sutta Nipata* and other Pali writings into German and also began to write his *Abhidhamma Studies*. It was at Dehra Dun that he came to know Lama Govinda, another German internee, who had become a monk in the Tibetan Buddhist tradition. They explored the quite significant differences between Tibetan and Theravada Buddhism, and Nyanaponika learned Sanskrit from Govinda. On being released in 1946 he returned to Sri Lanka, to which he committed himself by becoming a citizen. In 1952 he was in Burma for the sixth Theravada Council at Rangoon, and stayed on to study with the great meditation master, Mahasi Sayadaw. It was as a result of this, and of years of practice of satipatthana (mindfulness) meditation, that he wrote *The Heart of Buddhist Meditation*, the English edition coming out in 1962 and being translated into seven other languages.

This is the method of meditation that I learned from him and try fitfully and with very imperfect success to practise. 'Mindfulness' is not just a special moment achieved in meditation but a state of mind that can come to pervade one's life. Attempting to express in my own way what I learned from Nyanaponika, the basic premise is that the ordinary consciousness of most of us most of the time is a distorted consciousness. I experience everything from my own particular and unique point of view, and thus as welcome or unwelcome, acceptable or threatening, fulfilling or frustrating my desires, and I am continually distracted by memories of the past and hopes and fears of the future. This constitutes my own subjective ego-centred world. But the world itself is devoid of the self-regarding valuations that we project upon it. And in the practice of mindfulness we can come to be part of the world's present moment, an element in its ever-changing transitoriness, experiencing each fleeting moment for its own sake. The result can be – and in people like Nyanaponika it visibly is – a serene happiness in release from self-concern into an openness towards all beings, and at the same time it carries them forward towards the ultimate goal of nirvana. It is a re-engagement with the world in a radically new way.

The technique of sattipathana meditation is very simple. You sit down comfortably, with a straight back, make a deliberate mental act of opening yourself to the greater reality in which 'we live and move and have our being', take several deep breaths, and then close your eyes and simply attend to your ordinary breathing, its coming in and going out. The mind wanders again and again and again, but you gently return to the breathing, continuing as long as you can without strain, the period increasing with practice. I myself find that the most favourable environment is sometimes the silence of the Friends' Meeting, because of the marked reinforcing effect of a number of people keeping silence together.

The exercise is relaxing and calming to both body and mind, and its effect continues after you stop. Whilst you are attending to the process of breathing, and nothing else, you are living in each passing moment, released from the distortions and anxieties of ego-concern. You may instead begin to become aware of the larger, ever-changing reality of which your own life is a part, and begin to feel surrounded by a friendly universe in which you can trust. But this, which is as far as I have got, is only the beginning. The continuing way is set forth in Nyanaponika's *The Heart of Buddhist Meditation* and in many other Buddhist writings.

In 1951 Nyanaponika had moved to the forest hermitage near Kandy. His mentor, Nyanatiloka, died in 1957. The next year Nyanaponika became one of the founders of the Buddhist Publication Society, and for as long as his strength continued he devoted a great deal of his time and energy to this. He also visited Switzerland once a year as spiritual adviser of Theravadins in Europe. Many Sri Lankans came to him at the hermitage for advice about their personal problems, which apparently he always dealt with patiently and helpfully – he said, 'If I err, may I err on the side of *karuna* (compassion).' Non-Buddhist visitors like myself also went to see him and he was willing to spend long periods in discussion about Buddhism. He occasionally came down to Kandy, and on one occasion came to a lecture that I gave at the British Council on Buddhism and Christianity, later inviting me to come to discuss it with him. He liked the spirit of what I had said, but firmly disagreed with criticisms that I had made of some aspects of Buddhist philosophy.

Because of his scholarly work – his translations and commentaries – he received academic recognition as an honorary fellow of the World Academy of Arts and Sciences, became an honorary member of the German Oriental Society, and received honorary doctorates from the Buddhist and Pali University of Sri Lanka and from Peradeniya University. And the Buddhist world conferred on him the title of *Amarapura Maha Mahopadhyaya Sasana Sobhana*, Great Mentor of the Amarapura Nikaya, Ornament of the Teaching.

The psychologist Erich Fromm, who read Nyanaponika's writings and visited him in Sri Lanka, wrote about him in 1976. He was struck by Nyanaponika's emphasis 'that peace and joy, not destruction and nihilism, are essential for the "feeling-world"', and he concludes, 'I am convinced that Nyanaponika Thera's work may become one of the most important contributions to the spiritual renewal of the West, if it can reach the knowledge of a sufficient number of people.'[18] This brief extract from Nyanaponika's writings will give the flavour of his teaching:

> Faith involves not merely a belief in the existence of a thing or in the truth of a credal formula, but also confidence in the power of its object. Religious faith is the belief and confidence in the power of the Supreme Good, and Buddhist faith, in particular, the belief in the incomparable power of the Noble Eightfold Path, the confidence in its purifying and liberating efficacy.
>
> Among those calling themselves 'believers' or 'religious people' or, in our case, Buddhists, there are still too few who have that kind of genuine faith in the actual power of the Good to transform and elevate the life of the individual and of society, to secure them against the resistance of the evil in themselves and in the world outside. Too few dare to entrust themselves to the powerful current of the Good, too many secretly believe, in spite of a vague sort of 'faith', that the power of the evil in themselves and the world is stronger – too strong to be contended with. Many politicians everywhere in the world seem to believe the same, particularly those who call themselves 'realists', obviously implying that only the evil is 'real'. They think that of necessity they have to submit to its greater power. If they are not willing to put it to the test, it is no wonder that they cannot achieve much good.[19]

What impressed me so much in Nyanaponika was a big personality and a powerful intellect which had nevertheless largely transcended the ego point of view. He was completely unselfconscious and unassuming: the information about his life which I have relayed comes from sources other than himself. Buddhists would say that the great compassion of buddhahood flowed through him.

Nyanaponika and Kushdeva are very different and yet essentially similar. They are different in that Kushdeva was an activist, Nyanaponika a contemplative. And yet even here, at a deeper level, they are similar. For whilst one worked to change the outer world in which we all live, the other worked to change the inner world in which we all live, for it is a Buddhist conviction that at a deep unconscious level our

18. Nyanaponika, 1994, p. xi.
19. Ibid., p. 304.

minds, our streams of thought and emotion, are in continuous interaction, so that 'loving-kindness meditation' affects the psychological climate of human life. The Buddha said, 'Here, monks, a disciple dwells pervading one direction with his heart filled with loving-kindness (*metta*), likewise the second, the third, and the fourth direction; so above, below and around; he dwells pervading the entire world everywhere and equally with his heart filled with loving-kindness, abundant, grown great, measureless, free from enmity and free from distress.'[20]

But even more deeply, the similarity between these two extraordinary individuals lies in their transcendence of the ego point of view, allowing a higher reality to manifest itself in their lives. Their significance to me is that in their presence I have also felt the power of that higher reality. Although one of them experienced it as God and the other as the Dharma, I am sure that if they had ever met, each would immediately have recognized the other as a kindred spirit. I see them as joint witnesses to ultimate reality and, in their differences, to the diversity of authentic human responses to that Reality.

20. *Digha Nikaya*, 13; Nyanaponika, 1994, p. 251.

PART VI

TIME PRESENT AND TIME FUTURE

24

WHAT WE DON'T NEED TO KNOW

THE BEGINNING AND THE END

The world religions generally profess to know everything, or at least everything really important – the nature of ultimate reality; the origin and structure of the universe; the purpose of human existence; what happens to us after death; angels and devils, heaven and hell. These speculations take different forms in different cultures and are generally expressed in mythic or metaphoric terms. People have always wanted to live within the framework of an explanatory story which enables them to feel that the world is not completely alien, but a place whose meaning or purpose they can understand.

So in response to the question of how the universe began, we have various well-known kinds of ancient stories: creation from chaos, found in various Indian and Near Eastern versions, including an early strand of Judaism; emergence from a cosmic egg; production by world-parents; 'earth-diver' myths, and many more. However in developed Judaism the original creation myth was superseded, as also in Christianity and Islam, by the belief that the universe began through a unique act of divine creation out of nothing (i.e. not out of anything). During the early centuries CE this ran alongside the Neoplatonist picture. In this the ultimate divine One, which is absolute Being, 'overflows' into non-being, thus giving rise to a universe compounded of being and non-being in a descending chain of forms of existence, from God at the top as perfect being which is also perfect goodness, down in diminishing degrees of being and goodness through the angelic realms, then humans, animals, plants, and finally minerals. Here there is no specific reason for creation. It is just the nature of infinite Being to overflow in this way.

But although the Neoplatonist picture was absorbed by a number of early Christian writers – including the very influential St Augustine – it occurs in their thought in tension with the different idea of a deliberate divine creation out of nothing, and it is this latter that eventually became the official doctrine. It provokes the question, 'Why did God create?' The motive is generally said to be love. God wanted to share existence, or wanted there to be created beings as objects of the divine love. However this initially attractive idea brings problems. For if – as the tradition also affirms – God was eternally perfect, lacking nothing, and hence incapable of being further enriched, God would have no need to create. On the other hand a God who *did* need to create would not be initially perfect. The dilemma can also affect the neighbouring doctrine of the Trinity. This is often held to explain how, 'prior' to creation, God can be love, the answer being that the three Persons of the Trinity eternally love one another. But if this mutual love within the divine society is sufficient then there is, once again, no need for further objects of love, no need to create. This popular version of the trinitarian doctrine thus undermines the equally popular idea of divine love as the motive for creation. It would seem more satisfactory simply to admit that we cannot conceive why an absolute and perfect God has created a universe.

A different response to this basic question comes from Hinduism. One of the most popular figures in Indian religious art is the dancing Shiva. The story of Shiva went through many developments and transformations, culminating in the lord Shiva as the ultimate power of life and death, saviour of the world by swallowing its poison, defeating the demons, overcoming death, teacher of yogic wisdom and source of all creativity, and yet at the same time terrible in his power, destroying as well as creating. The beginningless and endless life of the universe is Shiva's dance, a continuous act of creation and destruction as life gives way to death, and death to new life, in aeon after aeon. As dancing is an end in itself, done for its own sake and with no ulterior purpose, so the entire universe in both its creative and its destructive aspects is an end in itself. It is the eternal play of divine energy, the dance of life of which we are already a part, but in which we can also freely and gladly participate.

There are then different conceptions of the origin and hence the nature of the universe. The broad division among them is between those, mainly western, which think in terms of a divine creation out of nothing, thus defining the universe as being of a radically different order from the divine, and those others, mainly eastern, which think of the universe more pantheistically (i.e. all is God) or panentheistically (i.e. all is within God), as a beginningless and endless process which is itself an aspect of the divine life.

Both conceptions are speculations in which we impose our human categories on the unknown. We saw earlier (p. 27) that for scientific cosmology the existence of the universe is a sheer mystery, a mystery which science has in practice simply to ignore, starting instead with the given observable order of nature and proceeding from there. We may in the end have to conclude that, for religious thinking also, the existence of the universe is a sheer mystery to us. For why should we assume that we are capable of knowing everything?

And what about the end of things? Here again there are many different pictures, understood literally by some and mythologically by others. The different scriptures contain a vast range of accounts of heavens and hells, inhabited by a great variety of angelic and demonic beings. But the broad division among conceptions of the ultimate state is between notions, mainly but not solely western, of the eventual perfecting of human individuals, and hence ultimately of human society, in the presence of God, and notions, mainly but not solely eastern, of the eventual transcendence of individual selfhood as it merges into the divine life. More about all this in chapter 26. But,

> No one sees the beginning of things,
> but only the middle.
> Their end also is unseen.
> There is no reason to lament.[1]

THE BUDDHA'S 'UNANSWERED QUESTIONS'

The only major religion which acknowledges a large area of ignorance is Buddhism. I once had the opportunity to ask the Dalai Lama if there were any questions which Buddhism cannot answer. He smiled and said 'Yes,' offering as an example the question of why the universe exists, and he was not in the least embarrassed to confess ignorance about this. For an important part of the Buddha's teaching concerns the *avyakata*, the unanswered or undetermined questions. The list of ten propositions whose truth or falsity we do not know appears in Suttas 63 and 72 of the *Majjhima Nikaya* (and also elsewhere in the Pali canon):

1. *Bhagavad Gita* II, 28; Bolle, p. 25.

1. The universe is eternal.
2. The universe is not eternal.
3. The universe is (spatially) infinite.
4. The universe is not (spatially) infinite.
5. The soul (*jiva*) is identical with the body.
6. The soul is not identical with the body.
7. The Tathagata (i.e. a Buddha, or perfectly enlightened being) exists after death.
8. The Tathagata does not exist after death.
9. The Tathagata both exists and does not exist after death.
10. The Tathagata neither exists nor does not exist after death.

The questions which these propositions answer are live issues today: Was the big bang an absolute beginning, or part of an infinite series of expansions and contractions? Is the universe finite or infinite? Is the mind–brain identity theory correct or not? What is the ultimate fate of humanity when the creative process is finally completed? The Buddha said that we should not be concerned about these questions lest they distract us from the one great matter, which is to seek inner liberation. He told the parable of the man who has been pierced by a poisoned arrow but insists, before he will accept medical treatment, on knowing who shot the arrow, whether it was shot from a springbow or a crossbow, what the bow string and the shaft of the arrow are made of, from what kind of bird the feathers came . . . He is likely to die before he can get to know all this. And likewise, one who spends his time and energies seeking answers to the great metaphysical questions may well miss the pearl of great price, liberation, enlightenment, nirvana. For the quest for such knowledge 'is not connected with the goal, is not fundamental to the Brahma-faring, and does not conduce to turning away from, nor to dispassion, stopping, calming, super-knowledge, awakening, nor to nibbana'.[2]

Another issue is latent within the Buddha's unanswered questions, for they fall into two groups. One consists of those to which there is an answer, although we do not happen to know it. Thus the universe does or does not exist through infinite time, and either is or is not infinitely large, and the mind–brain identity theory either is or is not correct. But the other group consists of questions which have no correct answer because they are posed in terms which do not apply to this subject matter. Thus the question of whether a fully enlightened person exists after death is, according to the Buddha, posed in such a way that it has no correct answer. Note that this is not the question, 'What happens to you and me at death?' The Buddha's answer to that is the doctrine of

2. *Majjhima Nikaya* II, 63, 431; Horner, 1957, p. 101.

rebirth. The wrongly posed question is about *parinirvana*, final nirvana, beyond the series of earthly lives. The Buddha taught that the unenlightened mind lacks the experiential and conceptual resources with which to grasp this. This comes out in a conversation with a monk, Vacchagotta, who asks in what sphere an enlightened person arises after death:

> 'Arise', Vaccha, does not apply.
> Well then, good Gotama, does he not arise?[3]
> 'Does not arise', Vaccha, does not apply.
> Well then, good Gotama, does he both arise and not arise?
> 'Both arises and does not arise', Vaccha, does not apply.
> Well then, good Gotama, does he neither arise nor not arise?
> 'Neither arises nor does not arise', Vaccha, does not apply.

Vaccha then expresses his bewilderment and disappointment, and the Buddha replies, 'You ought to be at a loss, Vaccha, you ought to be bewildered. For, Vaccha, this *dhamma* [this truth] is deep, difficult to see, difficult to understand, peaceful, excellent, beyond dialectics, subtle, intelligible to the wise',[4] referring all the time to human destiny beyond the series of bounded lives. He illustrates the notion of a question which is so posed that it has no answer by asking Vaccha, 'When a flame is quenched, in which direction has the flame gone – north, south, east, or west?' Clearly not in any direction. Likewise none of the options that human thought can supply can answer the question, 'What happens to a perfectly enlightened being beyond death?' At first sight, the flame illustration would suggest that the Buddha is saying that the enlightened being does not go anywhere because he ceases to exist. But that this is not his meaning becomes clear when he goes on to say that 'Freed from denotation by consciousness is the Tathagata, Vaccha, he is deep, immeasurable, unfathomable as the great ocean'.[5] And elsewhere he explicitly rejects the non-existence option: 'There are some recluses and brahmans who misrepresent me untruly, vainly, falsely, not in accordance with fact, saying: "The recluse Gotama is a nihilist, he lays down the cutting off, the destruction, the disappearance of the existent entity". But as this, monks, is just what I am not, as this is just what I do not say, therefore these worthy recluses and brahmans misrepresent me untruly, vainly, falsely, and not in accordance with fact'.[6] *Parinirvana*, the final state, simply cannot be conceived in our present human terms.

3. The Buddha's personal name was Gautama (in Sanskrit), Gotama (in Pali).
4. *Majjhima Nikaya* II, 63, 487; Horner, 1957, p. 165.
5. Ibid., p. 166.
6. *Majjhima Nikaya* I, 22, 140; Horner, 1954, p. 180.

LIVING ON A NEED-TO-KNOW BASIS

We saw, in connection with our awareness of the physical world, that our senses only respond to those aspects of the environment that are relevant to us as vulnerable animal organisms seeking to survive and flourish. Vast ranges of cosmic radiation, of light and sound waves, and of chemical differences, are excluded by the inherent limitations of our sensory equipment. And so we live in an enormously simplified version of the world, the version in which we are equipped to live. In other words our cognitive equipment functions on a 'need-to-know' basis.

I suggest that the same is true of our nature as spiritual beings. According to the world religions we exist not only within our familiar natural environment but also within a supra-natural environment. As we saw earlier (pp. 37–8), because of its value-laden character we are able, as free personal beings, to shut this out of our consciousness. But even when we allow the fifth dimension of reality to enter our experience, much remains utterly mysterious to us. Going beyond questions about the origin and structure of the physical universe, we do not know what happens to us after death. All that we know, if our big picture is basically correct, is that nothing good that has been created in human life will ever be lost. But although we have guesses, hunches, theories about that fulfilment, we are very probably (as the Buddha suggested) incapable at present of conceiving its nature. We do not know how the sufferings and sorrows of life, the agonies and despairs, can become steps on a long journey leading eventually to that fulfilment, as they will if the cosmic optimism of the world religions is justified. We have our theories, but they are only theories.[7] However we do not need at this stage of our existence to know the solution to these mysteries. To become aware of the divine reality here and now by awakening to the fifth dimension of our own being is to begin to live in trust, trust in the (from our human point of view) friendly, serendipitous character of the vast process of the universe. This is not a faith wherein no harm can befall us in this present life, or those we love, but a faith that ultimately, in Lady Julian's words, 'all shall be well, and all shall be well, and all manner of thing shall be well'.

Notice that the 'conflicting truth-claims' of the different religions are concerned with questions to which, if we are entirely honest, we all know that we do not know the answers! Pretending however to knowledge that they cannot have, some traditions and sub-traditions affirm as certain that the universe began through an act of divine

7. I have developed such a theory in *Evil and the God of Love*.

creation out of nothing, others that it is a divine emanation, yet others that it is a beginningless and endless process. Again, some affirm that at death we are translated to heaven or hell or purgatory, others that we live again many times on earth or in other spheres of existence. Some affirm the eventual perfecting of the individual ego, others an eventual transcendence of ego-existence in union with the divine reality. Some affirm that all human souls will reach the final fulfilment, others that only a fortunate minority will. But if we can accept that these are speculations, we both allow others to have their own different speculations, and are also freed to apply critical intelligence to them all.

This involves a downgrading of religious dogmas to a less than absolute status. Here there is, once again, a thought-provoking teaching of the Buddha, that religious doctrines are not ends in themselves but are 'skilful means' (*upaya*) to aid us on our way to enlightenment. As such they will sooner or later have served their purpose and should be discarded. He told the parable of the raft, in which a traveller comes to a wide stretch of water. The side he is on is dangerous, but the other side is safe. However there is no bridge or boat. So he collects grass, sticks and branches to make a raft, and crosses to the other side. Because the raft has been so useful, he lifts it onto his head and carries it with him. But, says the Buddha, he should leave it behind. It has served its purpose and now can only be a hindrance. 'You, O monks, who understand the Teaching's similitude to a raft, you should let go even of good teachings, how much more of false ones.'[8]

This is something that is also well understood within Hinduism, in which the different stages of life are recognized, and in which it may be appropriate to direct one's devotion to different gods at different times and in different circumstances. Applying the principle within Christianity, at a certain stage of spiritual growth one may find it helpful, even necessary, to hold steadfastly to the idea of the incarnation, the Trinity, the atonement, the Virgin Birth, the bodily resurrection and ascension of Jesus and his second coming, the primacy of the Popes as successors to St Peter, or the absolute authority of Church or Bible, or the efficacy of prayer to Mary and the saints. But believers who are spiritually and intellectually alive find that their beliefs change over the decades. A different way of seeing things can gradually develop within us. Ideas that were important and sustaining in adolescence, in the first flush of conversion, in some life crisis, or whilst living within a particular community or a particular set of circumstances, may lose their grip and

8. *Majjhima Nikaya* I, 22, 135; Nyanaponika, 1994, p. 33.

be either discarded or (more often) allowed quietly to fall into the background. Although furiously attacked by fundamentalist believers as apostasy, this is normally a healthy and mind-expanding process of growth.

So because different religious beliefs may promote response to the Real in different people at different times, alien ideas should generally be tolerated by those who do not share them. But there is an important limit to this. Beliefs which, when acted upon, can cause harm to others should not be tolerated. To take two examples from the Christian tradition (for we are more entitled to criticize our own than others'), the teaching of the Dutch Reformed Church in South Africa in the apartheid era that black people are inherently inferior to whites, or the centuries-long Christian belief that the Jews are guilty of deicide and deserve punishment, have been morally intolerable. On a less immediately harmful level, there are deeply entrenched theological beliefs which imply the unique superiority of one's own religious community. There is the Christian belief that Christianity was founded directly by God in person and is thus God's own religion. There is the belief that the Jews are God's Chosen People, standing in a uniquely privileged relationship to God. There is the belief that the Qur'an is God's final and definitive revelation, so that other revelations are included and superseded, and non-theistic faiths totally false. There is the Hindu belief that the Vedas are the eternal truth, superior to all other truths. And there is the Buddhist belief that 'this is the only Way. There is none other for the purity of vision,'[9] with the implication that other ways are useless or at least inferior. Of course by no means all adherents of each religion treat their own as uniquely superior. There are Christians who regard the idea that Jesus was the Son of God as a metaphorical, not a literal, truth; Jews who hold that all peoples are in their different ways God's chosen people; Muslims who not only affirm the status of the other People of the Book (Jews and Christians), but who see the sacred scriptures of the east as expressions of the divine Word as well as the Arabic Qur'an received through the prophet Muhammad; Hindus who regard all religions as 'different paths up the same mountain'; and Buddhists (such as, for example, the present Dalai Lama) who see the other world religions also as ways to enlightenment. Nevertheless the absolute and exclusive aspect of the official beliefs of the different traditions continues to divide communities and families and continues to provide a religious justification for human conflict.

9. *Dhammapada* 20; Narada, p. 221.

WHAT THEN *DO* WE NEED TO KNOW?

What we need to know is how to live here and now. And it is noticeable that whereas the metaphysical questions about which we can only speculate divide the religions, their basic moral principles unite them. I am speaking here of their *basic* ethical teachings, not of the detailed codes that have been created within different societies at different times and in different cultural, economic, political and climatic circumstances. These inevitably reflect those circumstances and should be allowed to change as the circumstances change. But because these commandments are usually embodied in sacred scriptures, it is very difficult to revise them, and more often they are officially retained whilst being in practice reinterpreted. And even this process of making them mean something other than what they say is usually a generation or more behind the change of moral outlook that has prompted the reinterpretation.

In contrast to this, it is the basic teaching of *all* the world religions that we should behave towards others as we would wish others to behave towards us. This has appealed to the human conscience in every part of the world and in every generation: 'One should never do that to another which one regards as injurious to oneself' (the Hindu *Mahabharata*, Anushana parva, 113:7); One should go about 'treating all creatures in the world as he himself would be treated' (the Jain *Kritanga Sutra*, I, 11:33); 'As a mother cares for her son, all her days, so towards all living things a man's mind should be all-embracing' (the Buddhist *Sutta Nipata*, 149); 'Do not do to others what you would not like yourself' (the *Analects* of Confucius, XII: 2); A good man should 'regard others' gains as if they were his own, and their losses in the same way' (the Taoist *Thai Shang*, 3); 'That nature only is good when it shall not do to unto another whatever is not good for its own self' (The Zoroastrian *Dadistan-i-dinik*, 94: 5); 'As ye would that men should do to you, do ye also to them likewise' (Jesus in Luke 6:31); 'What is hateful to yourself do not do to your fellow man. That is the whole of the Torah' (*Babylonian Talmud*, Shabbath 31a); 'No man is a true believer unless he desires for his brother that which he desires for himself' (Muhammad in the Hadith *Ibn Madja*, Introduction, 9); 'Lay not on any soul a load which ye would not wish to be laid upon you, and desire not for anyone the things ye would not desire for yourselves' (the Bahá'í *Gleanings from the Writings of Bahá'u'lláh*, 66, 127); and going behind the post-axial faiths to 'primal' religion, 'Grandfather Great Spirit, all over the world the faces of living ones are alike. With tenderness they have come up out of the ground. Give us the strength to understand, and the eyes to see. Teach us to walk the soft Earth as relatives to all that live' (Sioux prayer, in Roberts, p. 184).

This is the common moral outlook of the great traditions. The difficulties come when it is translated into the specific norms and laws of a particular society. For there are different ways of being human, some (mostly western and northern) more individualistic, others (mostly eastern and southern) more communal. Again, metaphysical convictions affect such life-and-death issues as birth-control, abortion, euthanasia. So the gradual formation of a much-to-be-desired global ethic will be extremely difficult. It will obviously have to go beyond the basic principle of valuing others as one values oneself to a range of middle-level principles. But the more concrete these become the more they will encounter presently unresolvable ground-level differences of moral insight and judgement. It is much easier to formulate universal 'Thou shalt nots' (ruling out, for example, murder, torture, exploitation) than to formulate universal 'Thou shalts'. However this is not a treatise on ethics, and I have to resist the temptation to pursue these issues further here.[10]

10. To pursue these issues further see, for example, Hans Küng and Jurgen Moltmann, eds., *The Ethics of World Religions and Human Rights* (London: SCM Press and Philadelphia: Trinity Press International, 1990); Hans Küng and Karl-Josef Kuschel, eds., *A Global Ethic* (London: SCM Press, 1993); and Hans Küng, ed., *Yes to a Global Ethic* (London: SCM Press, 1996).

25

LIVING WITHIN A TRUE MYTH

MYTH AND METAPHOR

In ordinary conversation to say that something is a myth is to say that it is not true. Someone might say, for example, that it is a myth that tall people are more intelligent than short people; or that economic circumstances determined the outcome of the American civil war. The point now is not whether these propositions are true or false – which is why I have chosen one that is clearly false and one that is quite possibly true – but that this is how the word 'myth' is commonly used. And so it is assumed that when a biblical story, or a religious belief, is declared to be a myth it is being dismissed as bunk. But this is not how the word has come to be used by anthropologists, sociologists, psychologists, theologians and philosophers of religion, although there is no one agreed way in which they all use it. But in the sense in which I shall use it here, there are true as well as false myths.

I mean by a true myth a story, or a description, that is not literally true but that nevertheless expresses and tends to evoke an appropriate attitude towards the subject of the myth. As a trivial example, 'The devil got into him', said about a small boy caught kicking the cat, is not asserted as being literally true. It is however, in the sense in which I am using the term, mythologically true. Again, 'You're a genius' might be said to someone who has discovered how to work the video-cassette recorder: it does not literally take a genius to do this, but nevertheless the description successfully expresses the admiration and thanks that it is meant to express.

Turning now to well-known religious myths, the stories of the creation of the world in seven days, and of the fall of Adam and Eve and their expulsion from the Garden of Eden, are not literally true, but may nevertheless be mythologically true as a way of saying that the world is a divine creation and that humans are very imperfect beings living in a very imperfect world. In these cases what the myth says can also be said in literal terms, though not so vividly. Again, Hinduism is rich in mythology. Its central myth is that of the sacred mountain, Mount Meru (or sometimes a sacred banyan tree), at the centre of the world. This both separates and joins heaven, earth and the realm beneath the earth. There is no such literal mountain, or tree, but the idea points to a universal connectedness of the whole of reality, in contrast to the monotheistic dualism of a creator God and a created universe. In each case the value of the myth is that it speaks in a concrete and visualizable way that appeals to the imagination and can thus seep into the mind, usually affecting our attitudes more powerfully and pervasively than an abstract statement. Thus far then, we can say that the significance of myths lies in their presentational power rather than in uttering truths which cannot be otherwise expressed.

There is, however, a sense in which myths do communicate something that cannot be otherwise expressed, for myths are expanded metaphors. The literal statement that in kicking the cat the boy was being cruel can be expressed by the metaphorical statement that such behaviour is devilish, which can in turn be developed into the brief story of the devil getting into him. Metaphors involve a crossing over of meaning: one term is illuminated by attaching to it some of the associations of another. Thus 'The chairman ploughed through the agenda' says more than just that the committee successively discussed its various items. The picture of the chairman *ploughing* through the agenda can indicate to many a dogged determination to move the meeting forward, holding fast to the agenda. (This could of course be either true, in the sense of being an appropriate picture, or false.) Thus far the metaphorical statement can be spelled out, more lengthily, in literal terms. But we must note that ploughing may have partially different associations for different people, so that the statement may evoke a range of differing responses. This openness of the web of associations prevents metaphors from being definitively translated into literal terms, for we cannot limit their field of possible associations. As expanded metaphors, myths thus lack fixed semantic boundaries and so cannot be fully substituted by literal statements. But this is the only sense in which myths are irreducibly mythical. It is a mistake to think –

as many vaguely do – that myths can express deep truths that cannot be expressed in any other way. Their mysteriousness consists simply in the indeterminate range of associations that they may trigger, preventing them from being pinned down to a single literal translation.

THE USE AND MISUSE OF MYTHS

Myths, accepted as such, can be extremely valuable if, or in so far as, they are true, and extremely dangerous if, or in so far as, they are false. For example the idea of America, God's own country, the Land of the Free, has united a vast and disparate nation and stirred a healthy devotion to it. On the other hand this same mythic idea added patriotic fervour to such episodes as the McCarthy witchhunts of the 1950s and was used to drum up support for the disastrous Vietnam war from the early 1960s to the early 1970s. Again the idea of Britannia, proudly ruling the waves and guiding the world, has inspired a patriotic dedication to public service, but was also used to glorify colonial exploitation and oppression.

In many cases no harm is done if religious people believe, mistakenly, that their myths are literal truth. But in some cases a great deal of harm is done. This typically happens in connection with the ownership of sacred sites whose sanctity is guaranteed by ancient myths. For example the Hindu mythological epic the *Ramayana* contains many stories about the hero Rama or Ram who in due course came to be seen as an incarnation of Vishnu. In Mogul times a number of mosques were built on the sites of Hindu temples, and one in particular, in Ayodhya, has come to be identified as Ram's birthplace. In modern times this myth has been seized upon by extreme Hindu nationalists – the same group of people who were responsible for the assassination of Gandhi – as an opportunity to incite Hindus to hatred against their Muslim neighbours. In 1992 they succeeded in inciting a vast mob to attack and destroy the mosque. This naturally alarmed the religious minorities – Sikhs and Christians as well as Muslims – and greatly exacerbated communal tension throughout the country. The political leaders who incited the mob were probably well aware of the mythical status of the story, but because the mass of their followers accepted it as historical fact, they could exploit it to undermine the secular and pluralist character of India as established in its constitution and to promote instead their own Hindu supremacist agenda.

Again, further west, it is very possible that Abraham, revered as their great ancestral figure by Jews, Christians and Muslims alike, was not a historical individual. There may have been a particular person, some three thousand years ago, beyond the reach of firm historical evidence, who constituted a grain of fact around which the Abraham saga developed. But insistence on the historical character of the stories, guaranteeing the sacred character of Hebron as Abraham's supposed burial place, has provided a focus for ever renewed Jewish–Muslim enmity, the worst moment being the murder by Baruch Goldstein of twenty-nine Muslim worshippers in the Cave of the Patriarchs in 1995.

But the figure of Abraham, thus available for use by literalists as a point of division and strife, can also be used as a point of meeting and reconciliation. For Abraham, as the common mythic ancestor of Judaism, Christianity and Islam, can be a powerful symbol of their kinship and a patron of friendly dialogue between them. Karl-Josef Kuschel has recently used the figure of Abraham in this way. He is clear that the value of the symbol does not depend upon any historical thesis. 'Anyone who wants to "grasp" Abraham purely historically', he says, 'will not understand anything about him . . . The Abraham stories are the stories of the faith of a people which is explaining to itself God's relationship with it by means of these stories . . . The Abraham stories in the Hebrew bible . . . are "proclamations", not historiography.'[1] For Kuschel it is thus irrelevant whether, or to what extent, the Abraham saga is historical, which is usually a way of acknowledging, without directly saying so, that it is probably not historical. What is important is the healing and uniting power of the myth. And its healing power is enhanced by the openness of myth to selective use. We can use it to convey a central idea without having to give equal weight to any irrelevant or unhelpful elements in the story.

THE JEWISH MYTH

A major example of a true myth is the central story in the Hebrew scriptures of their deliverance from slavery in Egypt, their long wandering in the wilderness, and their settlement in the promised land. It is a story of God's miraculous interventions on behalf of his specially treasured people. Behind it there probably lies the historical fact of a relatively small Hebrew group coming out of Egypt and settling in Palestine, gradually establishing themselves by a mixture of battles and alliances, and eventually coalescing with other Hebrew tribes who were already there. But the great imaginative epic, developed by generations of priestly storytellers, became the unifying myth of the people, expressing their faith in God. It is this myth that religious Jews celebrate

1. Kuschel, pp. 4–5.

year by year in the great feasts of Passover, Shavuot, Sukkot, Purim, Rosh Hashanah, Yom Kippur. But to what extent do Jews have to believe in the historical accuracy of the ancient story? For many, probably most, its historicity – except in the general sense that the ancient Hebrews did settle successfully in Palestine – is not to be insisted on. What is important is their belief in God's calling, protection and guidance. The power of the myth lies in the present, not the past, as the great festivals come round again and again as moments of encounter with God in the community's life today. A leading rabbi, Irving Greenberg, says that 'the Exodus inaugurated the biblical era of the Jewish people's history. In Judaism's teaching, the Exodus is not a one-time event but a norm by which all of life should be judged and guided. The Exodus is an "orienting event" – an event that sets in motion and guides the Jewish way (and, ultimately, humanity's way) towards the Promised Land – an earth set free and perfected.'[2]

If our big picture is basically correct, this Jewish way of life, developed by the rabbis over the centuries, is life within a true myth, a myth that has its own distinctive spiritual beauty and sustaining power. It is a true myth because it enables the community to become conscious, above all on the high holy days, of living in God's presence. But within the myth the rabbis have exercised the freedom that myth bestows, playing with its themes, splitting hairs in their interpretations of the Torah, telling sometimes humorous stories about God, laughing at themselves and at one another.

But when Jews take their story literally it can have disastrous consequences. Accepting it as myth, the appalling examples that it includes can be tacitly set aside. But taking the narrative literally, Jews have to believe that God inflicted plague after plague upon innocent Egyptian families, slaughtering all their first-born children, with the added horror that God had deliberately caused Pharaoh to refuse to let the Hebrews go in order to punish both him and his subjects: 'I have hardened his heart and the heart of his servants, that I may show these signs of mine among them, and that you may tell in the hearing of your son and of your son's son how I have made sport of the Egyptians and what signs I have done among them; that you may know that I am the Lord.'[3] Such a god is a role model for ruthless tyrants but not a 'light to lighten the gentiles'. The story then proceeds to the merciless genocide of the inhabitants of Palestine. The Lord commands Saul to 'go and smite Amalek, and utterly destroy all that they have; do not spare them, but kill both man and woman, infant and suckling, ox and sheep, camel and ass',[4] and causes the sun to stand still for a whole day in order to

2. Greenberg, pp. 17, 25.
3. Exodus 10:1–2.
4. I Samuel 15:3.

give the Israelites more time to slaughter their enemies.[5] It was this passage that Yigal Amir, who in 1995 assassinated Yitzhak Rabin, the peace-making prime minister of Israel, cited in his defence: 'Amir explained that he would have no problem killing babies and children as it is written in [the Book of] Joshua, in the name of conquering land for Israel.'[6] Indeed the entire Jewish supremacist movement in modern Israel takes its inspiration from a literal construal of the myth of the Chosen People and their Promised Land.

We see in Judaism then both the wonderful life-sustaining power and beauty of myth and also the appalling danger that can come from taking it literally.

THE CHRISTIAN MYTH

The same is true of Christianity. We have our own narrative of the human story, beginning with creation, continuing through redemption, with the cross of Christ as its pivotal point, and proceeding to the End, God's grand finale. To say that this is myth, formed by the religious imagination in response to the person of Jesus, is not to say that Jesus never existed, but that the way in which his significance has been understood has been an exercise in mythological thinking. It is certain that there was a Jesus of Nazareth, living in the first third of the first century CE. Some of the stories about what he said and did must be historically true, some partly so, others not at all, and there has long been an academic industry devoted to sorting them into these categories. Such weighing of probabilities is the kind of work that lends itself to keen argument and debate, to the formation of rival schools of thought and to changing fashions of opinion. So the following picture can only reflect what I personally regard as the most reliable New Testament scholarship since the critical rediscovery of the Jewishness of Jesus in the 1970s.[7]

It seems likely that during the two or three years of his public ministry Jesus was one of several itinerant Galilean preachers and healers who stressed God's fatherly love and were critical of the more legalistic religion of the priesthood at the Jerusalem Temple. He was intensely conscious of God's holy and loving presence, a presence that was as real to him as the hills and lake of Galilee. To live in this consciousness is already to be in God's kingdom or rule, and he sought to bring others to share that consciousness and to live the life of the Kingdom in the here and now. He shared the contemporary Jewish

5. Joshua 10:13–14.
6. *Los Angeles Times*, 24 January 1996.
7. Some of the works by New Testament scholars on which I have relied most (listed in the bibliography) are Sanders 1985 and 1993, Schillebeeckx, Fredriksen, Houlden, Charlesworth, Casey.

apocalyptic sense of existing in a moment of supreme crisis, expecting God soon to intervene decisively in human history, bringing the present phase to an end and instituting the divine kingdom on earth: 'Jesus came into Galilee, preaching the gospel of God, and saying, "The time is fulfilled, and the kingdom of God is at hand; repent, and believe in the gospel.'[8] It seems that he felt called by God to the unique role of the final prophet before the impending Day of the Lord, a role that gave him a central place in God's providence. It did not however amount to his being God incarnate. Jesus did not think of himself as God, and can have had no conception of the later Christian doctrine according to which he was the second person of a divine Trinity. This would have been impossible to a faithful Jew. 'Why do you call me good?' he is reported to have said, 'No one is good but God alone.'[9]

But did not Jesus make a claim to deity when he said, 'He who has seen me has seen the Father' (John 14:9) and 'I and the Father are one' (John 10:30)? The answer of modern New Testament scholarship is 'No'. These enormously influential sayings were put into his mouth some sixty or more years later by a Christian writer expressing the developed theology of his part of the church. Even very conservative scholars today agree that the deity-claiming sayings of the fourth gospel should not be attributed to the historical Jesus. But again, was not Jesus the Son of God? Here again, modern historical scholarship has thrown a flood of light. The term 'son of God', which seems to the modern mind so momentous, was familiar throughout the ancient world. It was applied to pharaohs and emperors, to great philosophers and great heroes; and within Judaism it was a familiar metaphor for anyone who was a special servant of God. 'Son of' meant 'in the spirit of' or 'specially blessed by'. And so Adam was God's son, the Hebrew people as a whole were God's son, their ancient kings were enthroned as son of God – hence the enthronement formula, 'You are my son, today I have begotten you';[10] and indeed any truly pious Jew could be called a son of God. But within Judaism the term was always used metaphorically.

Jesus then was wholly human. But he was one of the most remarkable, charismatic and God-filled human beings we know. His intense awareness of God was so powerful that in his presence people began, often for the first time, to be genuinely conscious of God as a living reality. And in his moral teaching he spelled out what it is to live consciously in God's presence, trusting God's loving providence and giving oneself freely as an agent of the divine love.

But the message that God was about to sweep away all earthly rule

8. Mark 1:15.
9. Mark 10:18.
10. Psalm 2:7.

– proclaimed by a popular preacher to whom the crowds flocked – was alarming both to the Roman authorities and to their clients, the Jewish leaders in Jerusalem. This was a volatile period of intermittent revolts which Rome was accustomed to squash without mercy. So when Jesus went up to Jerusalem to challenge the Temple priests in the name of God, they collaborated with the Romans in arresting and trying him, and Roman soldiers executed him by the standard method for insurrectionists, public crucifixion.

But the powerful memory of Jesus and his teaching continued to inspire many of his followers, who now constituted a small 'new religious movement' within diverse first-century Judaism. They fervently awaited Jesus' return in glory as God's agent instituting the kingdom on earth. But as this was delayed year after year the expectation faded, and Jesus was gradually transformed in their thinking from the prophet of a future historical salvation to the agent of a present inner salvation. His spirit within them, the spirit of his life and teachings, was objectified as the Holy Spirit, the third member of a divine Trinity. And the Jesus cult developed into the cult of the risen Christ, transfigured and deified.

With this the Christian myth was born. God had descended in the person of his son to be born on earth as a child, had died to atone for our sins, and had risen to continued life on earth and then up into heaven, to return again in majesty on the last day. In familiar words from the creeds (which date from the fourth century), it is the story of God Almighty, maker of heaven and earth, and of his only Son Jesus Christ our Lord, who existed before all ages and was born on earth of the Holy Spirit and the Virgin Mary. He suffered under Pontius Pilate, was crucified for the remission of sins, rose again on the third day, ascended into heaven where he sits at the right hand of God the Father, thence to come again to judge the living and the dead. And revolving around this central story are many sub-themes – the revolt of Satan; the fall of Adam and Eve; the work of angels, kings and prophets, saints and martyrs; and the continuing holiness of the church and its hierarchy.

In the early days, whilst the spirit of Jesus was still strong – in the form of memories of his personal presence and influence – the Jesus movement constituted a powerful stream of new life, liberating men and women from the endemic fear of demons and giving them new hope and confidence. But the establishment of Christianity in the fourth century as the religion of the empire, and the church's institutionalization as partner of the state, changed its character. Through the long medieval period, the divine authority of Christ the King was mediated through the emperor as his civil representative on earth. The picture of Jesus as our brother and teacher was overlaid by the picture of Christ sitting on the throne of judgement, with the torments of hell as a terrible possibility for the disobedient.[11] But beginning around the fourteenth century the church's absolute authority began to be shaken by intellectual influences from the Renaissance and later the Enlightenment. In the new mental climate Jesus again became in the public consciousness the symbol of love, the embodiment of divine grace and mercy. And so the Christian myth is now for most of us the story that God so loved the world that he sent his son to redeem it by entering the depths of our human suffering and rising triumphantly beyond it. Secure in the knowledge of God's love we are made free to love one another. And if our big picture is basically correct, this is a true myth, drawing us from natural self-centredness towards a radical re-centring in the love and service of the heavenly Father, who is the authentic manifestation to us of the Ultimate, the Real.

However, when the Christian myth is taken literally its central theme develops dangerous implications. For if Jesus was literally God, in the sense of being the second Person of the Godhead living a human life, it follows that Christianity alone among the world religions was founded by God in person, and is thus God's own religion, uniquely superior to all others. This conviction was used to validate Europe's conquest of most of what today we call the Third World, carrying off many of its inhabitants as slaves, exploiting its economies and destroying its cultures. The idea that Jesus was God likewise validated the Christian persecution of the Jews, who were held guilty of deicide, thus creating a deep-seated prejudice within the European psyche which continued in the secular anti-Semitism of the nineteenth and twentieth centuries, culminating in the Holocaust of the 1940s. When taken literally, the Christian myth becomes a supremacist ideology which, in conjunction with human greed, pride and prejudice, has used the name of Christ to justify profoundly unchristlike acts.

LIVING CONSCIOUSLY WITHIN A TRUE MYTH

Yet the Christian myth has also proved in century after century to be powerfully salvific. Can we then continue to live within it whilst being aware of its mythic character?

Let us take the two high points of the Christian year, Christmas and Easter. The Christmas readings and prayers, hymns and carols, language

11. For more about this period see, for example, Nineham, 1993.

and greetings, customs and decorations, celebrate a beautiful, inspiring, uplifting picture, but not literal history. It is unlikely that Jesus was born on 25 December (which was the date of a pre-Christian winter festival), or that he was born in 1 CE (more probably 4 or 5 BCE), or that he was born at Bethlehem (probably brought into the story to fulfil a supposed prophecy), or that shepherds came to worship at his cradle, or that wise men from the east followed a miraculous star to greet him (the entire traditional birth narrative being a product of pious imagination), or that he had no human father (a mythic theme that attached itself to many great figures in the ancient world), or that he was God incarnate (an idea that he would have regarded as blasphemous). Given all this, how is one to respond to the Christmas event? One can either opt out, because the Christmas story is not literally true, or one can opt in, accepting the myth as evocative poetry, stirring the emotions, expanding the imagination, warming the heart, and all in the direction of an enhanced sense of the gracious and loving presence of the heavenly Father, who is our human face of the ultimately Real. Probably a majority today within the officially Christian populations, at least of Europe, North America and Australasia, already read the Christmas story in this way. But in order consciously to celebrate Christmas in this spirit we have to learn how to embrace and rejoice in true myth. For the habit of binary thinking has so restricted us to the alternatives of straight fact or straight fiction that we find it difficult to feast on poetry, allowing emotion free rein, rejoicing in the magical powers of the imagination, and glorying in a great mythic story as our human way of relating to that which transcends all human thought.

Similarly, at Easter the readings, hymns, prayers and greetings celebrate the renewal of life, light after darkness, joy after pain, resurrection after death. It is unlikely that Jesus came physically back to life after his crucifixion, that he walked around Galilee and Judea for forty days, and then ascended bodily into the sky; or (for this is likewise part of the gospel story) that at the same time 'the tombs also were opened, and many bodies of the saints who had fallen asleep [i.e. had died] were raised, and coming out of the tombs after his resurrection they went into the holy city [Jerusalem] and appeared to many'.[12] This part of the story is interesting because the writer does not hesitate to claim that the event was seen by many, in spite of the fact that if such an earth-shakingly extraordinary thing had indeed happened it would certainly have registered in the consciousness and records of the time. But it was possible for a Christian scribe, writing forty to fifty years after Jesus' death, to accept without question the miraculous stories that

12. Matthew 27:52–3.

had developed within his community. The earliest resurrection experience of which we have a first-hand account is that of St Paul on the Damascus road, two or three years after Jesus' crucifixion, when he was blinded by a bright light and heard a voice (probably inwardly: 'those who were with me saw the light but did not hear the voice',[13]) but did not see any resurrected body.[14] This non-physical experience was equated by Paul with the appearances to Peter and the twelve,[15] and Barnabas likewise described this Damascus road experience as Paul's 'seeing of Jesus'.[16] It therefore seems probable that the original experience was of the same kind. But the glory of Easter does not depend on knowing the exact nature of the event that came to be called Jesus' resurrection. Its glory is the celebration of the priority of life and goodness over death and evil. As such it is a central aspect of the Christian myth, and if our big picture is correct, this is a true myth, opening us to the reality of the Transcendent.

But can 'ordinary believers' be expected to move from a literal to a metaphorical understanding of some of the central themes of the Christian story? Many have already done so in relation to the biblical creation myth, although the change was originally a matter of profound alarm and bitter controversy. But can Christians now be expected to come to see Jesus, no longer as God incarnate, but as our brother, one of us although far ahead of the rest of us in his openness to God? There are two questions here: 'Can this happen today?' and, 'Can it happen gradually during the next fifty to a hundred years?' As to the first question, the fact is that some church members can, and others, including most of the church leaders, cannot. But it is very difficult to know what is going on in other people's minds. It is one thing to join wholeheartedly on Sunday in traditional Christian worship, with the ancient absolutist language still enshrined in sacred liturgy and song, and another thing to hold seriously, so as to be prepared to justify in the broad daylight of ordinary life, the idea that the historical Jesus of Nazareth was literally God. If asked in a survey, many people will say 'Yes' to the official formulation; but if pressed to say what this means – whether, for example, Jesus was God's son in the literal sense that half of his chromosomes came from Mary and half from God the Father – they are likely to have doubts and, if questioned further, to retreat, or advance, through a further series of qualifications which eventually empty the original formulation of its content. But of course very many church members do not ask themselves what the traditional language means, and there are always clergy and theologians ready to assure them that they need not trouble themselves about such questions. So it

13. Acts 22:9.
14. Acts 9:3–8; 22:6–11; 26:12–18.
15. I Corinthians 15:8.
16. Acts 9:27.

may be too much to ask the core church members in the present generation to see the Christian story as a true myth. But will Christians in fifty or a hundred years time look back and see that the understanding of divine incarnation as a true myth gradually spread in the same way that the idea of evolution, and hence of the mythic character of many Bible narratives, gradually spread so as to become generally accepted? My guess is that just as the evolution debate left, in effect, two Christianities – one fundamentalist-evangelical and the other liberal-progressive – so the debate about the unique superiority of Christianity as having been founded personally by God will develop and intensify that division. Fundamentalist-evangelical Christianity will continue to appeal strongly to believers who need a simple black-and-white certainty, but liberal-progressive Christianity, if it can reconfigure itself so as to be religiously realistic, has the possibility of appealing to that large section of the secular world that is nevertheless open to the signals of transcendence which are all about us. But as to what will in fact happen, we can only wait and see!

26

DEATH AND BEYOND

OUR CONTEMPORARY CONFUSION

The modern west has largely lost the belief, once so powerful, in a life after death. Even theologians today usually try to avoid the subject. This is not just due to a healthy agnosticism about the form that any such life might take, but often, more basically, because they often fail to appreciate the logical connection between this and their other beliefs.

But any big picture which includes the Transcendent and affirms that the ultimately Real is (from our human point of view) benign must involve a conception of the structure of the universe that is compatible with this. For the religious claim is that human life, with all its pain and suffering as well as all its pleasures and joys, is part of a cosmic process in which the suffering will finally have become, retrospectively, an element in a process moving, on a vast scale, to a limitlessly good future. This is not compatible with the complete obliteration of moral and spiritual beings – human beings – at the end of their present earthly life.

But, it is often asked, is not the desire to survive death a selfish desire? Should we not seek fulfilment in this present life, accepting its brief and fleeting character and living it to the full while it lasts? Surely the happy and self-fulfilled do not need to crave immortality. And it has indeed been found that generally those who have lived a full and satisfying life are least concerned by the approach of death.[1]

Many of us, including those who read and who write such books as this, are glad to be alive, whether or not we shall cease to exist at death. We may even approach Marcus Aurelius' ideal of 'the soul which, at

1. The full pattern of attitudes to death is however complex. For the modern psychological research see, for example, Schulz, 1985.

whatever moment the call comes for release from the body, is equally ready to face extinction, dispersion, or survival'.[2] But it does not follow from this that a religious interpretation of the universe need not involve any conception of further life beyond death. To think otherwise is, consciously or unconsciously, to occupy an elitist position that forgets that large numbers of our fellow humans have been much less fortunate than ourselves in the lottery of life. This is the point that I made earlier in commenting on humanism and on non-realist forms of religion. Millions of men, women and children who have died early of malnutrition, or have been devoured by famine or plague, slaughtered in war or genocide, ground down in slavery, gravely damaged by abuse in childhood, or otherwise deprived of the development of the human potential within them, have been unable to rejoice with us in the goodness of this life, as also are the multitudes who suffer these evils now. When we look beyond our own personal circumstances to the condition of humanity as a whole through the past millennia and today, we have to face the fact that belief in a loving God, or in a benign universe, is inherently committed to some kind of continuation of the human story beyond the point of bodily death.

TRADITIONAL POSSIBILITIES

The question then for a religious big picture, is 'What kind of continuation?' The answer is by no means obvious and a number of rival conceptions offer themselves.

Within Judaism, Christianity and Islam there is the belief that the soul, as the present conscious self, continues to exist after the death of the body, either living for ever as spirit, or being at some stage reunited with its physical body, or acquiring a new 'spiritual' body. The conclusion of the human story, according to these traditions, is eternal life in heaven, or in heaven via an intermediate state, or in hell.

This conception involves immense difficulties which no doubt account for the fact that so many people within the three monotheistic traditions no longer seriously believe it. The faithful echo it in liturgies, hymns and ecclesiastical rhetoric, particularly within funeral services, but it does not, for most, form part of the operative set of convictions by which they live. They can see, on reflection, that if there is a loving God, this life, which has been so unsatisfactory and so incomplete for so many, cannot be all. But they have nothing to support this other than the familiar imagery, which cannot be taken literally, and so the whole idea of further life falls by default out of their minds.

2. Aurelius, p. 75.

In saying that the traditional doctrine of an eternal heaven and hell presents great difficulties I am not invoking the naturalistic assumption that we are purely physical organisms who perish totally at death. I have already (chapter 1) rejected this materialist view. But the idea of a finite human self existing endlessly is itself problematic. The present 'me' is a product of twentieth-century western civilization. Am I to be eternally a white male twentieth-century Englishman with my particular genetic inheritance, formed by my particular education and other shaping influences? Would these attributes be appropriate in heaven? In eternity will the different cultures and historical epochs still divide human beings? Will we develop a common language or continue to speak a hundred different tongues? Or will we, as heavenly beings, leave behind our earthly cultural identity? And if so, will we still be the same persons?

Again, our self-identity depends, from our own point of view, mainly on our memory. It is because I remember enough of my past that I am, subjectively, still the same person. But could I, in the distant future long after the end of this earthly life, remember back over millions, and then millions of millions, of years? Is there no limit to the memory capacity of a finite being? Or it is perhaps enough that we can remember back over a limited period of, say, about a century? We could then be the same person as yesterday, or fifty years ago, although not subjectively the same person as a million years ago. Perhaps we are, as the philosopher Derek Parfit has suggested, a series of persons merging successively into one another, so that we can speak of our former selves and our future selves.[3] This possibility begins to approach the idea, to which I shall come presently, of our deeper self living many lives, each in turn arising out of our accumulated past.

Despite such questions, the eternal finite self may perhaps be logically possible, even though we cannot spell out the possibility in any satisfactory way. But is logical possibility, combined with extreme implausibility, enough to make us believe it?

Another suggestion is that we are eternally remembered by God. This comes from the 'process' theology propounded most famously by Charles Hartshorne.[4] It appeals to many because it avoids the problems of continuing personal identity. For on this view we do not live on after death in the sense of continuing as conscious agents having new experiences and doing new things. Instead our life, completed at death, is perpetually retained in the divine memory. In so far as we have done well we will then have enriched the divine life, and in so far as we have committed evil we will either have besmirched it or (in another version)

3. Parfit, part III.
4. Hartshorne, chapter 10.

our evil deeds will be selectively filtered out of the divine memory. But the positive possibility can give meaning and value to our present life: we have the opportunity to contribute something to the eternal consciousness of God.

Clearly this is not a conception of life after death, and it does not make human fulfilment possible, for it does not permit any further spiritual growth in response to new experiences and new challenges. Nevertheless this is, once again, a logically possible, if religiously unsatisfying, scenario.

The Buddhist and Hindu traditions have a different approach which seems to me to offer more plausible options than either the eternal perpetuation of the present self or its eternal storing within the divine memory. The two ideas that I want to adopt also occur in western, but more centrally and in more developed forms, in eastern thought.

MANY LIVES

The fact that our life has a beginning and an end is an essential aspect of what we are. Life has a shape, a curve starting at birth, rising through childhood and youth, spanning the long maturity of the middle decades, and then descending as the body wears out, terminating in death. For we exist as part of the universal interdependent temporal process, within which everything, including ourselves, changes slowly or rapidly from moment to moment. This fleeting character of life has gripped the imagination of poets in every generation, Shakespeare as usual expressing it as memorably as anyone:

> Like as the waves make towards the pebbled shore,
> So do our minutes hasten to their end;
> Each changing place with that which goes before,
> In sequent toil all forwards do contend.
> Nativity, once in the main of light,
> Crawls to maturity, wherewith being crown'd,
> Crooked eclipses 'gainst his glory fight,
> And Time that gave doth now his gift confound.
> Time doth transfix the flourish set on youth
> And delves the parallels in beauty's brow,
> Feeds on the rarities of nature's truth.
> And nothing stands but for his scythe to mow. (Sonnet 60)

One can see this as depressing, with our life slipping away towards its inevitable end, so that when death approaches,

> Do not go gentle into that good night.
> Old age should burn and rage at close of day;
> Rage, rage, against the dying of the light. (Dylan Thomas)

Or one can be reconciled to mortality by seeing its creative function within the cosmic picture presented by the world religions. For the function of mortality is to make time precious. The boundaries of birth and death exert a pressure that gives urgent meaning to our lives. Because we do not live for ever we have to get on with whatever we are going to do. And because we are ever-changing creatures we have the possibility of ever fuller realizations of the potentialities latent within us.

But who fully realizes those potentialities before they die? None whom I, for one, have ever known. If there is a continuation of life after death, providing opportunity for further spiritual growth, it seems likely that this continuation takes the form of another finite, mortal span of life. And if one is not enough, then more than one, perhaps a long succession of further lives. It would also seem that these must be embodied existences – though not necessarily in the matter or forms that we know – in which we interact with other people and in which moral choices have continually to be made.

Where could such further lives be lived? The eastern religions assume that they are in this world. Whilst there are, according to them, many other spheres of existence, it is only in earthly embodiments that spiritual progress can be made – hence reincarnation, or rebirth, in this world. But other possibilities are suggested by modern astronomy and cosmology. The astronomers tell us that in the vastness of the universe there may be other, and if so probably many other, planets sustaining life. It is possible then that there are other worlds in which personal–spiritual life is lived. But further, the astrophysicists speak of the possibility of other universes independent of our own. Quantum theory points to the possibility of multiple space-time systems. According to some interpretations 'these other universes actually exist and are every bit as real as the one we inhabit'.[5] Or again it is possible that 'the constants of nature vary from region to region, so that each region of the universe is a kind of subuniverse'.[6] We are here in the realm of genuine possibilities, not of certainties. All we can say at present is that the idea of multiple embodied lives, whether in this or other worlds, is an open possibility.

5. Davies, p. 136.
6. Weinberg, p. 176.

WHAT REINCARNATES?

But what part or aspect of us might live again, perhaps many times? The popular conception of reincarnation as repeated rebirths of the present conscious self involves serious difficulties. If Mary dies at the age of eighty, and is reborn a year later as a baby called Jane, it is clear that Jane does not have the consciousness of the eighty-year-old Mary. She does not have Mary's memories, including her knowledge, wisdom, prejudices, skills. Thus Mary at the end of her life is in every observable respect a different personality from Jane at the beginning of hers. Baby Jane, then, is not Mary in any simple, straightforward sense. Mary's memories may perhaps exist latently within her, and Mary's most basic character traits may be influencing Jane's character development. But this will require a more complex understanding of reincarnation than the popular one. The simplest picture of reincarnation as like going to sleep in one body and waking later in another is not sustainable.

The Hindu and Buddhist philosophers have in fact thought out the more complex conception that is needed. They distinguish between the self-conscious ego, the 'I' who is now composing this sentence, and a deeper entity or process of which the ego is a temporary vehicle. Simplifying this down to its barest essentials, Vedantic Hinduism speaks of the *jiva* or, roughly, soul which is embodied in my present self.[7] The *jiva* registers and thus 'embodies' the moral, aesthetic, intellectual and spiritual dispositions that have been built up in the course of living a human life, or rather a succession of such lives. To appreciate this idea we have to conceive of thoughts, emotions, desires as things, and indeed as things that are capable of existing apart from consciousness as dispositional energies able, when linked with consciousness, to guide action. Through like grouping with like in mutual reinforcement, such dispositions form relatively stable and enduring structures which constitute the basic character of the individual through whom they express themselves, and by whose choices they are being continuously modified. Such dispositional structures survive the extinction of consciousness in death and continue as realities which will later become linked with a new psycho-physical organism. Thus Mary and Jane are different people who are however successive incarnations of the same continuing psychic structure. This process continues until it has served its purpose with the continually reincarnating deeper self, the *jiva* or soul, attaining in its last incarnation to the verge of complete union with the ultimate reality of Brahman.

7. This is a great simplication. For the complexities, see my *Death and Eternal Life*, part 4.

Buddhists usually speak of rebirth rather than of reincarnation, because there is no continuing entity that is successively reincarnated. One of the Buddha's basic teachings is that there is no eternal self, soul, *atman*. Even the empirical self, or ego, is not an enduring entity but is (as David Hume argued) a succession of moments of consciousness linked together by the fact that the later moments are affected by and include memory of the earlier moments. Within this causal continuity, according to the doctrine of karma, all our actions (including mental actions) affect both our own future and that of others. As we read in the *Dhammapada*, 'If one speaks or acts with wicked mind, because of that, suffering follows one, even as the wheel follows the hoof of the draught-ox . . . If one speaks or acts with pure mind, because of that, happiness follows one, even as one's shadow that never leaves.'[8] And this karmic influence continues beyond our present life until we attain to final enlightenment, awakening, nirvana. Accordingly we are repeatedly reborn, not in the sense that the present conscious self lives again, but in the sense that the continuing karmic pattern forms a succession of empirical selves.

Philosophical Hinduism and Buddhism thus agree that that which lives many times is not the present conscious 'I' but an underlying reality which is expressed through a succession of selves, each existing only for a limited period of time.

The other contribution of eastern thought, already evident within this scenario, is that a human personality, in the sense in which we are each conscious of being one, is not eternal. It is essentially mortal, a fleeting episode within a much longer story. It is not something complete, fit to endure for ever, but a fragment, finite in time as well as space. Only the fifth dimension of our existence – the divine image within us, the universal *atman* in the depths of our being, or the eternal buddha nature in which we all participate – is beyond mortality. And the series of human personalities of which I, this present conscious self, am one, is directed towards the presently inconceivable state of union with the Divine, the Ultimate, the Real.

In each case the main tradition holds that the memories of each successive life exist within that which continues and that the fully realized person is able at will to recover them. Thus during the long meditation of his enlightenment the Buddha reviewed his many previous lives. And according to some Hindu and Buddhist teachers the memory of our whole series of previous lives, which exists latently within us, is subject to occasional leakages into consciousness, such as are reported by those who appear to remember, either spontaneously or under hypnosis, fragments of a previous life. There is now a large literature of

8. *Dhammapada*, 1; Narada, p. 1.

such 'memories'. The reports remain at present, however, for me in the fifty-fifty probability category. I do not feel entitled to be sure either that some of them or that none of them are indeed fragmentary memories of a previous life. They may be, but it is difficult to be certain.

The fact of our mortality can be either alarming or liberating. So long as I cling to my fragmentary and very imperfect ego, its approaching demise is the worst possible news, and I will go to great lengths to shut it out of my mind. If on the other hand I can see myself as the present moment within a long creative process, and if I trust in the value of that process, I can accept my mortality without fear or resentment and can try to live to the full within my present finite span. For everything that I do is contributing, positively or negatively, to the future selves who will continue the project presently embodied in me. I am like a runner in a relay race: the torch has been handed to me, and for a short while the whole project depends upon me. My life thus has urgent meaning. I am contributing something unique, however slight, not only to the world that will continue after my death, but also to the future selves who will, one after another, embody the basic dispositional character-structure – the soul, or *jiva*, or the karmic nexus – which I have inherited and which I am all the time modifying in small ways for good or for ill.

Both eastern and western thinkers have tried to work out theories of the mechanism by which multiple lives are thus linked by an underlying dispositional structure or pattern. But to almost every question that we ask there are several possible answers. For example, does the present conscious personality cease to exist at the moment of bodily death, or does it persist for a certain time? Some strands of Buddhism teach that rebirth begins the moment the present life ends. Other strands, as in the *Bardo Thodol*, or Tibetan Book of the Dead, teach that the present self continues through a *bardo*, or in-between, period. At death we are confronted by the Clear Light of Reality, but if we cannot bear that Light we move into a series of psychoanalytic-like experiences, sometimes terrifying and sometimes comforting, which reveal the limitations and weaknesses that require further life. And then in the process of rebirth the former personality ceases and a new personality begins to form.

Such evidence as there is of communication between the living and the dead – in mediumship, apparitions, etc. – would suggest at least a limited period of personal survival, and this is certainly a possibility. I was for many years a member of the (London) Society for Psychical Research, studying its reports, as well those of other researchers, and I have come to see a limited personal survival as a more than fifty-fifty probability.[9] However I do not want to base anything on that evidence here – it can all too easily minister to that clinging to the ego from which a genuinely accepted religious understanding of the universe frees us. To cling to the surface personality is to shut out the infinitely greater reality that is all the time above and around and within us. True religion is focused in the present moment, for it is here and now that the Real, the Ultimate, is present to us; it is here and now that we have the opportunity to open ourselves to that Reality.

I shall therefore say here rather little about existence after bodily death. But according to our big picture, the spiritual project that is now taking place in and through our lives will continue in many more lives. The present conscious 'I' is mortal. But in all that I think and do I am affecting positively or negatively the ongoing dispositional structure which is my deeper self. And so nothing good that my life creates will ever finally be wasted. As to whether even this deeper self will have an endless separate existence, or will finally become one with the eternal Reality, we at present neither know nor need to know.

DYING

Whilst it seems appropriate to say no more here about post-mortem existence (in spite of having published a five-hundred-page book on the subject[10]), it is nevertheless appropriate to say something about the process of dying. A very interesting development of the last twenty or so years has been the recording of 'near-death experiences', made more frequent by advances in the resuscitation of people who were apparently dead, their hearts and breathing having stopped. Many of those who have been in this state for several minutes, and have then been resuscitated, report experiences which, whilst presenting a range of variations, nevertheless fall partly or wholly within a distinct pattern. There is the sensation of moving through a dark tunnel and emerging into bright light in a state of immense freedom and euphoria, and then of encountering a 'being of light' who is felt to be totally loving and accepting. They are however then drawn back reluctantly into the body, regaining normal consciousness on the operating table or wherever their 'death' occurred. But the memory of the experience remains vividly with them and very often frees them from any fear of death.

This is a greatly simplified summary of a wide range of phenomena. These can be pursued in the literature, as also can the debate between

9. The literature is immense but for a survey of the entire field of parapsychological research, see Wolman, 1977. For fascinating philosophical discussions, see Price, 1995.
10. Hick, 1994.

those who attribute the experience simply to lack of oxygen in the dying brain and those who argue that whilst there are major similarities with the known effects of oxygen starvation there are also major differences which do not fit that explanation.[11] I myself remain at present agnostic about the significance of near-death experiences. But the point that I would make at the moment is not affected by one's conclusion about that. For whether these experiences constitute a fleeting glimpse across the boundary between this life and a next phase of existence, or are simply chemically induced hallucinations, they are nearly always highly positive in character. And so, if that is what awaits us, it is not anything to dread, but on the contrary something to look forward to!

But the process of dying, prior to the loss of ordinary consciousness, is too often not something to look forward to. It can sometimes be a harrowingly painful experience – agonizing mentally and emotionally as well as physically – both for dying persons and for their loved ones. And so it raises the question of whether medically assisted patient-requested euthanasia should be legally permitted. This is not the place for an extended discussion of this difficult issue. But we are at the point at which more public debate is needed, and I would like to further this by expressing a point of view.

It is already widely agreed that it can be right to close down the artificial life-support system in the case of someone who is irreparably brain-damaged and in a persistent vegetative state. In addition to this there are two other sets of circumstances in which it seems to me that medically assisted patient-requested euthanasia should be legalized. (The generally used term 'voluntary euthanasia' seems to me too weak: what we are talking about is patient-requested euthanasia.)

The severe pain that sometimes afflicts a terminally ill patient can usually, given the necessary expertise and care, be satisfactorily controlled, although sometimes only by a morphine dosage that will terminate life. But in addition to severe pain there can be severe discomfort, such as a very distressing and frightening difficulty in breathing or in swallowing, or the terror that can be caused by being paralysed and helpless. Specialized treatment in a hospice or a hospital ward dedicated to the care of the dying can be very helpful, but there are not nearly enough such places, or enough expert home care, available or likely to be available for all in the foreseeable future, even in the most wealthy countries. It therefore seems unrealistic to resist patient-requested euthanasia on the grounds that unacceptable pain can, in theory, be prevented. No doctor or nurse should of course be

11. The modern discussion of near-death experiences began with Moody, 1975. For the most recent arguments for a naturalistic explanation, see Blackmore, 1993, and for a critical response to these arguments, see Fenwick, 1995. See also Ring, 1980, Kellehear, 1996 and Badham, 1997.

required against their conscience to provide the means to a painless death. But after an independent second (and perhaps third) medical opinion that the painful condition is terminal, and after an independent legally defined confirmation that the patient genuinely and freely wants it, euthanasia should, in my judgement, be permitted.

The other type of case is that of someone, usually elderly, who is slipping into dementia, Alzheimer's or other, and being aware of this wishes – the wish being, again, independently confirmed – to receive euthanasia when the brain has deteriorated too far for him or her to request it. Deep dementia is probably the most undignified and pitiful state in which a human can be. Again, no doctor or nurse should be obliged to assist in euthanasia when it has been requested in an advance directive, although when in carefully defined circumstances this is made legal, enough doctors and nurses will undoubtedly be willing to honour their patient's wish in this way.

There are two main objections to the legalization of patient-requested euthanasia, one reasonable, the other unreasonable.

The unreasonable one is that only God can properly decide when someone is to die and that human interventions are therefore always sinful; or in secular terms, that we should not interfere in the ordinary course of nature. That God decides when everyone dies, other than by sinful human action, would entail that God has decreed the deaths of all who die of diseases or in famines, earthquakes, droughts, fatal accidents, etc., and this is surely an unacceptable implication. And that we should not interfere in the course of nature entails that the practice of medicine and surgery should be abandoned and all hospitals closed – again, this is not an acceptable implication.

The reasonable objection is that if euthanasia were legalized some people would feel under pressure to request it in order to cease to be a burden upon those they love, or, worse, they might be put under that pressure by unscrupulous relatives wanting to inherit from them, or just wanting to be rid of the burden of looking after them. Legally, the latter case would be excluded by a strong system of independent confirmation of the patient's genuine and free request, but it must be admitted that this law would probably, like almost all other laws, sometimes be successfully broken. Legislatures, in passing the new law, would have had to weigh this fact against the desire of so many people for the legalization of patient-requested euthanasia for the terminally ill. Another kind of case is that in which there is no external pressure, but in which the individual himself or herself wishes to shorten the process not only to avoid further severe pain and further deep mental anguish, but also to spare others the burden and pain of looking after them. My own view is that this would be a reasonable consideration for a dying person to take into account, if he or she so wishes; for it is after all part of the reality of the situation. I would therefore treat the genuine desire of the dying person, based on whatever considerations, as paramount. I therefore do not see this objection, serious and legitimate though it is, as outweighing the benefit to many of legalized patient-requested euthanasia in the case of terminally ill individuals.

At present it is known that euthanasia, shortening the process of dying, occurs in reality in ordinary medical practice. It is justified by the technicality that the physician is prescribing the massive dose of morphine, or whatever, to treat the patient's pain even though knowing the dosage to be fatal. But should not doctors be relieved of the responsibility to grant or refuse a patient's request to avoid weeks or months of needless pain and distress by a quick and painless death; or to avoid years of dehumanized existence, physically alive but with at best occasional faint and fleeting moments of something approaching self-awareness? Physiological life simply as such is not important; its importance is as supporting personal life. But each individual, rather than the state or the medical profession, should – in my opinion – have the right to make the final decision in this area.

CONCLUSION

This has been a fairly wide-ranging discussion. How can we summarize its conclusions?

This is not a book which professes to know everything. We have to learn to live on a 'need-to-know' basis, trusting the fifth or spiritual dimension of our own nature as it responds – if for most of us only in fleeting and fragmentary ways – to the fifth dimension of the total reality around us.

Our life as finite vulnerable egos is a pursuit of security in the form of possessions and power of various kinds, inevitably in competition with others. This universal self-centredness is the root of both individual unhappiness and structural violence, injustice, crime, exploitation and cruelty, in fact most of the suffering in human life. It is diagnosed by the religions either (in the west) as 'fallen' and sinful or (in the east) as the false consciousness of the self-regarding ego. But the religions also teach that a limitlessly better existence is possible, and can be approached now along a variety of spiritual paths. Philosophy can help us to understand and appropriate this. For the naturalistic or materialist assumption – the assumption that nothing exists but matter/energy, including human brains and their activity – has come to pervade modern western consciousness. It is however only an assumption, and it is challenged by many signals of transcendence in the universe and in human life.

It is entirely rational and sane to regard the religious experience of humanity not simply as imaginative projection but as a range of responses involving the imagination to an ultimate reality that is both within us and beyond us. But because of the nature of consciousness, the forms taken by our responses are selected by the sets of ideas, and the corresponding spiritual practices, taught by the different religious cultures, the two key concepts involved being the idea of deity – our own nature as personal beings enlarged to infinity – and the idea of a non-personal ultimate.

However, the transcendent reality in itself is beyond all these forms, even personality and impersonality. It is transcategorial (ineffable), not describable in our human terms. But because the fifth dimension of our own being responds to the reality underlying and transcending everything, we are able to be aware of that reality, though always in the forms made possible by our cultural resources.

The world religions all report that, as it affects humanity, the Real or Ultimate is benign and that we live in what is finally, from our point of view, a serendipitous universe. To become conscious in some degree of the eternally Real, through one of its humanly experienceable manifestations, is in that degree to be liberated from the anxious, grasping ego, and freed to love one's neighbour, who is anyone and everyone. We see something of the extraordinary possibilities of our own nature, when it becomes open to the Transcendent, in the lives of the saints or mahatmas of every tradition. In the modern world, we find that the typical form of saintliness has increasingly become politically concerned and engaged; hence the case study of Mahatma Gandhi.

The metaphysical dogmas about which the different religions differ so strongly, and sometimes violently, are legitimate speculations, but should not be absolutized as infallible dogmas. In each religious and also non-religious worldview, in so far as it is in alignment with the Real, we live within a true myth – a cosmic story which is not literally true but which nevertheless evokes an appropriate life response to the Real.

Because we experience the Real in benign forms we can be confident that the human potential is destined to be fulfilled and that this present life is therefore an episode within a much longer process. A series of further finite lives awaits us in which our deeper self, living through a series of conscious egos, is formed in response to the contingencies of finite existence. In all that we do we are affecting, positively or negatively, our own future selves. Perhaps ultimately, with the fulfilment of the creative process, finite personality will have served its purpose and become one with the eternal Reality, but we do not at present need to know the final future.

What we do need to know is how to live now. This is the way of love, witnessed to by the saints and mystics of all the great traditions.

BIBLIOGRAPHY

Al 'Arabi, Ibn, 1990, *The Bezels of Wisdom*, New York: Paulist Press and London: SCM Press.

Al-Ghazali, A.H., 1987, *Ninety-Nine Names of God*, trans. Robert Stade, Ibadan: Daystar Press.

— 1994, *The Faith and Practice of Al-Ghazali*, trans. Montgomery Watt, Oxford: Oneworld Publications.

Ali, Ahmed (trans.), 1988, *Al-Qur'ān: A Contemporary Translation*, Princeton, NJ: Princeton University Press.

Alston, William, 1991, *Perceiving God*, Ithaca, NY and London: Cornell University Press.

Ambler, Rex, 1989, 'Gandhi's Concept of Truth', in John Hick and Lamont C. Hempel (eds.), *Gandhi's Significance for Today*, London: Macmillan and New York: SUNY Press.

Ansari, Khwaja Abdullah, 1978, *Intimate Conversations*, 1, trans. Wheeler M. Thackston, New York: Paulist Press and London: SPCK.

Aquinas, Thomas, 1945, *Basic Writings of Saint Thomas Aquinas*, Anton Pegis (ed.), New York: Random House.

Armstrong, D.M., 1987, 'Mind–Body Problem: Philosophical Theories', in Richard Gregory (ed.), *The Oxford Companion to the Mind*, Oxford and New York: Oxford University Press.

Athanasius, P., 1957, P. Schaff and H. Wace (eds.), *Nicene and Post-Nicene Fathers*, Series Two, Vol. IV, Grand Rapids, MI: Eerdman.

Augustine, St, 1955, *Enchiridion*, trans. Albert Outler, in *Augustine: Confessions and Enchiridion*, Philadelphia: Westminster Press.

Aurelius, Marcus, 1995, *Meditations*, Harmondsworth: Penguin Books.

Badham, Paul, 1997, *Religious and Near-Death Experiences in Relation to Belief in a Future Life*, Oxford: Religious Experience Research Unit.

Barker, Eileen, 1990, 'New Lines in the Supra-market: How Much can we Buy?', in Ian Hamnett (ed.), *Religious Unbelief and Pluralism*, London and New York: Routledge.

Beardsworth, Timothy, 1977, *A Sense of Presence*, Oxford: Religious Experience Research Unit.

Bergson, Henri, 1911, *Matter and Memory*, London: Macmillan.

Blackmore, Susan, 1993, *Dying to Live: Science and the Near-Death Experience*, London: Grafton.

Blumenthal, David R., 1978–82, *Understanding Jewish Mysticism*, 2 vols., New York: Ktav Publishing House.

Boase, T.S.R., 1972, *Death in the Middle Ages*, London: Thames Hudson.

Bodhi, Bikkhu (ed.), 1995, *Nyanaponika: A Farewell Tribute*, Kandy: Buddhist Publication Society.

Bolle, Kees, 1979, *The Bhagavadgita: A New Translation*, Los Angeles: University of California Press.

Bowker, John, 1987, *Licensed Insanities*, London: Darton, Longman & Todd.

Broad, C.D., 1953, *Religion, Philosophy and Psychical Research*, London: Routledge & Kegan Paul.

Brown, Judith, 1989, *Gandhi: Prisoner of Hope*, New Haven and London: Yale University Press.

Bruck, Michael von, 1991, *The Unity of Reality* (1986), trans. James Zeitz, New York: Paulist Press.

Bucke, Richard Maurice, 1969, *Cosmic Consciousness* (1901), New York: E.P. Dutton.

Butler, Cuthbert, 1967, *Western Mysticism*, London: Constable.

Carter, Rita, 1998, *Mapping the Mind*, London: Weidenfeld & Nicolson.

Casey, Maurice, 1991, *From Jewish Prophet to Gentile God*, Cambridge: James Clarke and Louisville, KY: Westminster/John Knox.

Catherine of Genoa, 1979, *Catherine of Genoa: Purgation and Purgatory, The Spiritual Dialogue*, trans. Serge Hughes, London: SPCK.

Chadha, Yogesh, 1997, *Rediscovering Gandhi*, London: Century.

Charlesworth, James H. (ed.), 1991, *Jesus' Jewishness*, New York: Crossroads.

Chatterjee, Margaret, 1983, *Gandhi's Religious Thought*, London: Macmillan and Notre Dame, IN: Notre Dame University Press.

Chittick, William, 1983, *The Sufi Path of Love: The Spiritual Teachings of Rumi*, Albany: State University of New York.

Clark, Mary, 1987, 'Neoplatonism', in Mircea Eliade (ed.), *The Encyclopedia of Religion*, Vol. 10, New York: Macmillan and London: Collier Macmillan.

Clement of Alexandria, 1956, A. Roberts and J. Donaldson (eds.), *The Ante-Nicene Fathers*, Vol. II, Grand Rapids: Eerdmans.

Cloud of Unknowing, 1978, *The Cloud of Unknowing and Other Works*, trans. Clifton Walters, London: Penguin Books.

Cohen, J.M. and Phipps, J-F., 1979, *The Common Experience*, London: Rider.

Cohn-Sherbok, Dan and Lavinia, 1987, 'Death and Immortality in the Jewish Tradition', in Paul and Linda Badham (eds.), *Death and Immortality in the Religions of the World*, New York: Paragon Press.

— 1994, *Jewish and Christian Mysticism*, New York: Continuum.

— 1995, *Mysticism and Sex*, Loughborough: Loughborough University.

Conze, Edward, 1975, *Buddhism, Its Essence and Development*, New York and London: Harper & Row.

Copley, Anthony and Paxton, George (eds.), 1997, *Gandhi and the Contemporary World*, Chennai: Indo-British Historical Society.

Cupitt, Don, 1998, *Mysticism After Modernity*, Oxford and Malden, MA: Blackwell.

Dasgupta, Surendranath, 1975, *A History of Indian Philosophy*, Vol. II, Delhi: Motil Banarsidass.

Davids, C.A.F. Rhys, 1964, *Therigatha*, trans. as *Psalms of the Early Buddhists*, London: Luzac.

Davids, T.W. and C.A.F., (trans), 1959, *Dialogues of the Buddha*, 4th edn., London: Luzac & Co.

Davies, Paul, 1980, *Other Worlds: Space, Superspace and the Quantum Universe*, London: J.M. Dent.

Dennett, Daniel C., 1996, *Kinds of Mind: Towards an Understanding of Consciousness*, London: Weidenfeld & Nicolson.

Denny, Frederick, 1988, 'Prophet and Wali: Sainthood in Islam', in Kieckheffer and Bond (eds.), *Sainthood: Its Manifestations in World Religions*, Berkeley and London: University of California Press.

Desmond, Adrian, 1997, *Huxley: Evolution's High Priest*, London: Michael Joseph.

Dhavamony, Mariasusai, 1971, *Love of God according to Saiva Siddhanta*, Oxford: Clarendon Press.

Dublin, Louis I., 1965, *Factbook on Man – from Birth to Death*, 2nd edn., London: Collier Macmillan and New York: Macmillan.

Dupré, Louis, 1987, 'Mysticism', in Mircea Eliade (ed.), *The Encyclopedia of Religion*, Vol. 10, New York: Macmillan and London: Collier Macmillan.

Eckhart, Meister, 1941, *Meister Eckhart: A Modern Translation*, trans. Raymond Blakney, New York and London: Harper Torchbooks.

— 1981, *Meister Eckhart: The Essential Sermons, Commentaries, Treatises, and Defense*, trans. Edmund Colledge and Bernard McGinn, Mahwah, NJ: Paulist Press.

Edwards, Jonathan, 1959, *Religious Affections* (1746), New Haven: Yale University Press.

Eliade, Mircea, 1978, *A History of Religious Ideas*, Vol. I, trans. Willard Trask, Chicago and London: Chicago University Press.

— 1987, (general ed.), *Encyclopedia of Religion*, 16 vols., New York: Macmillan and London: Collier Macmillan.

Evans-Wentz, W.Y. (ed.), 1960, *The Tibetan Book of the Dead*, London and New York: Oxford University Press.

Fenwick, Peter and Elizabeth, 1995, *The Truth in the Light*, London: Headline.

Fischer, Louis, 1950, *The Life of Mahatma Gandhi*, New York and London: Harper & Row.

Fox, George, 1924, *The Journal of George Fox* (1694), London: J.M. Dent and New York: E.P. Dutton.

Fredriksen, Paula, 1988, *From Jesus to Christ*, New Haven and London: Yale University Press.

French, Patrick, 1997, *Liberty or Death: India's Journey to Independence and Division*, London: HarperCollins.

Friedlander, Shems and Al-Hajj Shaikh Muzaffereddin, 1978, *The Ninety-Nine Names of Allah*, London: Wildwood House.

Gandhi, M.K., 1945, *Gandhi's Correspondence with the Government 1942–4*, 2nd edn., Ahmedabad: Navajivan Publishing House.

— 1968, *The Selected Works of Mahatma Gandhi*, 6 vols., Ahmedabad: Navajivan Publishing House.

Gidwani, Sushila, 1989, 'Gandhian Feminism', in John Hick and Lamont C. Hempel (eds.), *Gandhi's Significance for Today*, London: Macmillan and New York: SUNY Press.

Goulder, Michael and Hick, John, 1994, *Why Believe in God?* (1983), London: SCM Xpress Reprints.

Greenberg, Irving, 1988, *The Jewish Way*, New York and London: Summit Books.

Gregory, R.L., 1978, *Eye and Brain*, 3rd edn., London: Weidenfeld & Nicolson and New York: McGraw-Hill.

Happold, F.C., 1970, *Mysticism*, Harmondsworth: Penguin.

Harbans Singh, 1969, *Guru Nanak and Origins of the Sikh Faith*, Bombay, London and New York: Asia Publishing House.

Hardy, Alister, 1979, *The Spiritual Nature of Man: A Study of Contemporary Religious Experience*, Oxford: Clarendon Press.

Harries, Richard, 1985, 'On the Brink of Universalism', in Robert Llewelyn (ed.), *Julian, Woman of Our Day*, London: Darton, Longman & Todd.

Hartshorne, Charles, 1962, 'Time, Death, and Everlasting Life', in *The Logic of Perfection*, Lasalle, ILL: Open Court Publishing Company.

Hawking, Stephen, 1988, *A Brief History of Time*, London and New York: Bantam Press.

Hay, David, 1982, *Exploring Inner Space*, Harmondsworth and New York: Penguin Books.

— 1990, *Religious Experience Today*, London: Mowbray.

Hempel, Lamont C., 1989, 'Overview: The Elusive Legacy', in John Hick and Lamont C. Hempel (eds.), *Gandhi's Significance for Today*, London: Macmillan and New York: SUNY Press.

Hick, John, 1970, *Arguments for the Existence of God*, London: Macmillan and New York: Herder & Herder.

— 1985, *Evil and the God of Love*, 2nd edn., London: Macmillan and New York: Harper & Row (1978).

— 1987, 'The Non-Absoluteness of Christianity', in John Hick and Paul Knitter (eds.), *The Myth of Christian Uniqueness*, New York: Orbis Books and London: SCM Press.

— 1989, *An Interpretation of Religion*, London: Macmillan and New Haven: Yale University Press.

— 1990, *Philosophy of Religion*, 4th edn., Englewood Cliffs, NJ: Prentice Hall and London: Prentice-Hall International.

— 1993, *The Metaphor of God Incarnate*, London: SCM Press and Louisville, KY: Westminster/John Knox.

— 1994, *Death and Eternal Life*, (1985), reissue, Louisville, KY: Westminster/John Knox and London: Macmillan.

Hick, John and Hempel, Lamont C. (eds.), 1989, *Gandhi's Significance for Today*, London: Macmillan and New York: SUNY Press.

Hobsbawm, Eric, 1994, *The Age of Extremes: The Short Twentieth Century*, London: Michael Joseph.

Hoda, Surur, 1997, 'Schumacher on Gandhi', in Anthony Copley and George Paxton (eds.), *Gandhi and the Contemporary World*, Chennai: Indo-British Historical Society.

Horner, I.B., 1954, *Majjhima Nikaya* I, trans. as *The Collection of Middle Length Sayings*, Vol. I, London: Luzac.

— 1957, *Majjhima Nikaya* II, trans. as *The Collection of Middle Length Sayings*, Vol. II, London: Luzac.

— 1963, *Vinaya Pitaka, Cullavagga*, trans. as *The Book of the Discipline*, Vol. V, London: Luzac.

Houlden, Leslie, 1992, *Jesus: A Question of Identity*, London: SPCK.

Huxley, Aldous, 1977, *The Doors of Perception* and *Heaven and Hell* (1954), London: Grafton.

Ibn 'Ata'Illah, 1978, *The Book of Wisdom*, trans. Victor Danner, New York: Paulist Press and London: SPCK.

Idel, Moshe, 1988, *Kabbalah: New Perspectives*, New Haven and London: Yale University Press.

Inge, W.R., 1899, *Christian Mysticism*, London: Methuen.

Irenaeus, 1952, *Proof of the Apostolic Preaching*, chap. 12, trans. Joseph P. Smith, *Ancient Christian Writers*, Vol. 16, London: Longmans, Green & Co.

— 1956, A. Roberts and J. Donaldson, (eds.), *The Ante-Nicene Fathers*, Vol. I, Grand Rapids, MI: Eerdman.

Isherwood, Christopher, 1965, *Ramakrishna and his Disciples*, London: Methuen.

Iyer, Raghavan (ed.), 1986, *The Moral and Political Writings of Mahatma Gandhi*, 3 vols., Oxford and New York: Clarendon Press.

James, Lawrence, 1997, *Raj: The Making and Unmaking of British India*, London: Little, Brown & Co.

James, William, 1979, *The Varieties of Religious Experience* (1902), London: Collins Fount.

Jantzen, Grace, 1987, *Julian of Norwich*, London: SPCK.

— 1995, *Power, Gender and Christian Mysticism*, Cambridge and New York: Cambridge University Press.

Jordan, G. Ray, 1972, 'LSD and Mystical Experiences', in John White (ed.), *The Highest State of Consciousness*, New York: Anchor Books.

Julian of Norwich, 1978, *Julian of Norwich: Showings* (Short and Long Texts), trans. Edmund Colledge and James Walsh, New York: Paulist Press and London: SPCK.

Kabir, 1977, *Songs of Kabir*, trans. Rabindranath Tagore, New York: Samuel Weiser.

Katz, Steven T., 1978, 'Language, Epistemology, and Mysticism', in Steven Katz (ed.), *Mysticism and Philosophical Analysis*, New York: Oxford University Press and London: Sheldon Press.

Kellehear, Allan, 1996, *Experiences Near Death: Beyond Science and Religion*, Oxford and New York: Oxford University Press.

Kempe, Margery, 1995, *The Book of Margery Kempe*, trans. Tony D. Triggs, London: Burns & Oates.

Kendrick, T.D., 1956, *The Lisbon Earthquake*, London: Methuen.

Kieckheffer, Richard, and Bond, George (eds.), 1988, *Sainthood: Its Manifestations in World Religions*, Berkeley and London: University of California Press.

Klostermaier, Klaus, 1969, *Hindu and Christian in Vrindaban*, London: SCM Press.

Kluckhohn, Clyde, 1979, 'Preface' to William Lessa and Evon Vogt, *Reader in Comparative Religion*, New York: Harper & Row.

Kushdeva Singh, 1973, *Love Is Stronger Than Hate*, Patiala: Guru Nanak Mission.

— 1974, *In Dedication*, 2nd edn., Patiala: Guru Nanak Mission.

— 1982, *Bhagat Kabir*, Patiala: Guru Nanak Mission.

— 1983, *Mahatma Gandhi*, Patiala: Rotary Club.

Kuschel, Karl-Josef, 1995, *Abraham*, trans. John Bowden, London: SCM Press.

Lane, Robert E., 1995, in *Demos Quarterly*, No. 5.

Lerner, Monroe, 1970, 'When, Why, and Where People Die', in Brim, Freeman, Levine and Scotch (eds.), *The Dying Patient*, New York: Russell Sage Foundation.

Lewis, J.M., 1989, *Ecstatic Religion*, London: Routledge.

Lipner, Julius, 1994, *Hindus: Their Religious Beliefs and Practices*, London and New York: Routledge.

Lorenzen, David N., 1987, 'Sankara', in Mircea Eliade (ed.), *The Encyclopedia of Religion*, Vol. 13, New York: Macmillan and London: Collier Macmillan.

Lovejoy, Arthur, 1960, *The Great Chain of Being* (1936), New York and London: Harper Torchbooks.

Lyall, Leonard A. (trans.), 1932, *Mencius*, London and New York: Longmans, Green.

MacKenna, S., 1969, *Plotinus* (English translation of *Enneads*), 4th edn., London: Faber & Faber.

MacMullen, Ramsay, 1997, *Christianity and Paganism in the Fourth to Eighth Centuries*, New Haven and London: Yale University Press.

Macquarrie, John, 1995, *The Mediators*, London: SCM Press.

Magee, Bryan, 1997, *Confessions of a Philosopher*, London: Weidenfeld & Nicolson.
Marett, R.R., 1932, *Sacraments of Simple Folks*, Oxford: Clarendon Press.
Maxwell, Meg and Tschudin, Verena (eds.), 1990, *Seeing the Invisible*, London and New York: Penguin Books.
McGinn, Bernard, 1991, *The Foundations of Mysticism*, London: SCM Press.
— 1994, *The Growth of Mysticism*, London: SCM Press.
Merton, Thomas, 1975, *The Asian Journal of Thomas Merton*, New York: New Directions.
Middlemiss, David, 1996, *Interpreting Charismatic Experience*, London: SCM Press.
Mill, John Stuart, 1875, *Nature and the Utility of Religion*, 4th edn., London: Longmans, Green, Reader & Dyer.
Moody, Raymond A, Jr., 1975, *Life After Life*, Atlanta: Mockingbird Books.
Morris, James, 1973, *Heaven's Command*, London: Faber & Faber.
Murti, T.R.V., 1980, *The Central Philosophy of Buddhism*, 2nd edn., London: Unwin, Mandala Books.
Narada Mahathera (trans.), 1972, *The Dhammapada*, 2nd edn., Colombo: Vajiranama.
Nasr, Seyyed Hossein, 1981, *Knowledge and the Sacred*, Edinburgh: Edinburgh University Press.
Newman, Cardinal John Henry, 1947, *A Grammar of Assent*, 5th edn. 1882, C.F. Harrold (ed.), New York and London: Longmans, Green.
Nicholas of Cusa, 1990, *Nicholas of Cusa on Interreligious Harmony (De Pace Fidei)*, James Buchler and H. Lawrence Bond (eds.), Lewiston, NY: Edward Mellen Press.
Nicholson, R.A., 1963, *The Mystics of Islam*, London and Boston: Routledge & Kegan Paul.
Nineham, Dennis, 1977, in John Hick (ed.), *The Myth of God Incarnate*, London: SCM Press and Philadelphia: Westminster Press.
— 1993, *Christianity Mediaeval and Modern*, London: SCM Press.
Nyanaponika Mahathera, 1969, *The Heart of Buddhist Meditation*, 2nd edn., London: Rider.
— 1994, *The Vision of Dhamma*, 2nd edn., Kandy: Buddhist Publication Society.
Ornstein, Robert, and Naranjo, Claudio, 1972, *On the Psychology of Meditation*, London: Allen & Unwin.

Otto, Rudolph, 1957, *Mysticism East and West* (1926), trans. Bertha Bracey and Richenda Payne, New York: Meridian Books.

— 1958, *The Idea of the Holy* (1917), trans. John Harvey, New York: Oxford University Press.

Paffard, Michael, 1976, *The Unattended Moment*, London: SCM Press.

Pahnke, Walter N., 1972, 'Drugs and Mysticism', in John White (ed.), *The Highest State of Consciousness*, New York: Anchor Books.

Parfit, Derek, 1986, *Reasons and Persons*, Oxford and New York: Oxford University Press.

Pansikar, V.L., 1978, *Srimad-Balmiki-Maharsi-Panitah Yogava'sistha*, 2nd edn., Bombay: Tukaram Javaji.

Pascal, Blaise, 1947, *Pensées* (1670), trans. W.F. Trotter, London: J.M. Dent and New York: E.P. Dutton.

Payne, Robert, 1969, *The Life and Death of Mahatma Gandhi*, New York: E.P. Dutton.

Peers, Alison, (trans.), St John of the Cross, *Ascent of Mount Carmel*, 3rd edn., New York: Doubleday.

Pelikan, Jaroslav, 1985, *Jesus Through the Centuries*, New York and London: Harper & Row.

— 1987, 'The Odyssey of Dionysian Spirituality', in *Pseudo-Dionysius: The Complete Works*, trans. Colm Luibheid, New York: Paulist Press.

Pike, Nelson, 1992, *Mystic Union*, Ithaca, NY and London: Cornell University Press.

Plantinga, Alvin, 1983, 'Reason and Belief in God', in Alvin Plantinga and Nicholas Wolsterstorff (eds.), *Faith and Rationality*, Notre Dame and London: University of Notre Dame Press.

— 1997, 'Reformed Epistemology', in Philip Quinn and Charles Taliaferro (eds.), *A Companion to Philosophy of Religion*, Oxford and Cambridge, MA: Blackwell.

Plotinus, 1969, *Enneads*, trans. Stephen MacKenna, 4th edn., London: Faber & Faber.

Prabhavananda, Swami, (trans.), n.d., *Srimad Bhagavatam*, Madras: Sri Ramakrishna Math.

Pseudo-Dionysius, 1987, *Pseudo-Dionysius: The Complete Works*, trans. Colm Luibheid, New York: Paulist Press.

Price, H.H., 1995, *Philosophical Interactions with Parapsychology*, Frank Dilley (ed.), London: Macmillan and New York: St Martin's Press.

Radhakrishnan, Sarvepalli (trans.), 1953, *The Principal Upanishads*, London: Allen & Unwin and New York: Humanities Press.

Ring, Kenneth, 1980, *Life at Death: A Scientific Account of the Near-Death Experience*, New York: Coward McCann and Geohagen.

Roberts, A. and Donaldson, J. (eds.), 1956, *Ante-Nicene Fathers*, 2 vols, Grand Rapids, MI: Eerdmans.

Roberts, Elizabeth and Amidon, Elias (eds.), 1991, *Earth Prayers*, San Francisco: HarperSanFrancisco.

Robinson, Edward, 1977, *The Original Vision*, Oxford: Religious Experience Research Unit.

— 1978, *Living the Question*, Oxford: Religious Experience Research Unit.

Roy, Ranjit Kumar, 1997, 'Gandhi on Women: Their Role in the World of Politics', in Anthony Copley and George Paxton (eds.), *Gandhi and the Contemporary World*, Chennai: Indo-British Historical Society.

Royle, Trevor, 1997, *The Last Days of the Raj*, London: John Murray.

Rumi, Jalaluldin, 1979, *Teachings of Rumi*, trans. E.H. Whinfield, London: Octagon Press.

— 1983, *The Sufi Path of Love: The Spiritual Teachings of Rumi*, trans. William Chittick, Albany: State University of New York.

— 1995, *Rumi: Poet and Mystic*, trans. R.A. Nicholson, Oxford: Oneworld.

Runciman, Steven, 1954, *A History of the Crusades*, Vol. III, Cambridge: Cambridge University Press.

Russell, Bertrand, 1918, *Mysticism and Logic and Other Essays*, London: Edward Arnold.

— 1948, *Human Knowledge: Its Scope and Limits*, London: Allen & Unwin.

— 1969, *Autobiography*, Vol. III, London: Allen & Unwin.

Russell, Jeffrey Burton, 1987, 'Witchcraft', in Mircea Eliade (ed.), *The Encyclopedia of Religion*, Vol. 15, New York: Macmillan and London: Collier Macmillan.

Ruusbroec, John, 1985, *John Ruusbroec: The Spiritual Espousals and Other Works*, trans. James Wiseman, New York: Paulist Press.

Sanders, E.P., 1985, *Jesus and Judaism*, London: SCM Press.

— 1993, *The Historical Figure of Jesus*, London: Allen Lane.

Schaff, P. and Wace, H. (eds.), 1957, *Nicene and Post-Nicene Fathers*, Grand Rapids, MI: Eerdman.

Schillebeeckx, Edward, 1979, *Jesus: An Experiment in Christology* (1974), London: Collins.

Scholem, G.G., 1955, *Major Trends in Jewish Mysticism*, London: Thames & Hudson.

— 1980, 'General Characteristics of Jewish Mysticism', in Richard

Woods (ed.), *Understanding Mysticism*, New York: Doubleday.

Schulz, Richard, 1985, 'Thinking about Death: Death Anxiety Research', in Sandra Wilcox and Marilyn Sutton (eds.), *Understanding Death and Dying: An Interdisciplinary Approach*, Palo Alto, CA and London: Mayfield Publishing Company.

Schumann, Hans Wolfgang, 1973, *Buddhism*, trans. Georg Fenerstein, London: Rider.

Scotney, Norman, 1997, 'Gandhi's Lifeline–Belief: Towards Religious Pluralism', in Anthony Copley and George Paxton (eds.), *Gandhi and the Contemporary World*, Chennai: Indo-British Historical Society.

Shankara, 1978, *Crest-Jewell of Discrimination*, trans. Swami Prabhavananda and Christopher Isherwood, 3rd edn., Hollywood, CA: Vedanta Press.

Sharma, Arvind, 1989, 'Gandhi and Celibacy', in John Hick and Lamont C. Hempel (eds.), *Gandhi's Significance for Today*, London: Macmillan and New York: SUNY Press.

— (ed.), 1993, *Our Religions*, San Francisco: HarperSanFrancisco.

Shinran, 1979, *Notes on 'Essentials of Faith Alone'*, Kyoto: Hongwanji International Center.

Shirer, William L., 1960, *The Rise and Fall of the Third Reich*, New York: Simon & Schuster.

Slotkin, J.S., 1952, 'Menomini Peyotism: A Study of Individual Variations in a Primary Group with a Homogeneous Culture', in *Transactions of the American Philosophical Society*, NS Vol. 42, Part 4.

Smart, Ninian, 1965, 'Interpretation and Mystical Experience', *Religious Studies*, Vol. 1, No. 1.

Smith, Wilfred Cantwell, 1978, *The Meaning and End of Religion* (1962), New York and London: Harper & Row.

Sohan Singh, 1969, 'Sikhism Among World Religions' in Kirpal Singh Narang (ed.), *Sikhism*, Patiala: Punjabi University.

Stanner, W.E.H., 1979, 'The Dreaming', in William Lessa and Evon Vogt (eds.), *Reader in Comparative Religion: An Anthropological Approach*, 4th edn., New York: Harper & Row.

Stark, Rodney, 1998, 'On Theory-Driven Methods', in Jon R. Stone (ed.), *The Craft of Religious Studies*, London: Macmillan and New York: St Martin's Press.

Storr, Anthony, 1996, *Feet of Clay*, London: HarperCollins.

Suzuki, D.T., 1964, *An Introduction to Zen Buddhism*, New York: Grove Press.

— 1982, 'The Buddhist Conception of Reality', in Frederick Franck

(ed.), *The Buddha Eye*, New York: Crossroad.
Swanson, R.N., 1995, *Religion and Devotion in Europe, c. 1215–c.1515*, Cambridge and New York: Cambridge University Press.
Swinburne, Richard, 1979, *The Existence of God*, Oxford: Clarendon Press.
— 1996, *Is There a God?*, Oxford: Oxford University Press.
Takeuchi Yoshinori, 1983, *The Heart of Buddhism*, trans. James Heisig, New York: Crossroads.
Tart, Charles T., 1975, *States of Consciousness*, New York: E.P. Dutton.
Tendulkar, D.G., 1951, 'Mahatma: Life of Mohandas Karamchand Gandhi', Delhi: Government of India Publications Division, Vol. I.
Teresa of Avila, St, 1960, *The Autobiography of St. Teresa of Avila*, trans. Alison Peers, New York: Image Books.
— 1995, *The Interior Castle*, trans. Benedict Zimmerman et al. London: HarperCollins Fount.
Theologia Germanica, 1937, trans. Susanna Winkworth, London: Macmillan.
Thompson, Nehemiah, 1998, 'The Search for a Methodist Theology of Religious Pluralism', in Mark Heim (ed.), *Grounds for Understanding*, Grand Rapids, MI and Cambridge, UK: Eerdman.
Toulmin, Stephen, 1982, *The Return to Cosmology*, Berkeley and London: University of California Press.
Tracy, David, 1988, *Plurality and Ambiguity*, London: SCM Press.
Trilochan Singh et al. (eds.), 1965, *Selections from the Sacred Writings of the Sikhs*, London: George Allen & Unwin.
Turner, Denys, 1995, *The Darkness of God: Negativity in Christian Mysticism*, Cambridge: Cambridge University Press.
Underhill, Evelyn, 1999, *Mysticism* (1910), Oxford: Oneworld Publications.
von Balthasar, Urs, 1965, 'The Metaphysics and Mystical Theology of Evagrius', *Monastic Studies*, Vol. 3.
von Hugel, Friedrich, 1927, *The Mystical Element of Religion*, 2 vols., London: J.M. Dent and New York: E.P. Dutton.
Weinberg, Steven, 1993, *Dreams of a Final Theory*, London: Hutchinson.
White, John (ed.), 1972, *The Highest State of Consciousness*, New York: Anchor Books.
Whitehead, A.N., 1929, *Process and Reality*, Cambridge and New York: Cambridge University Press.
Wiener, Norbert, 1968, *The Human Use of Human Beings*, London:

Sphere Books and New York: Avon Books.
Williams, Rowan, 1991, *Teresa of Avila*, London: Geoffrey Chapman.
Wingfield, E.H. (trans.), 1979, *Teachings of Rumi*, London: Octagon Press.
Wittgenstein, Ludwig, 1953, *Philosophical Investigations*, trans. G.E.M. Anscombe, Oxford: Blackwell.
Wolman, Benjamin B. (ed.), 1977, *Handbook of Parapsychology*, New York and London: Van Nostrand Reinhold.
Woods, Richard (ed.), 1980, *Understanding Mysticism*, New York: Doubleday.
Woodward, Frank L., 1948, *Udana*, trans. as *The Minor Anthologies of the Pali Canon*, London: Oxford University Press.
— 1956, *Samyutta Nikaya* IV, trans. as *The Book of Kindred Sayings*, Part 4, London: Luzac.
Zaehner, R.C., 1957, *Mysticism Sacred and Profane*, Oxford and New York: Oxford University Press.

INDEX

Abulafia, Abraham 151
afterlife 3, 4, 8, 64–5, 66, 70, 77, 133, 219, 222–3, 224, 225, 241–9: annihilation 69, 241, 253; in divine memory 243–4; Hades, Sheol 4, 64; heaven and hell 4, 53–4, 58, 65, 68–9, 70, 71, 72–3, 110, 135, 219, 221, 225, 237, 242–3; immortality of the soul 65, 242; rebirth/reincarnation 38, 56, 57, 61, 139, 223, 225, 245, 246–9, 254; resurrection 65, 66, 238, 242; unity with the Real 38, 53, 58, 151–2, 247, 254
Al-'Arabi 43, 90
Al-Ghazali 41, 153
Al-Hallaj 152, 153
Al-Junayd 43
Ansari, Abdullah 73
Aquinas, Thomas 43, 79
Athanasius 148
Augustine, St 68, 83, 130, 131, 132, 133, 148–9, 220
axial age 5–6
Bahá'í religion 79, 227; *Gleanings from the Writings of Bahá'u'lláh* 227
Bahá'u'lláh 79
Baker, Augustine 120
Bernard of Clairvaux, St 148, 149
Bible 112, 231–2: Hebrew (Old Testament) 4, 6, 149; New Testament 6, 67, 73, 79, 160, 227, 235, 238
Boehme, Jabob 148
Bridget of Sweden 118, 123
Buddha, Buddhas 5, 6–7, 42, 59, 60, 62, 94–5, 176–7, 201, 216, 222–3, 224, 225, 247: Gautama 5, 59, 61, 95, 164, 173; Maitreya 95
Buddhism 4, 6–7, 19, 51, 56, 59–63, 78, 94–6, 103, 157, 165, 173, 211–15, 216, 221–3, 226, 227, 246–7: Amida 94; *anatta* (no substantial self) 59; *avyakata* (unanswered questions) 221–3; *Bardo Thodol* 38, 248; *bodhisattva* 164, 173, 177;

buddha nature (*buddhata*) 7, 24, 41, 51, 53, 60, 62, 94, 115, 132, 168, 247; *Dhammapada* 62, 247; Dharma/*dharma* 61, 165; Dharmakaya/*dharmakhaya* 42, 60, 94, 115; *dukkha* 6–7, 8, 60. 61; Four Noble Truths 6; *karuna* (compassion) 7, 62, 142, 214; liberation 61–2, 222; Madhyamika 95; Mahayana 5n., 59, 94, 95, 134, 173; *metta* (loving-kindness) 7, 62, 142, 216; *nibbana*/nirvana 10, 53, 59, 60, 62–3, 114–15, 134, 142, 213, 222, 247; Noble Eightfold Path 62, 215; Pali scriptures 60, 213, 221; *parinirvana* 142, 223; Pure Land 94, 95; Sambhogakaya 94; *samsara* (everyday life, rebirth) 59, 61, 134; satipatthana meditation 213–14; *satori* (enlightenment) 114, 115; *sunyata* (emptiness) 60, 62, 94, 95, 115; *Sutta Nipata* 213, 227; Tathagata (enlightened one, Buddha) 222, 223; Theravada 59, 60, 62, 173, 211, 213; Three Refuges 213; Tibetan 213; Trikaya 94; western adoption of 59; Zen 60, 105, 107, 114–15

Catherine of Bologna 118
Catherine of Genoa 118, 142, 164, 176
Catherine of Siena 118, 123, 176
China, Chinese religion 5, 15: Chinese Buddhism 59, 165; Confucianism 173
Christianity 4, 5, 8, 18, 24, 42, 59, 66–70, 78, 79–90, 129–30, 203, 219, 225–6, 234–40: charismatic 160–1; conversion 69, 159; exclusivism 166, 226, 237; fundamentalism 66–7; heresy 69, 84–5, 119, 120, 123, 129–35, 159, 166; hysterical manifestations 160; incarnation 86, 87, 225, 235, 238, 239, 240; Inquisition 85, 159; mysticism 69, 70, 79–88, 89, 118–35, 137, 138, 144–51, 153; persecution and violence 158–9, 226, 237; Reformation 66–7, 68, 84; sacraments 69; Schism 84, 123; second coming 67–8; Trinity 10, 68, 69, 78, 86–8, 89, 166, 220, 225, 235, 236
Clement of Alexandria 148, 149
Cloud of Unknowing 118, 120, 123, 132n.
Collette of Corbie 118
Confucius 5, 174, 201: *Analects* 227
consciousness 6–7, 10, 14, 15, 28–9, 113, 154, 213, 246, 254: altered states of 99–109, 110; of one's environment 39–40; false 6, 7, 8; group 5, 6; individual 6, 246; mind–brain identity theory 28, 222; self-consciousness 28
cosmic optimism 21, 51–73, 224: in Buddhism 59–63; in Christianity 66–70; in Hinduism 55–9; in Islam 70–3; in Judaism 64–6; of Julian of Norwich 133–5

cosmic pessimism 20–1, 22–5, 53
creation 6, 24, 83, 219–20
critical realism 32–43, 111, 151: cognitive freedom 35–8
cults and sects 155–7: Aum Shinrikyo 155; Branch Davidian 155; Children of God (Family of Love) 156; Hari Krishnas (International Society for Krishna Consciousness) 156; Heaven's Gate 155–6; Jonestown 155; Moonies (Unification Church) 156; Mormons 156–7; Order of the Solar Temple 155

dark side: of cults 155–7; of great religions 157–9, 226
death 248, 249–2: euthanasia 250–2; near-death experiences 249–50: see also afterlife
determinism 13–14, 126

Ebner, Margaret and Christina 118
Eckhart, Meister 41, 61, 88–90, 118, 132, 147, 163–4, 166
environmental issues 8, 70, 201–2, 204
Evagrius 145–6, 166
evil 6, 8, 23, 24, 131, 133–4, 157

fifth dimension 2, 8, 31, 38, 167, 169, 224, 247, 253, 254: *see also* transcendence
Fox, George 113–14, 132, 166
Francis de Sales 150
free will 13–14, 37–8, 126, 134
Friends of God 118

Gandhi, Mahatma (Mohandas Karamchand) 94, 140, 175, 177, 180–204, 205, 208, 254: *ahimsa* (non-violence) 141, 180, 182, 183, 185–7, 188, 190, 195–8, 199–201, 203, 204; and Hinduism 193–5; intellectual legacy 199–204; personality 182–90; political activism 180–1, 182, 183–4, 185–6, 187, 190, 192–3, 195, 196–7, 198, 199, 203; and the poor 186–7, 192, 199, 202; *satya* (Truth) 175, 188, 189, 191–3, 200; *satyagraha* 196, 203; *swaraj* 193, 196, 199; and untouchability 187, 193
Gautama: *see* Buddha
God 8, 9, 14, 15, 21, 38–9, 51–2, 53, 64, 70, 73, 78, 85–6, 88, 89, 123, 137, 173, 191–2, 216, 219–20, 251: as active in the world 17–19, 64, 232–3, 235, 251; Allah 10, 42, 51, 70, 78; anthropomorphic conception of 16, 18, 25, 59, 92, 125–6; as Brahman 10, 14, 15, 21, 51, 53, 56, 78, 91–2, 110, 126, 168, 176; as the Dharma 10, 14, 15, 110, 218; as Dharmakaya 21, 78; existence of 16, 52; feminine imagery 82, 125–6, 135, 150; human experiences of 15, 19, 40, 41, 42, 53, 78, 95, 100, 104–5, 107, 108, 110–17, 119, 124–8, 133–4, 136, 141, 150, 161–2, 165, 168, 169–70, 176, 177–8, 216, 254; ineffability of 9, 77, 80–4, 86–7, 88, 89, 91, 94, 126, 142, 191, 254; Jahweh 78;

pluralist conceptions of 77–9, 80; the Real 9, 10, 18, 25, 37, 38, 41, 77, 78, 94, 173, 249, 254; relationship with human beings 37, 41, 64, 70, 233; as the Tao 10, 14, 15, 78, 110; the Transcendent 8, 9, 10, 26, 30, 51, 52, 53, 59, 81, 86, 87, 104, 108, 112, 155, 169, 176, 177, 241; the Ultimate 8, 9, 10, 18, 30, 43, 51–2, 70, 77, 81, 82, 95, 117, 173, 192, 249, 254; the ultimate reality 9, 10, 51, 86, 91
guilt 6, 8, 51, 132, 135: *see also* sin
Guyon, Madam 164, 166

Hadewijch of Antwerp 118
Hawking, Stephen 16
Hilton, Walter 118, 120, 123
Hinduism 6, 41, 55–9, 91–4, 125–6, 128, 139, 173, 176, 188, 192, 193–5, 201, 204, 220, 225, 226, 227, 230, 231, 246: advaita Vedanta 51, 91, 92, 103, 137–42, 165, 194; Alvars 92; Arjuna 168; *atman*/Atman 8, 24, 41, 57, 132, 137, 140, 194, 195; *avidya* (spiritual blindness) 6, 51, 137, 253; *Bhagavad Gita* 5, 42, 51, 57, 112, 140, 192, 194–5; *Bhagavata Purana* 92; *bhakti* 56, 57; *bhakti* yoga 192; Brahma 91; Brahman 10, 14, 15, 21, 51, 56, 57, 58, 80, 91–2, 126, 137–8, 139, 140, 141, 142, 176, 191, 246; cosmic dance 56, 128, 220; Dharma 10; gods 56, 58; Ishwara 91, 94; *jiva* (the self) 246, 248; *jivanmukta* (liberated soul) 57, 141; *Jnana* yoga 192; karma 56–7, 193; *karma* yoga 192; Krishna 41, 56, 168; liberation (*moksha*) 57, 58, 138, 139, 189; *Mahabharata* 227; *maya* (illusion) 6, 132, 138, 188; *nirguna* Brahman 91–2, 94; Rama 56, 191, 231; *Ramayana* 231; *saguna* Brahman 91–2, 94; *samsara* (rebirth) 51, 56, 57, 58, 139; *sat* (real) 9, 56; Shaivism, Shiva 10, 56, 78, 91, 128, 191, 204, 220; Sita 191; Upanishads 5, 55, 59, 140; Vaishnavism, Vishnu 10, 42, 51, 56, 78, 91, 168, 191, 203; Vedas 55, 56, 91, 203, 226
humanism: *see* naturalism
Huxley, Aldous 102, 105, 106, 108
Huxley, T. H. 15

Ibn 'Ata'Illah 38, 71–2
Ignatius Loyola 164
India 5, 6, 55, 58, 71, 78–9, 100, 139, 140, 143, 157, 165, 200, 202–3, 219: caste 55, 56, 58, 59, 92, 193; communal violence 156, 177, 181, 187–8, 200, 205–7, 208, 209, 231; partition 157, 177, 181, 183, 206; struggle for independence 180–1, 183–4 195–8, 205: *see also* Buddhism; Hinduism; Jainism; Sikhism

Irenaeus 131, 149
Isaac of Acre 151–2
Islam 5, 18, 24, 42, 78, 219, 226: *baga* (life in God) 153; concept of God 51, 70, 89–90; *dhikr* (prayer) 152; exclusivism 226; *fana* (self-naughting) 152; Hadiths 227; *al-Haqq* (the real) 9, 89; Jewish–Muslim enmity 157, 232; paradise 70; 'People of the Book' 71, 226; revelation 71; Sufism (mysticism) 38, 71–2, 89–90, 132, 132n., 137, 138, 152–4, 173, 177, 203; *wali* 173

Jainism 5, 55, 78, 195, 204, 227: *anekantavada* 204; *Kritanga Sutra* 227; Mahavira 5, 173
Jesus 66, 123, 157, 165, 174, 175, 234–6: incarnation 86, 87, 225, 235, 238, 239, 240; Jewishness of 234, 235; life of 234, 238; Passion of 124, 126, 127, 128, 133; second coming of 67–8, 225, 236; teachings of 67, 68, 154, 200; 201, 227; in visions 124–8, 133, 168, 176
Joan of Arc 118
John of the Cross, St 147–8, 164, 166, 176
Judaism 5, 10, 18, 24, 64–6, 219, 226, 227, 235: Chosen People concept 226, 234; concept of God 51, 64; covenant 64; immortality of the soul 65, 242; Jewish–Muslim enmity 157, 232; Kabbalah (mysticism) 65–6, 79, 89, 137, 151–2; prophets 5; rabbinic Judaism 5n., 10, 65; resurrection of the dead 65, 66; Shoah (Holocaust) 66, 158–9, 237; Talmud 65, 227; *tsaddiq* 173; *Zohar* 79, 80
Julian of Norwich 42, 53, 117, 119–35, 176, 224: heresies of 129–35; life of 119–23; and salvation 129–35; visions of 123–8, 176
Junayd of Baghdad 153

Kabir 92–3, 94, 203
Kant, Immanuel 32, 62, 92, 95
Kempe, Margery 118, 120
Koestler, Arthur 104–5
Kushdeva Singh 205–11

Lao-Tzu 5, 174
Lull, Ramon 118
Luther, Martin 84

mahatmas (saints) 8, 24, 30–1, 107, 163–7, 169, 173–216, 254: founders 173–4; joy 176, 183; living saints 174–5, 178–9; secular/political saints 170, 175, 178–9, 254
Maimonides 65
Mandela, Nelson 170, 178, 198, 200
Margaret of Porete 118
Masao Abe 115
materialism: *see* naturalism
meditation 19, 59, 62, 95, 107, 138–9, 213–14, 216
Mencius 5, 35
Mill, John Stuart 50
More, Gertrude 120

Moses 173
Muhammad 71, 165, 174, 226, 227
mysticism 2, 41, 78, 91–6, 99–170: altered states of consciousness 99–109, 110; Christian 41, 42, 69, 70, 79–88, 89, 118–35, 137, 138, 153; delusory experience 155–7; 'divine sparks' 41, 83, 132, 192, 195; divinization, deification 145–9; Hindu 92, 103; Islamic (Sufism) 38, 41, 42, 43, 71–2, 89–90, 132, 132n., 137, 138, 152–4, 177, 203; Jewish 65–6, 79, 89, 137, 151–2; joy 114, 115–16, 127, 139–40, 142, 176–8; love poetry 149–51; mystical experience 110–17, 121–8, 131, 141, 144, 145–8, 150–4, 168, 176–7; practical lives of mystics 163–5, 178, 192–3; unitive 136–54; visions 41, 42, 110, 118, 123–8, 165, 168, 176; women mystics 118–21
myths 229–40: Christian 234–40; Hindu 230, 231; Jewish 232–4; as metaphors 229, 230–1, 239; the true myth 233, 237–40, 254; use and misuse of 231–2, 233–4, 236–7

naive realism 42, 111, 150–1
Nanak, Guru 93, 94, 174, 203, 209
Narada Mahathera 60
naturalism 1–2, 4, 13–25, 27–9, 37, 52, 105, 111, 167–8, 243, 253
Neoplatonism 79, 80–4, 137, 144–49, 219–20: and eastern mysticism 142–4, 146; and monotheism 137, 145
Nicholas of Cusa 78, 89
Nyanaponika Mahathera 79, 211–16

Parsis 78, 204
Paul, St 67, 68, 79, 80, 160, 165, 239
Plato 5, 137, 148
Plotinus 41, 132, 145, 164
pluralism, religious 10, 18–19, 40, 43, 77–90, 92–3, 94, 96, 194, 203–4, 208, 216, 226
prejudice 7: anti-Semitism 7, 36, 158, 159, 237; homophobia 7; Islamophobia 7; racial prejudice 36, 188
primitive religion 4–5, 17: primal religion 227
Pseudo-Dionysius (Denys; the Pseudo-Areopagite) 41, 61, 79–88, 89, 123, 132, 146–8

Qur'an 6, 10, 42, 51, 70, 71, 72–3, 90, 112, 165, 226

Ramanuja 57
religious experience 99–170: delusory 38, 42–3, 155–7, 160–2, 163, 166, 167–8; veridical 163–70: *see also* God, human experiences of; mysticism; transcendence
revelation 71, 78
reward and punishment 4, 17, 65, 68, 130, 131–5: *see also* afterlife
Rolle, Richard 118, 120, 123, 176

Rumi, Jalaluldin 42, 72, 73, 132n., 152, 153–4, 165, 177
Russell, Bertrand, 20–1, 24
Ruusbroec 41, 118, 123, 147, 149, 176

saints: *see* mahatmas
Satan, the devil 6, 126–7, 133, 166–7
Schleiermacher, Friedrich 112, 129
science 14, 16–19, 27–8, 221: and religion 14–15, 17–19, 20–5, 26, 52
self 8, 24, 41, 213, 254: eternal 243, 247; mortality of 247–9; transcendence of 30, 52, 53, 57, 58, 59, 61–2, 70, 88, 103–5, 107, 112, 114–15, 117, 136, 138–9, 140, 141, 152–4, 176, 213–14, 215, 216, 221, 225
Shankara 57, 91, 138–41, 165, 176
Shinran 95
Sikhism 55, 78, 93–4, 209–11: *Adi Granth* 93; Sikh nationalism 208–9
sin 6, 8, 51, 130–4, 135, 253: evil inclination 6
spirits, demons 4–5
suffering 7–8, 16, 22–3, 52–3, 66, 127–8, 133, 134, 177, 224, 241, 253
Suso 41, 118, 123, 132, 147, 149
Suzuki, D.T. 114

Takeuchi Yoshinori 60
Taoism: the Tao 10, 14, 15, 78, 110, 227; *Thai Shang* 227
Tauler, John 41, 118, 123, 132, 163
Teresa of Avila, St 149, 150, 164, 166–7, 176
Theologia Germanica 118, 123, 142, 154
transcategorial reality 8–10, 40–1, 80–1, 86, 88, 91, 92, 94, 142, 254: *see also* God, ineffability of
transcendence 8–9, 26–31, 37, 40–1, 42, 51–2, 58, 62, 100–1, 110–17, 253–4: of the self 30, 52, 53, 57, 58, 59, 61–2, 70, 88, 103–5, 107, 112, 114–15, 117, 136, 138–9, 140, 141, 152–4, 176, 213–14, 215, 216, 221, 225
Transcendent: *see* God

Ultimate: *see* God
universe: ambiguity of 15–17, 32, 167, 169; conceptions of 5, 13, 15, 16–17, 20, 25, 26–7, 29, 50, 53–4, 57, 58, 60, 61, 66, 82–3, 86, 137, 219–221, 222, 224, 230, 241, 245, 254; interconnectedness of 60, 114, 230; meaning of 2, 33, 49–51; origins of 16–17, 27, 219–20, 224–5; spiritual dimension of 38, 167

Wittgenstein, Ludwig 3, 49
women: mystics 118–21; patriarchalism 119, 202–3; position of 202–3, 204

Zoroaster, Zoroastrianism 5, 173, 227: *Dadistan-i-dinik* 227